Cherokee Narratives

Cherokee Narratives
A Linguistic Study

Durbin Feeling
William Pulte
Gregory Pulte

Foreword by Bill John Baker

University of Oklahoma Press : Norman

Published through the Recovering Languages and Literacies of the Americas initiative, supported by the Andrew W. Mellon Foundation

Library of Congress Cataloging-in-Publication Data

Names: Feeling, Durbin, author. | Pulte, William John, 1941– editor, translator. | Pulte, Gregory, editor, translator.
Title: Cherokee narratives : a linguistic study / Durbin Feeling, William Pulte, Gregory Pulte ; foreword by Bill John Baker.
Description: Norman, OK : University of Oklahoma Press, [2018] | In English and Cherokee. | "Published through the Recovering Languages and Literacies of the Americas initiative, supported by the Andrew W. Mellon Foundation." | Includes bibliographical references.
Identifiers: LCCN 2017024953| ISBN 978-0-8061-5986-7 (hardcover : acid-free paper) | ISBN 978-0-8061-5987-4 (softcover : acid-free paper)
Subjects: LCSH: Cherokee language—Texts. | Cherokee Indians—Folklore.
Classification: LCC PM784.A2 F44 2017 | DDC 897/.55708—dc23
LC record available at https://lccn.loc.gov/2017024953

This book is published as part of the Recovering Languages and Literacies of the Americas initiative. Recovering Languages and Literacies is generously supported by the Andrew W. Mellon Foundation.

The paper in this book meets the guidelines for permanence and durability of the Committee on Production Guidelines for Book Longevity of the Council on Library Resources, Inc. ∞

1 2 3 4 5 6 7 8 9 10

To all students of Cherokee
and especially
those who study the Cherokee syllabary

Contents

Foreword

Osiyo,

I am honored to introduce you to a groundbreaking new book authored by my friend Durbin Feeling. Durbin has committed his life to preserving the culture and heritage of our people, and he is an inspiration to all Cherokees.

Preserving our history, culture, and language is of utmost importance to the future of our Nation. Expanding and utilizing the Cherokee language is a vital part of our mission. Language is how we educate, communicate, and celebrate in our daily lives. Sadly, the Cherokee Nation has faced a shortage of literature available in the Cherokee syllabary.

For decades, the only readily available literature in our language, aside from language workbooks, has been the New Testament. The New Testament is written in a way that is difficult for Cherokees who do not read the language to understand. Reading Cherokee may be difficult for even the most fluent Cherokee speakers.

However, with this book, Durbin has achieved something special in delivering a text that we can treasure. The following pages are an account, or retelling, of Cherokee stories as told by Cherokee elders. Durbin captured the voices of our elders. He transcribed those tales and presents them here in both English and Cherokee. Simply having these stories written and preserved is certainly significant, but Durbin went further. His accounts are written in a conversational style that is critical for Cherokee language learners.

Durbin broke down each word in the stories and grammatically and phonetically analyzed them, so readers can truly understand. It allows the reader the ability to see how sentences are structured and to think like a fluent Cherokee speaker. Think of it this way: If you want to learn to speak German or Spanish or Greek or any other language, there are endless supplies of literary materials that you can study. Additionally, there are speakers and experts of those languages to explain structure and meaning to you. Before now, this was not an option for the Cherokee language, because there was no literature written in the Cherokee language.

I hope you enjoy this book and learn from it. It represents a huge leap forward, possibly the biggest we have had in a generation, in Cherokee language revitalization.

Wado,
Cherokee Nation Principal Chief Bill John Baker

Acknowledgments

I want to thank my late wife, Kathleen Pulte, for the immense help and support she provided during the years of this project. Always patient and understanding, Kathleen never complained about the time I spent working on *Cherokee Narratives*. In fact, she even encouraged me to do more!

I also want to extend special thanks to Alban Mouse, who lived in Austin, Texas, when I was there in the late 1960s and who became my first Cherokee teacher. Had I not met him, later Cherokee projects might never have taken place. Thank you, Alban, you helped me with a great deal of patience.

My thanks to David Chard, dean of the Simmons School of Education and Human Development at Southern Methodist University, for his support during my last few years before retirement. Chard appreciated the importance of diversity and took steps to promote it. I also remember with gratitude the late Marsh Terry, a longtime SMU administrator and faculty member. Terry took every opportunity to encourage me and Durbin Feeling to continue our research on the Cherokee language. He also encouraged Durbin Feeling to continue with his poetry.

William Pulte

I wish to acknowledge my mother, Kathleen Pulte, for her encouragement to work on this project. She passed away before it could be completed. Her support and encouragement remained with us until her last days and beyond.

I wish to acknowledge my wife, Claudia Pulte, for her support and patience with this project, which took time away from our family life. Claudia never complained about the long hours I spent analyzing and transcribing, although it came at a great sacrifice to our family. Our daughter Graciela's wonderful smile provided the inspiration that motivated us to press onward. I would also like to acknowledge Rob Walker at the Central University Library at SMU for providing the authors a place to meet. Rob was extremely helpful.

Gregory Pulte

Cherokee Narratives

Introduction

Cherokee Narratives is the third in a series of studies of the Cherokee language by Durbin Feeling and William Pulte. The two previous volumes are the *Cherokee-English Dictionary* (1975a) and "An Outline of Cherokee Grammar" (1975b). These volumes provide extensive information about Cherokee vocabulary and the Cherokee grammatical system, particularly about the complex structure of the Cherokee verb.

The *Cherokee-English Dictionary* includes about two thousand words. An unusual feature of the dictionary is the extensive information included in entries for verbs, which include a large number of subentries. Illustrative sentences are also provided, showing how each word is used in context. "An Outline of Cherokee Grammar" provides detailed information about many aspects of Cherokee grammar. The meanings of Cherokee prefixes and suffixes are described in depth, as are the forms in which they appear. Complete verb conjugations are included. All major Cherokee word classes and word order in phrases and sentences are also described.

Cherokee Narratives complements the two previous studies by presenting analyzed written and spoken narratives representing a number of genres. We hope that this volume will be helpful to students learning Cherokee, to speakers of Cherokee who wish to deepen their knowledge of the language, and to linguists conducting research. The narratives are also a rich source of information for students of Cherokee history and culture, as well as for those who wish to deepen their knowledge of the Cherokee syllabary, the unique writing system developed by Sequoyah.

The stories found in *Cherokee Narratives* fall into two major categories: stories related by Durbin Feeling and stories told by others and recorded and transcribed by Feeling. The stories that Feeling documented are known to members of his family in the Locust Grove area of the Cherokee Nation in northeastern Oklahoma. The additional stories were collected by Feeling from a number of speakers at a variety of locations across the Cherokee Nation and were transcribed by Feeling. Some of the narratives were related by speakers of Eastern Cherokee, providing extensive grammatical and lexical information about that variety of the Cherokee language. Thematically, a number of genres are represented, including creative writing, a biblical narrative, a procedural narrative, humor, legal language, an origin myth, a trickster tale, an account about an earlier period, and unexplained phenomena. The latter theme appears often within the narratives, reflecting an openness of Cherokees to embrace the metaphysical or spiritual world. Unlike a medium making an attempt to invoke or conjure up the paranormal, Cherokees at times experience the supernatural spontaneously.

During the early 1970s, Native American language projects became a topic of great interest among linguists. The Indian Education Act was a major impetus for these projects during the administration of President Richard M. Nixon. Policies and actions proposed by Chief W. W. Keeler provided significant support for the use and preservation of the Cherokee language. During this period, Feeling and William Pulte began to work on a variety of Cherokee language projects, including the *Cherokee-English Dictionary* (published in 1975) and Cherokee educational tools and bilingual materials for community use. Feeling and Pulte received additional support from Anna Gritts Kilpatrick, who was an advocate for funding Cherokee Nation projects, including the Cherokee bilingual education program and their development of the dictionary:

> The *Cherokee-English Dictionary* was made possible primarily by the efforts of the late Anna Gritts Kilpatrick. Anna Kilpatrick was proficient in Cherokee and a highly skilled translator from Cherokee to English. She and her husband, Jack Kilpatrick, conducted extensive research on Cherokee folklore and on other aspects of Cherokee culture. The Kilpatricks coauthored a number of books and articles. . . .
>
> During her years of research, Anna Kilpatrick had come to realize that the Cherokee language was receding and that measures had to be taken if [the language was] to retain its vitality. One of these measures, in her view, was the development of a Cherokee dictionary. She envisioned the dictionary as an aid in language learning for Cherokees who did not speak their ancestral language and for non-Cherokees who might want to study Cherokee. She believed that the availability of a dictionary would increase pride

in their language among Cherokee speakers, especially young people [who] she hoped would continue to speak their native language. (Pulte and Feeling 2002, 60)

Durbin Feeling and William Pulte began their collaboration in 1972. At that time Feeling was attending Northeastern State University in Tahlequah, Oklahoma, and working part-time for the Cherokee bilingual program at the Cherokee Nation, where William Pulte was employed full-time as staff linguist under Herbert Bacon. This period was characterized by intensive efforts to develop practical projects involving the use of native languages by teams of linguists and native language specialists. The purpose of these projects was to increase native language vitality.

The interest in Cherokee language preservation continued into the 1980s. In 1987, Wilma Mankiller was elected chief of the Cherokee Nation. During her term, Mankiller was a strong advocate for the use of the Cherokee language. Chief Mankiller understood the Cherokee language, although she did not speak it fluently. She used Cherokee phrases and sentences in her speeches and official functions. In her autobiography, Mankiller included a discussion of the use of Cherokee in rural communities and a section on the development of the Cherokee writing system by Sequoyah and its importance for the Cherokee people. Chief Mankiller had a profound appreciation for the Cherokee syllabary and the tremendous work Sequoyah engaged in to create it. To the traditionalist, nothing is more encouraging than hearing and speaking the language. To those who knew Chief Mankiller in the early days of her administration, she spoke Cherokee, albeit haltingly. In the later years, however, there was a distinct improvement. One day many people, including traditionalists, gathered at Sequoyah's old home in Sallisaw. The purpose of the gathering was to dedicate a statue of Sequoyah, and the featured speaker was Chief Mankiller. As she stepped up to the podium to make her presentation, she pleasantly surprised the audience with these words: "Osiyo nigada! Hila yitsi' Tsalagi itsiwonisgi?": "Hello, everyone. How many of you speak Cherokee?" The audience responded with smiles and uplifted hands! Chief Mankiller was an inspirational figure in the development of this book.

The Feeling and Pulte collaboration extended to the completion of the *Cherokee-English Dictionary*, the publication of the "Outline of Cherokee Grammar," and the completion of *Cherokee Narratives*. This extensive collaboration, now in its fifth decade, constitutes a major activity for both collaborators throughout their careers.

The Format of the Narratives

Each narrative is presented in four sections. The first section is interlinear, with each line shown in three ways: in the Cherokee syllabary, in a practical Roman orthography, and in a free English translation. In this section Cherokee words are translated without analysis of morphemes, the meaningful components within words. The second section is also interlinear, and includes a line of text in the Roman orthography, followed by a second line presenting a detailed analysis of the morphemes found within each word. The third section shows the entire narrative in the Cherokee syllabary, and the fourth presents the entire narrative in a free English translation.

The Cherokee Syllabary

Sequoyah devised the Cherokee syllabary in the early nineteenth century. His achievement is one of the greatest feats in the history of literacy. Although Sequoyah apparently did not speak English, he observed non-Indians reading and realized that the printed symbols represented English words in a printed form. He then began to construct a writing system for Cherokee. He spent more than ten years developing his system, which he completed prior to 1820. As Loren Nussbaum points out, "His system differed from an alphabet in that each syllable, rather than each sound of the language, was symbolized. These efforts first brought him ridicule, scorn, and worse. In 1821 his writing system received public recognition and acceptance from Cherokees. In the following years, he received acclaim and admiration from whites in both America and Europe" (Feeling and Pulte 1975a, xvii). In *Cherokee Narratives*, each narrative is shown twice in the Cherokee syllabary: in the first interlinear section of each narrative and in the third section where the entire story is shown in a block in the syllabary, as noted above.

Pitch

Each syllable of a Cherokee word must be pronounced with a specific pitch. Pitch is shown in the Roman orthography in the morpheme-by-morpheme section of each narrative. The pitch of a given syllable is indicated by a raised number or numbers following that syllable.

Syllables that are not followed by raised numbers have a low-level pitch. Note that a 23 sequence indicates that the preceding syllable has a pitch that begins at the relatively low pitch represented by 2 and rises to the higher pitch represented by 3. The reverse sequence, 32, represents a pitch beginning at 3 and falling to 2. A syllable followed by 1 exhibits a pitch falling from the low-level pitch of 2 to a lower pitch. Pitches falling from 2 to 1 are indicated by 1; it should be noted that 1 occurs only as the end point of a fall from 2. High-level pitches are represented by 3, and extra-high pitches by 4.

It would have been possible to represent pitch in Cherokee by the use of diacritics rather than superscript numbers; however, the latter were employed in the *Cherokee-English Dictionary,* and we have continued their use here in *Cherokee Narratives.*

Long and Short Vowels

Cherokee vowels are either long or short. Throughout the narratives, short vowels are indicated by an underscore. Long vowels are not marked: a vowel without an underscore is long. In the two previous volumes, short vowels were marked by dots beneath the vowels. The underscores in this volume are used in the same way.

Labels and Abbreviations

The morpheme-by-morpheme literal English translation found in the second interlinear section of each narrative uses a number of labels for prefixes and suffixes. They are listed below.

Prefixes and Suffixes

The following prefixes and suffixes are used throughout the book. The meanings of some, which might not otherwise be clear, are provided as well.

Label	Meaning
1	first person
2	second person
3	third person
Aff	affirmative: affirms an answer to a question
Ag	agentive
Caus	causative
Comp	completive: indicates completion of the action of the verb
Dat	dative: shows that the action of the verb is undertaken on behalf of someone

Dir	directional
Dl	dual
Dst	distance with direction: used when the subject of the verb is standing some distance away, facing the speaker
Emp	emphatic
Ex	exclusive
exP	experienced past: used when the speaker directly experienced the action of the verb
Fut	future
Hab	habitual
imP	immediate past: indicates that an action referred to has just occurred
Imp	imperative
Inf	infinitive
Inst	instrumental
Lat	lateral: used when the person spoken of is positioned with his or her side turned to the speaker, or is moving left or right of the speaker
Loc	location
Neg	negative
nonF	nonfactual: used to negate a verb or to express conditionality
Num	numerical
Ord	ordinal
Pas	passive
Pl	plural
Pos	possessive
Pres	present
Prog	progressive
Pst	past tense prefix
Ques	question
recP	recent past
Refl	reflexive
Rel	relative: introduces a relative clause, as well as other kinds of subordinate clauses
Rep	repetitive
repP	reported past: employed when the speaker has learned indirectly about the action or state referred to by the verb

Spec	specified action: used when the activity expressed by the verb has been specified or is understood
Tr	translocative: indicates that the person spoken of is facing away, or moving away in verbs of motion

Note that the following abbreviations are used in the analysis of subject and object prefixes of verbs:

sub	subject
obj	object
sg	singular
pl	plural

Ball of Fire

Durbin Feeling

In "Ball of Fire," Durbin Feeling connects the human world to the animal world. The story reflects the sensitivity of animals to the spirit world and how animals inform humans of the spirit world.

ᏣᏉᏫᏘᏏᏛ	ᎢᎸᎭᏛᎸ	57	ᏧᏕᏘᏴᏌᏗᏓ	Ꮭ	ᎠᏏ	ᏗᏁᎦᎵᏍᎩ
jagwatvsidisv	ilvhdlv	57	judetiyvsadisv	hla	asi	dinagalisgi
when I was growing up	somewhere	57	the year of	not	yet	electricity

ᏲᏙᎩᏏᎳᏕ	ᎤᎨᏅᏒ	ᏒᏈᏍᏕ	ᎤᎩᎸᏇᏫᏗ	ᎡᏒ	ᎾᎢ
yidogisilade	ogenvsv	galhjode	ogilvkwdi	gesv	na?v
we had no wiring	in our home	house	we liked	was	near

ᎢᏐᎦᏓᎵ	ᏧᏁᎥᏒ	ᎤᎸᎳᏍᏗ	ᏗᏓᏴᎳᏢᏍᎩ	ᎤᏂᎲ	ᎠᎴ
ijogadali	junenvsv	wogedasdi	didayvlatvsgi	unihv	ale
apart	their home	for us to go there	television	they had	and

ᏧᎵᏏᎲᏓᎬ	ᎢᏳᏍᏗ	ᎢᎸᏍᎩ	ᎢᏯᏓᏁᎸ	ᎳᏁᏜᎶᏏᎲ
julisihnvdagwu	iyusdi	ilvsgi	iyadanelv	danadlosihihv
nightly just	almost	a few	families	they would come and gather

ᏗᏓᏴᎳᏢᏍᎩ	ᏧᏁᏚᏫᎯᏘᎢ	ᏌᏩ	ᏒᎦᎷᏗ
didayvlatvsgi	junagatostanihlv?i	sagwu	yuwagodi
television	for them to come	one	time

RZⰟ	⊖ⰻᎩMᏳ		KᏆᏙᏒ	ᎩᏓ	ᏫⰯS4ᏗⰉ	ᏂSⱲⰻE
svnoyi	wiʔogiluhja		jogenvsv	gitli	usgasehdigwu	nigawesgv
midnight	when we returned		at home	dog	fiercely	was uttering

ᏝⰏ⊖ⰻE	ⰒᏔⱱⰉ	ᎪⱣⰻᏗ	DⱲTB	ᏣᎪᏳᏗⰻᏗ
dasuhwisgv	utloyigwu	gohusdi	agwuʔiyv	jagowatisgo
it was barking	just as	something	here close by	as if he were seeing it

ⰒᏔⰟ	⊖ᏋᏆⱤ	DᏁᎷᏳⰻE	DᏆ
uhloyi	nadvnehv	anelugisgv	age
the same	he was doing	it was chasing after it	over there

TᎬⰟⰒᏏᏝ	ZⱲꝺ
iyudanvhida	nogwule
distance	and then

ᏗDCⱱⰻᏗ	DⱲTB	TSMAT
diʔajvsgo	agwuʔiyv	igaʔluhgoʔi
he would turn back	here close by	he would return

Dꝺ	ᏝⰏ⊖ⰻE	ᏂᎬᎪⰻVT
ale	dasuhwisgv	nigvwasdoʔi
and	his barking	it would continue

Ꮭ	ⰒCTS	ᏂᎪS4ⰻᏞᏗꝺ
hla	udliʔiga	yojagasesdanele
not	much	we didn't pay much attention to it

TEⰟ	iⱲᎩ	ꝗᏋᏁᏔ
igvyi	vsgi	nudvnela
at first	that	when it did that

ⰒᎩCᏞⱲᎩh	ⰒᏒ	ⰒᏔⰟ	ꝗᏋᏁᎦ	DᏁᎷᏳⰻᏗ	DᏆ
ugijvdasgini	usv	utloyi	nudvnelv	anelugisgo	age
but the next day	night	same	he did it	he would chase after it	over there

TGᏉᎣᎤᎤᏞ	ᏃᏬᎩ	ᏗᎠᏣᎥᏍᎪ	ᏃᏬᎩ	TᎠᏄᎷᎩᏍᎪ
iyudanvhida	nogwule	di?ajvsgo	nogwule	i?anelugisgo
distance	and then	he would turn back	and then	again he would chase after it

ᎤᏠᏱᎬ	GᏍᏈᏫ	ᏱᎦ	ᎤᏍᏓᏩᏗᏍᏗ?Ꭲ
utloyigwu	yuduliha	kilo	usdawadvsdi?i
just as though	if he wanted	someone	to follow him

TEᏎᏃ	ᎦᏌᏬ
igvyihno	wahgagwu
and at first	just a cow

DᎧᏎᏯ	ᎠᎠᏍᏗᎬᎤ	ᏝᏓᎦ	SᎠᏞT	ᏱᎡᏐᏫ	ᎣᎨᎵᏍᎥ?T
aleyigi	gohusdigwu	nudale	ganahla?i	yi?edoha	ogelisv?i
or	just something	something else	stock	it may be roaming	we all thought

ᏃᏬ	ᎤᏍᎼᎤᏃᎦ	RᎥᏞ	ᏪᎮᎡ	DᎣ	SGᏬ	ᎤᎡSᎠ
nogwu	ugatvhdanelv	edoda	jigesv	ale	galogwe	usvdena
then	it made him curious	my father	who was	and	gun	big barrel

ᎠᏴᏘ	SᏈKS	KᎠᏞᏞᎣCZ	DBZ	RᎥᏞᏍ
wuyvhv	galihjode	josdadahnvtlihno	ayvhno	edodale
he went and got	in the house	and my brother	and I	my dad also

ᏃᏬ	ᎣᎮᏍᎤᏞᎦᎼR	ᏱC	ᏱCZ	ᏃᏬ	ᎤᏍGᎵᎤ
nogwu	ojisdawadvsv	gitli	gitlihno	nogwu	udelohosa
then	we followed it	dog	and dog	whenever	when he realized

ᎣᎮᏍᎤᏞᎦSE		ᎠᎮᏍᎠTR	Ꮭ	ᏃᏬ	ᏎᎠᎣC4	DB
ojisdawadegv		winigaya?isv	hla	nogwu	yidi?ujvse	ayv
that we were following him		he kept going	no	now	he didn't turn back	I

ᏃᏬ	KT	TᎮᎮT	ᎣᎮᏍᎤᏞᎦᎼR	DᎣ
nogwu	jo?i	iyoji?i	ojisdawadvsv	ale
then	three	of us	we all followed him	and

ᎢᏳᎵᏛ	ᏩᏂᎤᏗ
ilvhdlv	ginutdi
somewhere around	one-fourth

ᎢᏳᏣᏟᏗ	ᎢᏳᏓᏅᎯᏓ	ᎤᏂᎩᏒ	ᎪᎱᏍᏗ	ᏣᎨᎯᏐ	ᎢᏳᏍᏗ
iyuhliloda	iyudanvhida	uhnigisv	gohusdi	jakehiso	iyusdi
of a mile	in distance	he went	something	as if he were chasing it	just as

ᎤᏔᎾ	ᏚᏍᎦ	ᎠᎴᎯᎬ	ᎤᏕᏲᎸ	ᎠᎴ	ᏇᎳᏗ	ᏔᏗᎭ	ᏪᏓᏑᏫᏍᎪ
utana	jusga	dluhgv	udeyolv	ale	galvladi	ididla	widasuwisgo
big	oak	tree	he went around	and	up	toward	he was barking

ᎤᎵᎪᎲᏍᏗᏃ	ᎨᏒ	ᎠᎴ	ᏧᎵᏍᏚᏬᏐᎲ	ᎨᏒ	ᏕᏕᎸᎬ	ᎠᎴ
uligohvsdihno	gesv	ale	julisduwosohnv	gesv	dedluhgv	ale
in the fall time	it was	and	leaves had fallen completely	it was	trees	and

ᏒᏃᏱ	ᎡᎯ	ᏅᏓ	ᎢᏍᎫ	ᏔᎦᎯ
svnoyi	ehi	nvda	vsgwu	igahi
midnight	sun	dweller	also	brightly

ᎤᏗᏍᏛꞋᎢ	ᎠᏎᏃ	ᏙᎦᏕᏲᎲ
utisdv?i	asehno	ogadeyohnv
it was shining	but	we went completely around

ᏚᏍᎦ	ᎠᎴᎯᎬ	ᎲᏃ	ᎢᏍᎫ	ᎪᎱᏍᏗ
jusga	dluhgv	hlano	vsgwu	gohusdi
oak	tree	and not	also	something

ᎤᎩᎸ	ᏲᏥᎪꞋᎡ	ᎩᏟᏃ
uki?lv	yojigo?e	gitlihno
perched on	we didn't see	and dog

ᏂᎬᏩᏍᏛ	ᎤᏍᎦᏎᏗ	ᏂᎦᏪᏍᎬ	ᏓᏑᎯᏍᎬꞋᎢ
nigvwasdv	usgasehdi	nigawesgv	dasuhwisgv?i
continued	fiercely	uttering	barking

ᎣᎦᏢᏲᎳᏃ	ᎪᎱᏍᏗ	ᎣᏥᎪᏩᏛᏗ	ᎡᏙᏓ	ᏥᎨᏒ	ᏃᏊ
ogatlvyolahno	gohusdi	ojigowahtvhdi	edoda	jigesv	nogwu
and when we gave up	something	for us to see	my dad	who was	then

ᏗᏡᎬ	ᎦᎸᎳᏗ	ᎢᏗᏢ	ᏫᏚᎵᏐᏍᏔᏅ	ᎤᏒᏕᎾ	ᎦᎶᏇ	ᎠᎴ
didluhgv	galvladi	ididlv	widulisostanv	usvdena	galogwe	ale
at tree	up	toward	he aimed	big barrel	gun	and

ᏫᏚᏍᏓᏲᏢ	ᎩᎳᏊᏃ	ᎢᏴᏓ	ᎦᏌᏆᎸ	ᎠᏓᏪᎳᎩᏍᎩ
widusdayohlv	kilagwuhno	iyvda	gasagwalv	adawelagisgi
he shot	and just then	you could say	around	flaming

ᎠᎳᏍᎦᎸᏗ	ᎢᎩᏓ	ᏭᎵᏌᎳᏓᏅ	ᎦᎸᎶ	ᎢᏗᏢ	ᎠᎴ	ᎢᎸᏍᎩᏊ
alasgalvdi	ikida	wulisaladanv	galvlo	ididlv	ale	ilvsgigwu
a ball the	size of	it went up	sky	toward	and	just a few

ᎢᎳᏏᏗ	ᎢᏴ	ᏭᏍᎪᎸᏨ	ᎾᎯᏳ	ᎤᏑᎵᎪᏨ	ᎩᏟ	ᎤᏍᎦᏎᏗ
ilasihdi	iyv	wusgolvjv	nahiyu	usuligojv	gitli	usgasehdi
feet	distance	it faded	from then on	he quit	dog	fiercely

ᏂᎦᏪᏍᎬ	ᏓᏑᏫᏍᎬᎢ
nigawesgv	dasuhwisgvʔi
uttering	his barking

Morpheme by Morpheme

j-agw-atvs-idis-v
Rel 1 grow-up Inc exP

ilvh^{3}dlv^{4} 57 j-u-deti̲yv^{3}sa̲di^{3}s-v^{4}
somewhere 57 Pst 3 year-of exP

hla^{3} asi^{3} di-n-agalis-g-i
not yet Pl Pl to-lighten Prog Ag

yi̲-d-o^{23}gi^{3}-sila̲d-e^{3}
nonF Pl they-and-I connect repP

og-env³s-v⁴ galhjo²³de ogi-lv²³kwdi ges-v³ naʔv³
they-and-I home exP house they-and-I like be exP near

ijo-gadali j-u-n-e³nvs-v w-og-edas-di di-d-a-yvlatvs-g-i
they-and-I apart Pl 3 Pl home exP Tr they-and-I go Inf Pl Pl 3 in-view Prog Ag

u-ni-h-v
3 Pl have exP

ạle³
and

julisihnvdạgwu iyu⁴sdi ịlv⁴sgi iyạdanelv d-a-n-ạdlosi²³hị³h-v³
nightly just almost a-few family Pl 3 Pl gather exP

di-d-a-yvlatvs-g-i
Pl Pl 3 in-view Prog Ag

j-u-n-agato²³s-tạ³n-ihl-v⁴ʔi sagwu³ iyụ³wagodi
Inf 3 Pl watch Inf come exP one time

svno²³yi wị³-ʔogi-luhj-a j-og-e³nvs-v
midnight Tr they-and-I arrive imP Pl they-and-I home exP

gitli
dog

usgasehdi²³-gwu nị-g-ạwes-g-v³
fiercely just Lat 3 utter Prog exP

d-a-sụhwis-g-v³ uhlo³yi-gwu gohu⁴sdi a³gwụiyv³ j-a-gowati²³s-g-o
Pl 3 bark Prog exP same just something close-by Rel 3 see Prog Hab

uhlo³yi n-a-dv³neh-v³ a³-n-elu²³gi³²s-g-v³ ạ³ge
same Spec 3 do exP 3 Pl chase Prog exP over-there

iyu³dạnvhi⁴d-a nogwụ³-le³ dị³-ạ-jv³s-g-o³
at-distance then and Dst 3 turn-back Prog Hab

agwuiyv   i^{23}-g-a$?^3$luh^{3}g-o-$?$i
here-close-by   Rep arrive Prog Hab

ale^3 d-a-suhwis-g-v^3 ni-g-v^{23}wa^{3}sd-o^{4}i   hla^3 udli$^{3;23}$i^{23}ga^4
and   Pl 3 bark Prog exP   Lat 1 continue Hab   not   much

y-oj-a^{3}gasesda^{32}n-el-e^3 igvyi^4
nonF they-and-I pay-attention Dat repP   at-first

vsgi   n-u-dv^{3}ne^{4}l-a
that   Spec 3 do recP

ugijv^{23}da-sgi^{3}ni   usv^4 uhlo^{4}yi   n-u^3-dv^{3}nel-v^3 a^3-n-elu^{23}gi^{32}s-g-o^3
next-day however   night   same   Spec 3 do exP   3 Pl chase Prog Hab

a^{3}ge^4 iyu^{3}danvhi^{4}da   di^3-$?$a-jv^{3}s-g-o^3
over-there   distance   Dst 3 turn-back Prog Hab

nogwu^3-le   i^3-$?$a^3-nelu^{23}gi^{32}s-g-o^3 uhlo^{3}yi-gwu   y-u-du^{3}li^{4}h-a
then and   Rep 3 chase Prog Hab   same just   nonF 3 want Pres

kilo^3 u-sdawadvs-di$^4?$i   igvyi^4-hno
someone   3 follow Inf   at-first and

wahga-gwu
cow just

ale^{3}yi^{4}gi   gohu^{23}sdi-gwu   nu^{23}da^{3}le   ganahla$^3?$i   yi^3-$?$e-do^{3}h-a
or   something just   different   livestock   nonF be-there Pres

og-eli^{32}s-v$^{23}?$i   no^{23}gwu   ug-advh-da^{32}n-el-v^3
they-and-I think exP   then   3 curious Caus Dat exP

e-doda   ji-ges-v^3 ale^3 galogwe^3 usvde^{4}na
1Pos father   Rel be exP   and   gun   big-barrel

w-u-yvh-v^3 galihjo^{23}de   j-osd-adahnv^{23}hli-hno   ayv^3-hno   e-doda^3-le^3
Tr 3 go-get exP   house-in   Pl he-and-I brother and   I and   1Pos father also

no^{23}gwu oji-sda^{32}w$\underline{a}$dv^{3}s-v^3
then   they-and-I follow exP

gitli gitli^3-hno no^{23}gwu
dog   dog and   whenever

u-deloho^{4}s-a   oji-sdaw$^{32}\underline{a}$de^3-g-v   w$\underline{i}$-n$\underline{i}$-g-aya^{3}ʔis-v
3 realize recP   they-and-I follow Prog exP   Tr Lat 3 go exP

hla^3 no^{23}gwu y$\underline{i}$-d$\underline{i}^3$-ʔujv^{3}s-e^3
no   now   nonF Dst turn repP

ayv   no^{23}gwu
I   then

j$\underline{o}$ʔi $\underline{i}$-yo^{3}ji^{4}ʔi   oji-sda^{32}w$\underline{a}$dv^{3}s-v^3
three   in-number   they-and-I follow Prog exP

ale   ilvh^{3}dlv   ginu^{4}tvdi
and   somewhere-around   one-fourth

iyu^{3}hlilo^{4}da iyu^{3}d$\underline{a}$nvhi^{4}da u-hn$\underline{i}^3$gis-v^3 gohu^{4}sdi j-a-ke^{23}hi^{32}s-o iyu^{4}sdi
of-a-mile   in-distance   3 start exP   something   as-if 3 chase   just-as
                                                                      Hab

u^{3}t$\underline{a}$na jusga dluh^{3}gv u-de^{23}yo^{32}l-v^3 $\underline{a}$le^3 g$\underline{a}$lv^{23}l$\underline{a}$di
big   oak   tree   3 go-around exP   and   up

$\underline{i}$di^{3}dla w$\underline{i}$-d-$\underline{a}$-s$\underline{u}^3$w$\underline{i}$s-g-o^3
toward   Tr Pl 3 bark Prog Hab

u-ligohvs-di-hno
3 fall-in Inf and

ges-v^3 ale   j-u-lisdu^{23}wo^{32}s-$\underline{o}$hn-v
be exP   and   Pst 3 fall Comp exP

ges-v   de-dluh^{3}gv   a̲le^3
be exP   Pl tree   and

svnoyi   eh-i   nvda
evening   be Ag   sun

vsgwu^3 iga^{4}hi   u-tisd-v^{23}ʔi   ase^{3}hno   og-ade^{3}y-ohn-v^3
also   brightly   3 shine exP   but   they-and-I go-around Comp exP

jusga
oak

dluh^{3}gv   hla̲-no^3 vsgwu^3 gohu^{4}sdi   uki?l-v^3 y-oji^3-ogo̲?-e^3
tree   not and   also   something   on exP   nonF they-and-I see repP

gitli^3-hno   ni̲-g-vwasd-v^3 usga^{3}sehdi   ni̲-g-a̲wes-g-v^3
dog and   ni 3 continue exP   fiercely   ni 3 utter Prog exP

d-a-suhwis-g-v^4?i   og-a̲hlvyo^{3}l-a̲-hno   gohu^{4}sdi
Pl 3 bark Prog exP   they-and-I give-up recP and   something

oji-gowahtvh^3-di
they-and-I see Inf

e-doda   ji̲ -ges-v^3 no^{23}gwu
1Pos father   Rel be exP   then

di̲dluh^{3}gv   galv^{3}la̲di   i̲di^{3}dlv   wi̲-d-u-li̲so^{23}sta̲^{3}n-v^3
tree   up   toward   Tr Pl 3 aim exP

usvde^{4}na   ga̲logwe^3
big-barrel   gun

ale   wi̲-d-u-sda̲yohl-v^3 kila̲-gwu^3-hno
and   Tr Pl 3 shoot exP   then just and

i̲yv^{4}da   gasa̲^{3}gwa̲lv
time-frame   round

a-da-welagis-g-i	alasgaldi	ikida
3 Refl flame Prog Ag	ball	size

w-u-lisalada^{32}n-v^{3}	galvlo^{3}	idi^{3}dlv	ale^{3}	ilv^{23}sgi-gwu
Tr 3 go-up exP	sky	toward	and	few just

i^{3}lasihdi	iyv^{3}	w-u-sgo^{23}lv^{32}j-v	nahi^{3}yu	u-suligo^{3}j-v^{3}
foot	distance	Tr 3 fade exP	thereafter	3 quit exP

gitli	usga^{3}sehdi
dog	fiercely

ni-g-awes-g-v^{3}	d-a-suhwis-g-v^{4}?i
ni 3 utter Prog exP	Pl 3 bark Prog exP

Syllabary

ᏣᏆᏛᏏᏗᏒ ᎢᎸᎵ 57 ᏧᎦᏘᏴᏌᏗᏒ Ꮭ ᎠᏏ ᏗᎾᎦᎵᏍᎩ ᏅᏙᎩᏏᎳᎦ ᎣᎨᎤᏒ ᎦᎵᏦᏕ ᎣᎩᏄᏉᏗ ᎨᏒ ᎾᎥ ᎢᏦᎦᏓᎵ ᏧᏁᎤᏒ ᏬᎨᏓᏍᏗ ᏗᏓᏴᎳᏛᏍᎩ ᎤᏂᎲ ᎠᎴ ᏧᎵᏏᎤᏓᏊ ᎢᏳᏍᏗ ᎢᎸᏍᎩ ᎢᏯᏓᏁᎸ ᏓᎾᏌᏏᎯᎲ ᏗᏓᏴᎳᏛᏍᎩ ᏧᎾᎦᏙᏍᎳᏂᎵᎢ ᏌᏊ ᎢᏳᏩᎪᏗ ᎡᏃᏅ ᏫᎣᎩᎷᏣ ᏦᎨᎤᏒ ᎩᏟ ᎤᏍᎦᏎᏗᏊ ᏂᎦᏪᏍᎬ ᏓᏑᏫᏍᎬ ᎤᏌᏅᏊ ᎪᎱᏍᏗ ᎠᏊᎢᏴ ᏣᎪᏩᏘᏍᎪ ᎤᏌᏅ ᎾᏛᏁᎲ ᎠᏁᎷᎩᏍᎬ ᎠᎨ ᎢᏳᏓᎤᎯᏓ ᏃᏊᎴ ᏗᎠᏨᏍᎪ ᎠᏊᎢᏴ ᎢᎦᎷᎪᎢ ᎠᎴ ᏓᏑᏫᏍᎬ ᏂᎬᏩᏍᏙᎢ Ꮭ ᎤᏟᎢᎦ ᏱᏟᎦᏎᏍᏓᏁᎴ ᎢᎬᏅ ᎥᏍᎩ ᏄᏛᏁᎳ ᎤᎩᏨᏓᏍᎩᏂ ᎤᏒ ᎤᏌᏅ ᏄᏛᏁᎸ ᎠᏁᎷᎩᏍᎪ ᎠᎨ ᎢᏳᏓᎤᎯᏓ ᏃᏊᎴ ᏗᎠᏨᏍᎪ ᏃᏊᎴ ᎢᎠᏁᎷᎩᏍᎪ ᎤᏌᏅᏊ ᏳᎦᎵᏐ ᎩᎶ ᎤᏍᏓᏩᏛᏍᏗᎢ ᎢᎬᏅᏃ ᏩᎦᏊ ᎠᎴᏅᎩ ᎪᎱᏍᏗᏊ ᏄᏓᎴ ᎦᎾᏝᎢ ᏅᎡᏙᏐ ᎣᎨᎵᏒᎢ ᏃᏊ ᎤᎦᏛᏓᏁᎸ ᎡᏙᏓ ᏥᎨᏒ ᎠᎴ ᎦᎶᏇ ᎤᏒᎦᎾ ᏭᏴᎲ ᎦᎵᏦᏕ ᏦᏍᏓᏓᎤᏟᏃ ᎠᏴᏃ ᎡᏙᏓᎴ ᏃᏊ ᎣᏥᏍᏓᏩᏛᏒ ᎩᏟ ᎩᏟᏃ ᏃᏊ ᎤᎦᎶᎰᏌ ᎣᏥᏍᏓᏩᎦᎬ ᏫᏂᎦᏯᎢᏒ Ꮭ ᏃᏊ ᏅᏗᎤᏨᏎ ᎠᏴ ᏃᏊ ᏦᎢ ᎢᏱᏥᎢ ᎣᏥᏍᏓᏩᏛᏒ ᎠᎴ ᎢᎸᎵ ᎩᏄᏛᏗ ᎢᏳᏟᎶᏓ ᎢᏳᏓᎤᎯᏓ ᎤᏂᎩᏒ ᎪᎱᏍᏗ ᏣᎨᎯᏐ ᎢᏳᏍᏗ ᎤᏔᎾ ᏧᏍᏚ ᏈᎬ ᎤᎦᏱᎸ ᎠᎴ ᎦᎸᎳᏗ ᎢᏗᎲ ᏫᏓᏑᏫᏍᎪ ᎤᎵᎪᎲᏍᏗᏃ ᎨᏒ ᎠᎴ ᏧᎵᏍᏚᏬᏐᎤ ᎨᏒ ᎦᎵᎬ ᎠᎴ ᎡᏃᏅ ᎡᎯ ᎤᏓ ᎥᏍᏊ ᎢᎦᎯ ᎤᏘᏍᏛᎢ ᎠᏎᏃ ᎣᎦᎦᏱᎤ ᏧᏍᏚ ᏈᎬ ᏝᏃ ᎥᏍᏊ ᎪᎱᏍᏗ ᎤᎩᎸ ᏱᏥᎪᎡ ᎩᏟᏃ ᏂᎬᏩᏍᏛ ᎤᏍᎦᏎᏗ ᏂᎦᏪᏍᎬ ᏓᏑᏫᏍᎬᎢ ᎣᎦᎵᏱᎳᏃ ᎪᎱᏍᏗ ᎣᏥᎪᏩᏛᏗ ᎡᏙᏓ ᏥᎨᏒ ᏃᏊ ᏗᏈᎬ ᎦᎸᎳᏗ ᎢᏗᏢ ᏫᏚᎵᏐᏍᏔᎤ ᎤᏒᎦᎾ ᎦᎶᏊ ᎠᎴ ᏫᏚᏍᏓᏱᎵ ᎩᎳᏊᏃ ᎢᏴᏓ ᎦᏌᏆᎸ ᎠᏓᏪᎳᎩᏍᎩ ᎠᎳᏍᎦᎸᏗ ᎢᎩᏓ ᏭᎵᏌᎳᏓᏅ ᎦᎸᎶ ᎢᏗᏢ ᎠᎴ ᎢᎸᏍᎩᏊ ᎢᎳᏏᏗ ᎢᏴ ᏭᏍᎪᎸᏨ ᎾᎯᏳ ᎤᏑᎵᎪᏨ ᎩᏟ ᎤᏍᎦᏎᏗ ᏂᎦᏪᏍᎬ ᏓᏑᏫᏍᎬᎢ

English

When I was growing up, I guess it was about the year 1957, we did not have electricity in our house yet. We really liked to visit our neighbors. They had a television, and we would go just about every evening. A few families would come to watch the television. One night when we returned home, our dog was barking fiercely as if he were barking at some animal close by. He would run after it and then run back, barking all along. We didn't pay much attention to him that first night. And the next night he did the same thing. He would bark, run after whatever it was, and then run back as if he wanted someone to follow him. At first we thought it was just a cow or some other animal. But when he did it the second time, my dad got curious and went in the house and got our shotgun. So, my dad, my brother, and I followed the dog. When the dog noticed that we were willing to follow him, he kept going and did not run back. We followed the dog for about a quarter mile, and he acted like he was after something; then suddenly he stopped at the big oak tree, and he barked as he circled the tree. It was in the fall, and the leaves had fallen, and the moon was shining brightly. We went around the oak tree, but we did not see anything up in the tree. The dog kept barking fiercely. When we could not see anything up there, my dad aimed up toward the branch and fired a shot. Instantly, a ball of fire about the size of a basketball lifted up from somewhere in the tree and faded out a few feet above the tree. After that, the dog did not bark like that anymore.

Cat Meowing

Durbin Feeling

In "Cat Meowing," Durbin Feeling tells of a cat who brought news that an old man was dying. This story demonstrates how the behavior of animals reflects their sensitivity to the paranormal spirit world.

ᎦᏅᏓᏗᏍᎪ	ᏌᏊ	ᎢᏳᏩᎪᏗ	ᏥᏧᏣᏊ	ᏥᎨᏒ	ᎩᎶ
ganvdadisgo	sagwu	iyuwakdi	jichujagwu	jigesv	kilo
I remember	one	time	I just a boy	it was	someone

ᎤᏛᏐᏅ	ᎤᏢᎬ	ᎢᎸᏍᎩ	ᏧᏒᎯᏓ	ᎤᏢᏨ	ᎠᎴ	ᏂᏚᎵᏏᏂᏒ
utvsohnv	udlvgv	ilvsgi	jusvhida	udlvjv	ale	nidulsihnisv
old man	he was sick	a few	days	he remained sick	and	every night

ᎤᏣᏙᎬ	ᏂᎬᏩᏍᏛ	ᎥᏍᎩᏕᎲ	Ꮩ	ᎠᏎ	ᏄᎵᏍᏔᏁ	ᏭᏲᎱᏒᎮᏃ
ujadogv	nigvwsdv	vsgidehv	do	ase	nulstane	wuyohus-vhehno
he got worse	it seemed	well that	truly	perhaps	it happened	because he died

ᎢᎸᏍᎩ	ᏫᏄᏒᏝ	ᎾᎯᏳᎮᏃ	ᏥᎨᏒ	ᎤᏟ	ᎢᎦ	ᎡᎳᏗᏊ
ilvsgi	winusvhla	nahiyuhehno	jigesv	udli	iga	eladigwu
a few	days later	back then	when it was	mostly	quantity	just on foot

ᎣᏤᏙᎯ	ᎨᏒ	ᎢᎸᏢ	ᏲᎨᎾ	ᎠᎴ	ᎥᏍᏊ	ᎩᎶ	ᏳᏢᏣ
ojedohi	gesv	iluhdlv	yogena	ale	vsgwu	kilo	yudlvja
we walked	was	somewhere	when he went	and	also	someone	when he got sick

ᏴᏫ	ᎾᎥ	ᏂᏚᎾᏓᎸ	ᏓᎾᏓᏩᏛᎯᏙᎲ
yvwi	na?v	nidunadalv	danadawatvhidohv
people	close	together	they visited each other

ᎠᎴᏱᎩ	ᏓᏂᏨᏓᏆᏍᎬ	ᎤᏢᎩ	ᎠᏂᎦᏘᏗᎯᎲ
aleyigi	danijvdagwasgv	udlvgi	aniktidihihv
or	they would stay night after night	sick person	they would come and stay with him

ᏗᏰᎦᏟ	ᏗᏆᏍᏙᏃ	ᏓᏂᏃᎯᎲ	ᎤᏢᎩ	ᏗᎦᏅᎬ
dihyegahli	digwsdohno	danihnohihv	udlvgi	diganvgv
quilts	pillows	they brought	sick person	where he lay

ᏒᏃᏱᏃ	ᏱᏄᎵᏍᏔᎾ	ᎤᎿᏊ	ᎠᏂᏟᏅᎬ	ᎢᎦᏓ
svnoyihno	yinulstana	uhnagwu	anihlinvgv	igada
and midnight	when it became	just there	they would sleep	some

ᎦᏙᎯᏊ	ᏓᏂᏰᏍᏛᎥᏍᎬ	ᎪᎩ	ᏱᎩ
gadohigwu	daniyesdv?vsgv	gogi	yigi
just on ground	they would bed down	summer	if it was

ᏚᏂᎦᏒᏍᏙᎢ	ᏱᎩ	ᏙᏌ
duniksvsdo?i	yigi	dosa
they would make smoke	maybe	mosquito

ᏚᏂᏖᏍᏙᎢ	ᏃᏊᎴ	ᏓᎾᏓᏁᏟᏴᏍᎬ	ᎠᏂᎦᏘᏗᏍᎬ
dunitesdv?i	nogwule	danadanedliyvsgv	aniktidisgv
as they repel them	and also	they would alternate	staying up with him

ᎤᏢᎩ	ᎥᏍᎩᏃ	ᏄᎵᏍᏔᏂᏙᎸ	ᎯᎠ	ᏥᏥᏃᎮᎭ	ᎡᎳᏗ
udlvgi	vsgihno	nulstanidolv	hi?a	jijinoheha	eladi
the sick person	and that is	it happened	this	what I am telling	on foot

ᎣᏣᏂᎩᏍᎬ	ᏧᏪᏅᏒ	ᎣᏤᎪ	ᎤᎿ	ᏗᎦᏅᎬ
ojanigisgv	juwenvsv	ojego	uhna	diganhgv
we would start out	his home	we would go	there	where he lay

ᏢᏃ
dlvhno
and somewhere

ᏔᎵ	ᎢᏳᏟᎶᏓ	ᎢᏳᏓᏅᎯᏓ	ᎨᏒ	ᏦᎨᏅᏒ	ᏂᏛᎯᎩᏓ
ta?li	iyudhliloda	iyudanvhida	gesv	jogenvsv	nidvhigida
two	miles	in distance	it was	our home	starting point

ᎦᏅᏓᏗᏍᎪᎢᏃ	ᏬᎩᏨᏓᏋ	Ꮲ	ᏔᎵᎭ	ᎢᏳᏩᎧᏗ
ganvdadisgo?ihno	wogijvdagwv	dlv	taliha	iyuwakdi
I remember	we spent the night	about	two	times

ᏃᏊᏃ	Ꮲ	ᏅᎩᏁ	ᏒᏃᏱ	Ꮭ	ᏲᎨᏅᏎ
nogwuhno	dlv	nvhgine	svnoyi	hla	yogenvse
and then	some time	the fourth	night	not	we did not go

ᎡᎵᏏᏍᎩᏂ	ᏧᏪᏅᏒ	ᎣᎨᏅᏒ	ᎠᎴ	ᎣᎩᏒᎸ
elisisgini	juwenvsv	ogenvsv	ale	ogisvlv
but grandmother	her home	we went	and	we spent the night

ᏃᏊᏃ	ᎡᎵᏏ	ᏥᎨᏒ
nogwuhno	elisi	jigesv
and then	grandmother	who was

ᎣᎦᏛᏅᎢᏍᏓᏁᎸ	ᎣᎩᏒᏍᏗ	ᏚᏰᏍᏛᏂᏙᎸ	ᎣᎦᏅᏢᏗ
ogadvnv?isdanelv	ogisvsdi	duyesdvnidolv	oganhdlvdi
she prepared for us	our beds	she laid pallets around	for us to bed down

ᎣᎦᏅᏢᎾᏃ	ᏃᏊ	Ꮩ	ᏃᎦᏛᏁᎳ	ᎠᏏ
oganhdlvnahno	nogwu	to	nogadvnela	asi
after we lay down	then	quiet	we became	before

ᏫᏃᎩᎵᏅᏨᎾᏊ	ᏂᎦᏓ	ᎣᎦᏛᎦᏅ	ᏪᏌ	ᏂᎦᏪᏍᎬ
winogilinvjvnagwu	nigada	ogatvganv	wesa	nigawesgv
just before we went to sleep	all	we heard	a cat	its meowing

ᏔᎵᏁ	ᎢᎣᎦᏛᎦᎾ
taline	i?oktvgana
second time	when we heard it

ᏂᎤᏪᏌ	ᏃᏊ	ᏍᏗᎩᏓ	ᎾᎥᏂᎨ	ᏂᎬᏩᏍᏛ
ni?uwesa	nogwu	sdikida	na?vhnige	nigvwsdv
when it meowed again	then	a little bit	closer	it seemed

ᏏᏊᎴ	ᏦᎢᏁ	ᏃᏊ	ᎥᎣᎦᏛᎦᏅ	ᏃᏊᏚ	ᎤᏙᎯᏳ
sigwule	jo?ine	nogwu	v?oktvganv	nogwudu	udohiyu
and again	the third time	then	we heard again	and now	very

ᎬᏂ	ᎨᏒ	ᎡᏍᎦ	ᏣᎢᏒ	ᎠᎴ	ᏂᎦᏪᏏᏒ	ᎠᏍᏓᏲᏍᎬ
kvhni	gesv	esga	tsa?isv	ale	nigawesisv	asdayosgv
clear	it was	in this direction	its walking	and	it meowed along	it got louder

ᏂᏓᎦᏪᏏᏒᏃ
nidagawesisvhno
and it was meowing along in this direction

ᏂᎦᏓ	ᏃᏊ	ᎣᏍᏓ	ᎣᎦᏛᏓᏍᏛ
nigada	nogwu	osda	oktvdasdv
all	then	good	we were all listening

ᎠᎴ	ᎡᏝᏪ	ᎣᏥᏅᏜᎥᎢ	ᎪᎯ	ᎢᏴ	ᏃᏊ
ale	ehlawe	ojinhdla?v?i	kohi	iyv	nogwu
and	quiet	we were lying there	after	a while	now then

ᎠᏊ	ᎢᏴ	ᏙᏱ	ᏗᏢ	ᏄᏪᏏᏢ	ᏃᏊ
agwu	iyv	doyi	didlv	nuwesihlv	nogwu
here	nearby	outside	toward	it came and meowed	then

ᎤᏕᏲᎸ ᏍᎦᎵᏦᏕ ᏃᏋ ᏧᎶᏒ   ᏔᏗᏜ ᎿᎶᏒ
udeyolv galhjode nogwu julosv   ididla wulosv
it circled house then where it came from   toward it returned

ᏏᏋ ᏂᎦᏪᏏᏐᎯᏊ   ᏪᎦᏩᏕᎵᏦᎲᏍᎩ ᏂᎦᏪᏏᏒᎯ
sigwu nigawesiso?igwu wigvwadelichohvsgi nigawesisv?i
still continued to meow along until it faded out it is meowing along

ᎡᎵᏏᎰᏃ   ᏃᏋ ᎠᏎ ᏔᏴ ᎤᏁᏨ ᎯᎠ
elisihno nogwu kohi iyv uhnejv hi?a
and my grandmother then after a while she spoke this

ᏄᏪᏒᎯ ᎪᎲᏗᏛ   ᏗᏓᏆᏂᏒ   ᏔᏴᏃᎯᏎᎭ
nuwesv?i gohusdidv didatvganisv igihnohiseha
she said something (affirmative) that we are going to hear it is telling us

ᎤᏥᎥᏓᎰᏃ   ᏃᏋ ᎯᎠᏴ ᎧᎸ   ᏅᏓ ᏃᏋ
ugijvdahno nogwu hi?ayv kalv nvdo nogwu
and the next morning then about this the position of sun then

ᎤᎷᏨ ᎾᎥ ᎢᏦᎦᏓᎵ ᎠᎴ ᎣᏘᏃᎯᏎᎸ
uluhjv na?v ijogadali ale ogihnohiselv
he came near apart from us and he told us

ᎾᎯᏳ ᏒᏃᏱ ᎠᎵᎯᎵᏒ ᎤᏲᎱᏎ
nahiyu svnoyi ahli?ilisv uyohuse
at that time midnight time he died

Ꮎ ᎤᏛᏠᏅ ᏧᏞᎸᎬᎣ
na utvsohnv judlvgv?o
that old man who was sick

Morpheme by Morpheme

ga-nvd<u>a</u>di^{32}s-g-o^3 kilo sagwu iyu^{3}wa^{3}gdi ji-chu^{3}ja-gwu
1 remember Prog Hab someone one time 1 boy just

ji-ges-v kilo
Pst be exP someone

utvsohnv   u-dlv^3-g-v^3 ilv^{4}sgi
old-man   3 sick Prog exP   a-few

j-usv^{3}hida   u-dlv^{3}j-v^3 ale   nidulsihni^{32}sv
Pl day   3 get-sick exP   and   every-night

u-jado^{32}-g-v   ni-g-vwsd-v^3 vsgi^3 d-eh-v^3 ilv^{4}sgi
3 worsen Prog exP   Spec 3 seem exP   that   Pl have exP   a-few

do   ase^3 n-u-lstan-e   w-u-yohus-v^{23}hehno   ilvsgi
really   perhaps   Spec 3 happen repP   Tr 3 die exP because   a-few

winusv^{4}hla   nahiyu^3-hehno   ji-ges-v   udli   i^{23}ga^4 eladi-gwu
days-later   then because   Pst be exP   more   quantity   on-foot just

oj-edo^{4}h-i   gesv   iluh^{3}dlv   y-og-e^{4}n-a   ale^3
they-and-I walk Ag   be exP   somewhere   nonF they-and-I go recP   and

vsgwu   kilo   y-u-dlv^{4}j-a   yvwi   na?v
also   someone   nonF 3 get-sick Pres   people   near

ni-d-u-n-ada^{3}l-v   d-a-n-ada-watvh-idoh-v   ale   y-i^{4}gi
Spec Pl 3 Pl apart exP   Pl 3 Pl Refl visit around exP   and   nonF be

d-a-n-ijvdagwa^{32}s-g-v
Pl 3 Pl stay-night-after-night Prog exP

u-dlv^3-g-i   a-n-iktidi^3-hih-v   dihyehgahli
3 sick Prog Ag   3 Pl stay-with come exP   quilt

di-gwsdo^3-hno   d-a-ni-hno^{23}hi^{3}h-v^3 svno^{23}yi-hno^3
Pl pillow and   Pl 3 Pl bring exP   at-midnight and

yi-n-u-l^{23}stan-a   uhna^3-gwu   a-n-ihlinv^3-g-v^3 iga^{3}da
nonF Spec 3 happen Pres   there just   3 Pl fall-asleep Prog exP   some

gado-hi-gwu   d-a-n-iyesdv^3?vs-g-v   gogi
ground on just   Pl 3 Pl spread Prog exP   summer

y-i^{4}gi   d-u^3-ni-ksv^{23}sd-o̱ʔi   y-i^{4}gi   dosa
nonF be   Pl 3 Pl make-smoke Hab   nonF be   mosquito

d-u-ni-te^{3}sd-v^{4}ʔi   nogwu̱^{3}-le   d-a-n-ada̱-ne^{23}dli^{3}yvs-g-v
Pl 3 Pl would exP   now and   Pl 3 Pl Refl alternate Prog exP

a-ni-ktidi^{32}s-g-v   u-dlv^4-g-i
3 Pl stay-up Prog exP   3 sick Prog Ag

vsgi-hno   n-u-lsta̱ni^{23}-do^{32}l-v   hi̱ʔa   ji̱-ji-nohe^{4}h-a   ela̱di
that and   Spec 3 happen around exP   this   Rel 1 live Pres   on-foot

oj-ani̱^{3}gis-g-v   j-u̱-we^{3}nvsv   oj-e^3-g-o^3 uhna
they-and-I start Prog exP   Pl 3 home   they-and-I go Prog Hab   there

di̱-g-anh^3-g-v   dlv^4-hno   ta^{3}ʔli
Dst 3 lie Prog exP   somewhere and   two

iyu̱^{3}dhlilo^{4}da   iyu̱^{3}da̱nvhi^{4}da   ges-v   j-oge^{3}nvs-v   ni̱dvhni̱gida
mile   in-distance   be exP   Pl they-and-I home exP   start

g-anvda̱dv^{32}s-g-o^{3}ʔi̱^{3}-hno   w-ogi-jvd-a̱^{3}-gwv^3
1 remember Prog Hab and   Tr they-and-I spend-night Pres just

dlv   ta̱li-ha   iyu̱wa^{4}kdi
about   two Num   time

nogwu^3-hno   dlv   nvhgi-ne^3 svnoyi   hla^3 y-og-e^{3}nvs-e^3
then and   sometime   four Ord   at-night   not   nonF they-and-I go repP

e-li^{3}si-sgi̱ni   j-u̱-we^{3}nvs-v   og-env^{3}s-v   a̱le^3
1Pos grandmother but   Pl 3 home exP   they-and-I go exP   and

vsgwu^3 uhna^3 w-ogi-svhl-v
also   there   Tr they-and-I spend-night exP

ij-ahni^{3}h-e^{3}sdi^3-gwu   sina^{3}le   wi-ji-los-v̱ʔi
2 Pl spend-night FutPr just   tomorrow   Tr 2 Pl go-back Imp

ogi-se^{23}l-v howa^{23}-hno udohiyu vsgi
they-and-I spend-night exP so and very that

n-og-a̱dv^{3}nel-v nogwu^3-hno e-li^{3}si
Spec they-and-I do exP then and 1Pos grandmother

ges-v og-a̱dvnv^{3}ʔisda^{32}-nel-v^3
be exP they-and-I prepare Dat exP

ogi-svsdi^3 d-u-yesdv^{3}ni-do^{3}l-v^3 og-anhdlv-di^3
they-and-I bed Pl 3 spread around exP they-and-I lie-down Inf

og-anhdlv^{3}n-a-hno nogwu to^3 n-og-a̱dv^{3}ne^{4}l-a a̱si^3
they-and-I lie-down Pres and then quiet Spec they-and-I do Pres before

wi̱-n-og-i^{3}hli̱nvj-v^3 na̱gwu niga^{4}da og-a̱tvga^{32}n-v^3
Tr Spec they-and-I fall-asleep exP then all they-and-I hear exP

wesa ni̱-g-a̱wes-g-v^3 i^{4}na
cat Spec 3 utter Prog exP far-away

ni-di-ga-^{3}wes-g-v w-ok-tvga^{32}n-v^3 ta̱li-ne^3 i̱^{3}ʔok-tv^{4}gan-a
Spec Pl 3 utter Prog exP Tr they-and-I hear exP two Ord Rep they-and-I
hear recP

ni̱-ga-wes-g-v nogwu sdi^{3}ki̱da naʔv-hni̱^{3}ge ni̱-g-vwsd-v^3
Spec 3 meow Prog exP then a-little close more Spec 3 seem exP

sigwu^3-le^3 jo̱ʔi-ne^3
again and three Ord

nogwu v̱^{3}-ʔok-tvga^{32}n-v^3 nogwu̱^{3}-dv udohiyu kv^{4}hni
now Rep they-and-I hear exP now Emp really clear

ges-v^3 e^{3}sga j-a-^{3}ʔis-v a̱le^3 ni̱-ga̱wes-i^{3}s-v
be exP this-way Pst 3 walk exP and Spec 3 meow-along exP

a-sdayos-g-v^3 ni̱da̱-g-a̱^{3}wesi^{3}s-v-hno
3 louder Prog exP   this-way 3 come-direction-of exP and

ni̱ga^{4}da   nogwu   o^{4}sda   ok-tvda^{32}sd-v^3
all   then   good   they-and-I hear exP

a̱le   ehla̱we^3 ojin-hdla̱^{3}?-v?i   kohi   iyu   nogwu
and   quiet   he-and-I lie exP   there   after a while   then

a^{3}gwu   iyu   doyi   di^{3}dlv   n-u-wes-i^{23}hl-v^3 nogwu
here   nearby   outside   toward   Spec 3 meow come exP   then

u-deyo^{32}l-v   galhjo^{23}de   nogwu   j-u-los-v
3 go-around exP   house   then   Dst 3 come exP

i̱di^{3}dla   w-u̱-^{3}los-v^3 sigwu   ni̱-g-a̱wes-i^{3}s-o^3?i̱^{3}-gwu
toward   Tr 3 go exP   still   Spec 3 meow continue Hab just

wi̱-gvw-a̱de^{23}li-chohvs-g-i   ni̱-g-a̱wes-i^{3}s-v^{23}?i
Tr 3 fade Comp Prog Ag   Spec 3 meow continue exP

e-li^{3}si̱-^{3}hno   nogwu   kohi^3 iyv^3 u-hne^{3}j-v^3 hi̱?a
1Pos grandmother and   then   after   a while   3 speak exP   this

n-u-wes-v^{23}?i   gohu^{23}sdi̱-dv^3 di-d-a̱-tv^{3}ganis-v   igi-hnohis-e^{3}h-a
Spec 3 say exP   something Emp   Pl Fut 3 hear exP   he/you Pl-and-me tell Dat
                                                                    Pres

ugijv^{23}da̱-hno   nogwu   hi̱?a-^{32}yv   ka^{3}lv   nvdo   nogwu
next-day and   then   this about   position-of   sun   then

u-luhj-v   na̱?v^3
3 come exP   near

ijo^3-gada^{4}li   a̱le   ogi-hnohi̱s-e^{23}l-v
you Pl-and-I apart   and   he/them-and-me tell Dat exP

nahi̱yu   svno^{23}yi   ahli̱^{3}?i̱^{3}li̱sv   u-yohus-e
then   midnight   time   3 die repP

na   utvso̱hnv   j-u-dlv^3-g-v^4?i̱
that   old-man   Rel 3 sick Prog exP

Syllabary

SOᏞᏓᏉA ᎭᏉ TGGᎠᎥ ᏒᏌGᏉ ᏒᏓR ᎩG ᎣᏋᏠᎣ ᎣᏢE TᏇᏉᎩ ᏤRᎪᏞ ᎣᏢC꞉
Dơ ᏏSᏢᏏᏒ ᎣᏣVE ᏏEGᏑᎷ iᏉᎩSᏛ V D4 ᏇᏢᏉWᏝ ᏬᏒᎡRᏢZ TᏇᏉᎩ ᎤᏇRᏞ
ᎾᎪGᏢZ ᏒᏒR ᎣᏣ TS RWᏝᏉ ᏁVVᎪ ᏒR TᏇᏢ ᏗᏝᎾ Dơ iᏉᏉ ᎩG GᏢC BᎾ Ꮎi
ᏏSᎾᏞᏇ ᏞᎾᏞGᎷᎪVᏛ DơᏁᎩ ᏞᏏCᏞᏓᏉE ᎣᏢᎩ DᏏSᎥᎥᎪᏛ ᎥBSC ᎥᎥᏉVZ
ᏞᏏZᎪᏛ ᎣᏢᎩ ᎥSᎣE RZᏁZ ᏁᏇᏢᏉWᎾ ᎣᏔᎣ DᏏCᎣE TSᏞ SVᎪᏉ ᏞᏏᏯᏉᎷiᏉE
AᎩ ᏁᎩ ᏏᏏSRᏉVT ᏁᎩ VᎠ ᏏᏞᏉVT ZᏉơ ᏞᎾᏞᏅCBᏉE DᏏSᎥᎥᏉE ᎣᏢᎩ
iᏉᎩZ ᏇᏢᏉWᏏVᏇ ᎪD ᏒᏒZᏢᏕ RWᎥ ᏁGᏏᎩᏉE ᏨᎱᎣR ᏁVA ᎣᏔ ᎥSᎣE PZ
WᏢ TGCGᏞ TGᏞᎣᏛᏞ ᏒR ᏒᏒᎣR ᏏᎷᏏᎩᏞ SOᏞᏓᏉATZ ᏌᎩCᏞᏕ P WᏢᏅ
TGGᎠᎥ ZᏉZ P ᎣᎩᏝ RZᏁ Ꮞ ᏗᏝᎣ4 RᏢᏏᏉᎩᏏ ᏨᎱᎣR ᏁᏒᎣR Dơ ᏁᎩRᏇ
ZᏉZ RᏢᏏ ᏒᏒR ᏁᏓᎷᎣTᏉᏞᏝᏇ ᏁᎩRᏉᎥ SBᏉᎷᏏVᏇ ᏁSᎣᏢᎥ ᏁSᎣᏢᎾZ
ZᏉ V ZSᎷᏝW DᏏ ᎾZᎩᏢᎣCᎾᏉ ᏏSᏞ ᏁᏓᎷᎣSᎣ ᏯᎡ ᏏSᏯᏉE WᏢᏝ TᏁᏓᎷSᎾ
ᏏᎣᏯᎡ ZᏉ ᏁᎥᎩᏞ ᎾiᏒᏒ ᏏEGᏑᎷ ᏏᏉơ KTᏝ ZᏉ iᏁᏓᎷSᎣ ZᏉơ ᎣVᎪG
EᏏ ᏒR RᏉᏏS GTR Dơ ᏏSᏯᏏR DᏉᏞᏗᏉE ᏏᏞSᏯᏏRZ ᏏSᏞ ZᏉ ᏁᏉᏞ ᏁᏓᎷᏞᏉᎷ
Dơ RᏞᏉᏯ ᏁᏒᎣᏏiT AᎪ TB ZᏉ DᏉ TB VᏁ ᎥP ᏇᏯᏏP ZᏉ ᎣᏏᏗᏇ SᏢKᏚ
ZᏉ ᏨGR TᎥᏍ ᏬGR ᏏᏉ ᏏSᏯᏏᏠTᏉ ᎾEGᏚᏢKᏛᏉᎩ ᏏSᏯᏏRT RᏢᏏZ ZᏉ AᎪ
TB ᎣᏝC꞉ ᎪD ᏇᏯRT AᎢᏉᎥᎷ ᎥᏞᎷᏏᏏR TᎩZᎪ4Ꮕ ᎣᎩCᏞZ ZᏉ ᎪDB ᏇᏇ ᎣV
ZᏉ ᎣᎷC꞉ Ꮎi TKSᏞP Dơ ᏁᎩZᎪ4Ꮗ ᎾᎪG RZᏁ DCTᏢR ᎣᏗᎡ4 Ꮎ ᎣᏋᏠᎣ
ᏨPET

English

I remember once when I was just a boy, there was an old man who had been sick for several days, and each day he seemed to get worse. I suppose it was true, because a few days later he died. Back then our mobility was by foot. When someone was sick, the people in the neighboring area would come and sit up with the sick. They would bring with them quilts and pillows, and when it got late, some would make their pallets on the ground and sleep. If it was during the summer, they would build a fire to produce smoke to repel the mosquitoes as they kept watch.

That is what had happened in this story that I am telling. We would start out on foot to go to his home. It was about two miles from our house. I remember we spent the night there a couple of times. About the fourth night we did not go, but instead we went to visit my grandmother. It got dark while we were there, so we decided to spend the night there. She prepared our beds for us, and we all went to bed, but before any of us fell asleep, we heard a faint meowing of a cat somewhere off in the distance.

When we heard it the second time, it seemed a little closer. We heard it again the third time, and we knew for sure it was coming toward us, as the meows were getting louder. As it came toward us, we all took notice and listened quietly. In a little while we heard it right outside, and as it went around the house it was meowing. It circled the house and then went back the way it came, still meowing as it went, until the meows faded in the distance. After a while my grandmother spoke up and said, "It's telling us that we will hear some news." The next day when the sun was up high, a neighbor came over and told us that the old man who had been sick had died that night.

The Invisible Companion Black Fox

Durbin Feeling

The following story reflects a prevalent Cherokee sentiment that some individuals can see what others cannot.

Ꮲ	ᎠᏎ	ᏓᎳᏚ	ᎢᏯᏆᏕᏘᏴᏓ
dlv	ase	daladu	iyagwadetiyvda
about	probably	sixteen	my age

ᎨᏎ	ᎩᎳᎢᏊ	ᎢᏳᏍᏗ	ᎠᎩᏁᏓ	ᎨᏒ
gese	kilaʔigwu	iyusdi	agineda	gesv
was	just recently	almost	I gotten	had

ᎠᏆᎵᏍᎪᎸᏓᏁᎯ	ᏓᏆᎴᎳ	ᎠᎩᎯᎵᏓᏍᏗ	ᎠᎴ
agwalsgolhdanehi	dagwalela	agihilidasdi	ale
which permits me	car	for me to drive	and

ᎠᎩᎸᏉᏗ	ᎨᏒ	ᏗᏓᎾᏅ	ᎾᎩᎶᎯᏍᏗ
agilvkwdi	gesv	didadnv	nagilohisdi
I liked	was	to the store	to go and return

ᎣᏏ	ᎠᎩᏰᎸᏒ	ᏓᏆᎴᎳ	ᎬᎩᎯᎵᏓᏍᏗ
osi	agiyelvsv	dagwalela	gvgihilidasdi
good	for me	car	for-me-to-drive

ᎨᏒᎢ	ᎡᎵᏃ	Ꮲ	ᏦᎢ	ᎢᏳᏟᎶᏓ	ᎢᏴ
gesvʔi	elihno	dlv	joʔi	iyutliloda	iyv
was	and possibly	about	three	miles	about

ᎠᏂᎩᏓ	ᏛᏓᎾᏅ	ᎤᏔᎾᏃ	ᏂᎦᏅᏅ
agnigida	dvdananv	utanahno	niganvhnv
in distance to	store	and big	there was a road

33	ᎪᏪᎵ	Ᏸ	ᎩᏄᏛᏗ	ᎢᏳᏟᎶᏓ
33	gohweli	dlv	ginutdi	iyutliloda
33	numbered	about	one-fourth	measure of

ᎠᏂᎩᏓ	ᏦᎨᏅᏒ	ᎠᏎᏃ	ᎠᎨ	ᎢᏴ
ahnigida	jogenvsv	asehno	age	iyv
in distance	our house	but	over there	about

ᏗᎦᏁᎶ	ᎾᎥ	ᎢᏦᎦᏓᎵ	ᎥᏍᎩᏃ
diganelo	na?v	ijogadali	vsgihno
he lived there	near	our neighbor	that and

ᏂᎪᎯᎸ	ᎠᎪᏩᏛᏗ	ᎨᏐ	ᎡᎳᏗ
nigohilv	agowahtvhdi	geso	eladi
all the time	him to see	was	on foot

ᎠᎢᏒ	ᎥᏍᎩᏃ	ᏄᎵᏍᏔᏂᏙᎸ	ᎾᎯᏳ
a?isv	vsgihno	nulstanidolv	nahiyu
as he walked along	that and	it happened	then

ᎩᎳ	ᎤᏒ	ᏗᏓᎾᎾ	ᎠᏇᏙᎸ
kila	usv	didanana	agwedolv
early	night	to the store	I had been

ᎥᎦᎢᏒ	ᏗᏇᏅᏒ	ᎢᏗᏜ	ᏃᏊᏃ
vga?isv	digwenvsv	ididla	nogwuhno
I was on my way back	my house	toward	and then

ᎠᏆᏞᏌ	33	ᎪᏪᎵ	ᎦᏅᏅ
agwadlesa	33	gohweli	ganvhnv
when I turned off	33	numbered	road

ᎠᎴ	ᏗᏇᏅᏒ	ᎢᏗᏜ	ᏫᎦᏅᏅ
ale	digwenvsv	ididla	wiganvhnv
and	my home	toward	down the road

ᏩᏆᏕᏙᎾ ᏓᏆᎴᎳ ᏚᏨᏍᏛ ᏫᏚᎸᏌᏓᏓ
wagwadetona dagwalela dujvstv widulvsadada
when I got on car lights they shined

ᏫᎦᏅᏅ ᏫᎦᏥᎪᎥ ᎠᏂᏔᎵ ᎠᏂᏍᎦᏯ
wiganvhnv wigajigoʔv anitaʔli anisgaya
down the road I saw them two of them men

ᏩᎾᎢᏒᎢ ᏌᏊᏃ ᎩᎳᏊ ᎢᏴᏓ
wanaʔisvʔi sagwuhno kilagwu iyvda
walking in the other direction and one immediately length of time

ᏥᏲᎵᏨ ᎾᎥ ᎢᏦᎦᏓᎵ ᎨᏒᎢ
jiyolijv naʔv ijogadali gesvʔi
I recognized him near neighbor was

ᎤᎾᎵᎪᏒᎢᏍᎩᏂ Ꮭ ᏱᏥᏲᎵᏤᎢ ᎠᏎᏃ
unaligosvʔisgini hla yijiyolijeʔi asehno
but his partner not I did not recognize him however

ᏫᎦᏥᏯᏢᏔᎭ ᎠᏆᎴᏪᏍᏔᏅ ᎤᎾᏦᏗ ᎤᎬᏩᏟ
wigajiyadlvtaha agwalehwistanv unajodi ugvwahli
when I caught up with them I stopped for them to get in purpose of

ᏓᏳᏍᏚᎢᏒᏃ ᎦᎶᎯᏍᏗ ᎠᎴ ᏓᏳᏣᏅᎢ
dayusduʔisvhno galohisdi ale dayujanvʔi
he opened and door and he got in

ᎤᏣᎾᏃ ᎤᏍᏚᏅ ᎦᎶᎯᏍᏗᎢ ᏍᏓᎵᎪᏒᎾᎲ
ujanahno usduhnv galohisdiʔi sdaligosvnahv
and when he got in he closed it door what about your partner

Ꮭ ᏱᏛᏣᏂ ᏥᏲᏎᎸ ᎡᏝᏪᎢᏊᏃ
hla yidvjani jiyoselv ehlaweʔigwuhno
no he is not getting in I said to him and silently

ᏓᏆᎧᎿᏅ ᏞᎦ ᏥᏍᎦᏍᏓᏁᏗ ᎦᏁᎸᏗᏍᎬ
dagwakahnanv hlega jisgasdanehdi ganelhdisgv
he looked at me awhile for me to scare him my trying

RⱠᏬE	D4Z	OⱱⲚG		ᏜᎫ	ᎩG
elisgv	asehno	uhneja		hladi	kilo
he thought	but	when he spoke		not	someone

ᏧᎩᎧᏪᎪ4	DᏪⱱ4Ꮇ		DBZ	ZᏬ
yoginaligose	agwoselv		ayvhno	nogwu
I wasn't with	he said to me		and I	then

DᏯᏬᏚᏬᏞᏔᏬ	OⱱᏒOⱱᏬ
aksgasdanehv	ulenvhv
my getting scared	started

Morpheme by Morpheme

dlv^3	a^{23}se	d̲aladu^3	iya̲^{3}gwadetiyv^{4}da
about	perhaps	sixteen	one-year-of-age

ges-e^3	k̲ila^{3}ʔ-igwu	iyu^{4}sdi	ag-ine^{4}d-a	ges-v^3
be exP	recently just	almost	1 get recP	be exP

agw-alsgolhd̲aneh-i
1 have-permission Ag

dagwale^{3}la	agi-h̲ili^{23}da^{32}s-di	ale^3
car	1 drive Inf	and

ag-ilv^{4}kwdi	ges-v^3	dida^{3}dnv
1 like	be exP	store

n-agi-loh̲is-di
Lat 1 go-return Inf

osi^3	ag-iyelv^{3}s-v^3	dagwale^{3}la	gv-gih̲ili^{23}das-di
good	1 think exP	car	nonF they/me drive Inf

ges-v^{4}ʔi	el̲i^4-hno	dlv^3	joʔi	iyu^{3}hl̲ilo^{4}da
be exP	possibly and	about	three	mile

iyv
about

ahni^{3}gi^{4}da dvda^{3}nanv^3 u^{23}tana^3-hno ni-g-anvhn-v^3
in-length store big and Lat 3 be-road exP

33 gohwe^{4}li dlv^3 ginu^{4}tdi iyu^{3}hlilo^{4}da
33 numbered about one-fourth one-mile

a^{23}hni^{3}gi^{4}da j-og-e^{3}nvsv ase^3-hno a^{3}ge i^{3}yv
in-length Pl they-and-I house but and over-there about

di-gane^{3}l-o^3
Dst live Hab

na?v
near

i^{23}jo^3-gada^{4}li vsgi-hno
they-and-I apart that and

nigo^{23}hi^{3}lv a-go^{23}hwahtvh-di ges-o^3
always 3 see Inf be Hab

eladi
on-ground

a^3-?is-v vsgi-hno^3 n-u-lstani^{23}do^{32}l-v^3 nahiyu^3
3 walk exP that and Spec 3 happen exP then

kila^3 usv^3 dida^{3}nana^3 agw-edol-v^3
early night store 1 be exP

v-^{23}g-a^3?i^{2}s-v^3 di^{23}-gw-e^{3}nvsv idi^{3}dla nogwu^3-hno
Rep 1 walk exP Pl 1 house toward then and

agw-adle^{3}s-a 33 gohwe^{4}li ganvhnv^3
1 turn-off recP 33 numbered road

ale^3 di-gw-e^{3}nvsv^3 idi^{3}dla   wi-g-anv^3-hnv
and   Pl 1 house   toward   Tr 3 road exP and

w-agw-a^{3}de^{23}ton-a   dagwale^{3}la   d-ujvstv
Tr 1 get-on recP   car   Pl light

wi-d-u^{23}-lv^{3}s<u>a</u>dad-a   wi-g-anvhn-v   a-ni-sgaya
Tr Pl 3 shine recP   Tr 1 down-road exP   3 Pl man

wi-g-ajigo?-v^3 a-ni^{23}-ta^3?li   w-a-n-a^3?isv^4?-i   sagwu^4-hno
Tr 1 see exP   3 Pl two   Tr 3 Pl walk Ag   one and

k<u>i</u>la-gwu   iyv^{4}da   ji-yolij-v^3 na?v
immediately just   length-of-time   1 recognize exP   near

ijo^3-g<u>a</u>da^{4}li   ges-v?i   u-n-ali^{3}gos-v^3?i-sg<u>i</u>ni
they-and-I apart   be exP   3 Pl be-partners exP but

hla^3 yi-ji^{23}y-o^{3}lije^3?i   ase^3-hno   wi-gaji^{3}y-adlv^{3}t<u>a</u>h-a   agw-alehwistan-v^3
no   nonF 1   but and   Tr I-them catch-up   1 stop exP
        recognize   recP

u-n-ajo-di   ugv^{23}wahli
3 Pl get-in Inf   purpose

d-a-yu^{23}sdu^3?is-v^{23}-hno   galohisdi
Pl 3 open exP and   door

ale^3 d-a-yu^{23}j<u>a</u>^{32}n-v^{23}?i
and   Pl 3 get-in exP

u-ja^{32}n<u>a</u>-hno   u-sdu^{32}-hnv^3 galohisdi^4?i   sd-ali^{3}gosv^3-nahv^3
3 get-in and   3 close exP   door   you/two partner what-about

hla^3 yi-d-v^{23}-ja^{32}n-i   ji-yos-e^{23}l-v^3 ehlawe^3?i-gwu^3-hno
no   nonF Pl 3 get-in Ag   1 say Dat exP   silently also and

d-agw-akahnan-v^{3}	hle^{4}ga	ji-sgasdaneh^{3}-di^{3}	g-anelh^{3}di^{23}s-g-v
Pl he/me look exP	awhile	1 scare Inf	1 try Prog exP

e-li^{32}s-g-v^{3}	ase^{3}hno	u-hne^{4}j-a	hladi^{3}
3 think Prog exP	but	3 speak recP	no

kilo	y-o^{23}-gi^{3}-naligos-e^{3}
someone	nonF they-and-I be-with repP

agw-os-el-v	ayv-hno^{3}	no^{23}gwu
he/me say Dat exP	I and	then

ak-sga^{3}sdaneh-v	u^{3}-lenvh-v^{3}
1 get-scared exP	3 start exP

Syllabary

Ꮲ ᎠᏎ ᏓᎳᏚ ᎢᏇᏆᎦᏗᏴᏓ ᎨᏎ ᎩᎳᎢᏊ ᎢᏳᏍᏗ ᎠᎩᏁᏓ ᎨᏒ ᎠᏆᎵᏍᎪᎸᏓᏁᎯ ᏓᏆᎴᎳ ᎠᎩᎯᎵᏓᏍᏗ ᎠᎴ ᎠᎩᎸᏉᏗ ᎨᏒ ᏗᏓᎾᏅ ᎾᎩᎶᎯᏍᏗ ᎣᏏ ᎠᎩᏰᎸᎡ ᏓᏆᎴᎳ ᎬᎩᎯᎵᏓᏍᏗ ᎨᏒᎢ ᎡᎵᏃ Ꮲ ᏦᎢ ᎢᏳᏟᎶᏓ ᎢᏴ ᎠᏂᎩᏓ ᏛᏓᎾᏅ ᎤᏔᎾᏃ ᏂᎦᏅᏅ 33 ᎪᏪᎵ Ꮲ ᎩᎸᏛᏗ ᎢᏳᏟᎶᏓ ᎠᏂᎩᏓ ᏦᎨᏅᎡ ᎠᏎᏃ ᎠᎨ ᎢᏴ ᏗᎦᏁᎶ ᎾᎥ ᎢᏦᎦᏓᎵ ᎥᏍᎩᏃ ᏂᎪᎯᎸ ᎠᎪᏩᏛᏗ ᎨᏖ ᎡᎳᏗ ᎠᎢᏒ ᎥᏍᎩᏃ ᎸᎵᏍᏔᏂᏙᎸ ᎾᎯᏳ ᎩᎳ ᎤᏒ ᏗᏓᎾᎾ ᎠᏬᏙᎸ ᎥᏚᎢᏒ ᏗᏬᏅᏒ ᎢᏗᏜ ᏃᏊᏃ ᎠᏆᏓᏌ 33 ᎪᏪᎵ ᎦᏅᏅ ᎠᎴ ᏗᏬᏅᏒ ᎢᏗᏜ ᏫᎦᏅᏅ ᏩᏆᎦᏙᎾ ᏓᏆᎴᎳ ᏚᏨᏍᏛ ᏫᏚᎸᏌᏓᏓ ᏫᎦᏅᏅ ᏫᎦᏥᎪᎥ ᎠᏂᏔᎵ ᎠᏂᏍᎦᏇ ᏩᎾᎢᏒᎢ ᏌᏊᏃ ᎩᎳᏊ ᎢᏴᏓ ᏥᏲᎵᏨ ᎾᎥ ᎢᏦᎦᏓᎵ ᎨᏒᎢ ᎤᎾᎵᎪᏒᎢᏍᎩᏂ Ꮭ ᏱᏥᏲᎵᏤᎢ ᎠᏎᏃ ᏫᎦᏥᏇᎵᏔᏖ ᎠᏆᎴᏫᏍᏔᏅ ᎤᎾᏦᏗ ᎤᎬᏩᏟ ᏓᏳᏍᏚᎢᏒᏃ ᎦᎶᎯᏍᏗ ᎠᎴ ᏓᏳᏨᏅᎢ ᎤᏨᎾᏃ ᎤᏍᏚᏅ ᎦᎶᎯᏍᏗᎢ ᏍᏓᎵᎪᎡᎾᎲ Ꮭ ᏱᏛᏟᏂ ᏥᏲᏎᎸ ᎡᏝᏪᎢᏊᏃ ᏓᏆᎧᎿᏅ ᏞᎦ ᏥᏍᎦᏍᏓᏁᏗ ᎦᏁᎸᏗᏍᎬ ᎡᎵᏍᎬ ᎠᏎᏃ ᎤᏁᏣ ᏝᏗ ᎩᎶ ᏲᎩᎾᎵᎪᏎ ᎠᏉᏎᎸ ᎠᏴᏃ ᏃᏊ ᎠᎩᏍᎦᏍᏓᏁᎲ ᎤᎴᏅᎲ

English

I guess I was about sixteen years old, and I had just gotten my operator's license. I really enjoyed going to the store because I liked to drive our car. The store was about three miles from where we lived. There was a state highway about a quarter of a mile from our house, and a neighbor lived just on the other side of us, and you would see him walking these roads all the time. One evening it had just gotten dark. I was driving back from the store going home. As I turned off the state highway and onto the dirt road, the lights of our car shined down the road, and

I saw two men walking. I recognized one of them immediately as our neighbor. But his partner I didn't recognize. As I caught up with them, I stopped the car to give them a ride. The door opened, and our neighbor got in and closed the door behind him.

"Isn't your friend going to ride with us?" I asked him. He looked at me puzzled. He thought I was trying to scare him. When he spoke, he said, "There was no one with me." Then I began to get scared.

Little People

Durbin Feeling

The Cherokee people have traditionally believed in a race of small, human-like beings called Little People. The Little People appear to humans at various times.

SOᏋᏞᏗᏇA	ᏗᎩSBᏒᏒ	ᏥᏒR	ZᏇᏠ	RSS		RᏒᏏZ
ganvdadisgo	digigayvlige	jigesv	nogwule	edudu		elishino
I remember	my parents	who were	and also	my grandfather		and my grandmother

ᏥᏒR	AᎩZᏗ4Ꭰ	ᏒR	KᏥᎮC	VSᏠᏏᎠᏗR	Ꮎ	BᎾ
jigesv	gogihnohisehi	gesv	jojiyohli	dogatvsidisv	na	yvwi
who were	they would tell us	were	we children	as we were growing up	those	people

ᏛᎾᏇᏗ	ᏥᏞZ4Ꮙ		ᏞZ	iᏇᏬ	ᏹhSᏒᏇᏗᏞᏇ	ᎩG
junsdi	jidanosehv		hlahno	vsgwu	yinigalsdihagwu	kilo
little ones	which they were called		and not	even	just any	someone

ᏛhAᏅᎪ	ᏹᏒ4	iᏇᎩᎾ	BᎾ	ᏛᎾᏇᏗ	RᏒᏇᎩh	TᏑᏇᎩ	Ꮎhi
junigohvhi	yigese	vsgina	yvwi	junsdi	elisgini	ilvsgi	nani?v
they have not seen	was	those	people	little ones	although	a few	of them

ᎩG	SᏥᎮᏒᎩ	OᏋᎾSGᏒRᎪ	ᏒR	AᎢᏇᏗ	D4Ꭹ	ᏒR
kilo	gajiyoligi	unadelohosvhi	gesv	gohusdi	asegi	gesv
someone	I know them	they had known about it	was	something	peculiar	was

hSⱤⱥWOⱼⱼⱥE Dơ ꭹУ OⱷⱰᎷSOⱼⱾ ⅠR ꭹG DhꝈhⱥE
nigalstanv?vsgv ale yigi unatvganvhi gesv kilo aniwonisgv
the happenings and maybe they had heard was some- their
          about it   one talking

D4ⱥУh ꭹG hᏝhAGⱼⱥEⱰ
asesgini kilo nidanigowhtisgvna
however someone but they not seeing them

ⱼⱥУZ TGⱤⱥWhⱯⱾ ꭹУ BⱰ
vsgihno iyulstanidolvhi yigi yvwi
and that it had happened if people

ꝺⱰⱥⱯT ᏞhᏉ4ⱷT ᏞZ ⱼⱥⱱ ⱼⱥSTⱥⱯ ꭹⱤ4
junsdi?i danihlosehv?i hlahno vsgwo disga?isdi yigese
little ones they blamed them and not also to fear them it was not

DⱰⱯⱥA ꭹShZⱤᏞ OⱷⱰᏝOⱼⱯPZ Dơ ⱥⱥᏝ
anadisgo yidunihnohehla unadanvtihehno ale osda
they say when they talked about because they are friendly and good
     them

ⅠR TGⱤⱥᏝⱯ BⱰ TGZ hᏝⱵPVⱷⱰ
gesv iyulsdahnehdi yvwi iyuhno nidasodlvjehvna
that which is to happen to him person if not to dare them

ꭹУ DⱰⱯⱥAT Dơ ꭹУ EGⱰᏝⱥSⱾⱯ ⅠR
yigi anadisgo?i ale yigi gvwanadasdelhdi gesv
if it they said and maybe they to help was

AⱦⱥⱯ SⱰBУ ꭹhꝺⱥⱯᏝⱰ ꮾSᏠ TⱯꙆ OⱷᏉꭹⱥ
gohusdi ganayegi yinijusdidana wvktv ididla uhloyigwu
something dangerous if it existed ahead toward same as

OⱼⱰWOⱼⱾ ꭹᏠꙆⱤⱯ ⱼhⱥZGⱼVⱾ ⱵⱤSEⱯꝉ BⱰ
unelanvhi yidvnelhdi dinikanowadidohi jidekdiha yvwi
God if you have faith in angels the ones he uses people

ᏓᏍᏕᎵᏍᎬ	ᎠᎭᏂ	ᎡᎶᎯ	ᎨᏒ	ᎾᏍᎩᏯ	ᏯᏛᎾ	ᏒᏍᎩᎾ	ᏴᏫ
dasdelisgv	ahani	elohi	gesv	nasgiya	yadvhna	vsgina	yvwi
his helping them	here	on earth	which is	that same	let's say	that	people

ᏧᎾᏍᏗᎢ	ᏥᏓᏃᏎᎲᎢ	ᎪᎱᏍᏗ	ᏴᎦᎵᏍᏔᏂᏓ	ᎨᏐ	ᎢᏳᏓᎵᎭ
junsdi?i	jidanosehv?i	gohusdi	yvgalstanida	geso	iyudaliha
little ones	which they are called	something	it might happen	it is	once in a while

ᏱᏅᎦᎦᎵᏍᏓᏊ	ᎦᏰᎵᏍᏗ	ᏒᏍᎩᏃ	ᏱᏄᎵᏍᏔᏂᏙᎳ
yinvgagalsdagwu	gayelisd	vsgihno	yinulstanidola
impossible to happen	one might think	and that	if that happens

ᎠᎾᏓᏍᏕᎵᏍᎪ	ᏴᏫ	ᏧᎾᏍᏗ	ᎠᎾᏗᏍᎩ	ᎨᏒ	ᏗᎩᎦᏴᎵᎨ	ᏥᎨᏒᎢ
anadasdelisgo	yvwi	junasdi	anadisgi	gesv	digigayvlige	jigesv?i
they help you	people	little ones	they would say	were	my parents	who were

ᏌᏊᏃ	ᎢᏳᏩᎪᏗ	ᎡᎵᏏ	ᎡᏚᏚᏃ	ᎤᏒ
sagwuhno	iyuwakdi	elisi	eduduhno	usv
and one	time	my grandmother	and my grandfather	night

ᎢᎠᎾᎢᏎ	ᏧᏁᏅᏒ	ᎢᏗᏢ	ᏧᏂᎳᏫᎢᏍᏗ
i?ana?ise	junenvsv	ididla	junilawi?isdi
they were walking back	their home	toward	church

ᎤᏁᏙᎸᎯ	ᎤᏍᏗᏃ	ᎦᏅᏅ
unedolvhi	usdihno	ganvhnv
they had been	and little	road

ᎠᎾᎢᏎ	ᎡᎵ	ᎢᎸᏍᎩ
ana?ise	eli	ilvsgi
they were walking	quite	a few

ᎢᏳᏩᎪᏗ	ᎤᏂᎶᏏᏙᎸ	ᎠᎴ	ᎤᏂᎩᏌᏓ	ᎠᎴ	ᎬᏁᎳᎩᏊ	ᏯᏛᎾ
iyuwakdi	unilosidolv	ale	unikisada	ale	gvnelagigwu	yadv
times	they had been through	and	they were used to it	and	by memory	yo

ᎤᎾᎠᏟ ᏓᏕᏲᎵᎬ ᎤᏍᏗ ᎦᏅᎥᏅ ᎠᏎᎰ ᎠᏎᎩ ᏄᎵᏍᏔᏁ
unanhte dadeyolegv usdi ganvhnv asehno asegi nulstane
they knew the curves little road however strange it happened

ᎠᎾᏗᏍᎪ ᎾᎯᏳ ᎠᎾᎢᏌᎥᎢ ᎭᎾ ᎠᏨᎢᏍᏙᏗ ᏯᏂᏝᏤ
anadisgo nahiyu ana?isv?i hlahno atsvisdodi yanihyehe
they say at that time as they and not light they did not have
walked

ᎠᏎᏍᎩᏂ ᎤᏂᎩᏌᏓ ᎨᏎ ᏓᏕᏲᎵᎬ ᎠᎪᎯᏍᎩᏂᏔ ᎨᏒ
asesgini unikisada gese dadeyolegv kohisgini gesv
however they used to it were the curves but this time which is

ᏚᏩᎢᏝ ᏫᏚᏂᏃᎵᏥᏝᎡᎢ ᎢᎸᏍᎩᎰ ᏄᎾᏁᎵᏔᏁ
duwa?ihlv widuninolhjihle?i ilvsgihno nunanelhtane
bushes they bumped into and a few times they tried

ᎤᎾᏕᏯᏍᏗ ᏚᏩᎢᏝ ᎠᏎᎰ ᏏᏆ ᎤᎾᏆ
unadeysdi duwa?ihlv asehno sigwu uhnagwu
for them to go around bushes but again just there

ᏫᏓᏂᏃᎵᏥᎯᏤ ᎠᎴ ᎤᎾᏕᏲᏁ ᏂᎬᏤᏍᏗ ᎠᎾᏗᏍᎪᎢ
widaninolhjihihe ale unadeyohne nigvwsde anadisgo?i
they would bump into and they circled it seemed they say

ᏃᏆᎰ ᏄᏂᎲᏩᏘᎥ ᎤᏓᎸᎥᏛ ᎤᏂᎦᏪᎵᏎ ᎠᎴ
nogwuhno wunihwahtvha udlanvdv uniktvlese ale
and then when they found it opening they went through and

ᎤᎾᏂᎩᏎ ᎤᏍᏗ ᎤᎦᏅᎥᎢᏔ ᎢᏃ ᎢᏴᏓ ᎤᎾᏂᎩᏓ
unahnigise usdi wiganvhnv?i gehno iyvda unahnigida
start out little down the road and over distance they had
there walked

ᎢᏗᏜ ᎤᎠᎾᎢᏎᎢ ᎢᎤᎾᏨᏒᎰ
ididla wi?ana?ise?i i?unajvsahno
toward they were walking and when they
turned around

ZᏇ	ᏬᎤᏝᏇ	ᏊhᏳ4	TᏘPTᏇ	ᎤhᏚhᏃᏢᏍᏢᎾ
nogwu	osdagwu	wunilose	ilvhdlvʔigwu	winiduninolhjihlvna
then	just good	they went through	without somewhere	them bumping into it

Morpheme by Morpheme

g-anvda̲di^{32}s-g-o^3 di-gi̲-ga̲yv^{23}li̲^{3}ge^3 ji̲-ges-v^3 no^{23}gwu̲^{3}le^3
remember Prog Hab   Pl 1 parent   Rel be exP   also

e-dudu^3 e-li^{3}si̲^{3}-hno   ji̲-ges-v^3 gogi-hnohi̲se^{4}h-i
1Pos grandfather   1pos grandmother and   Rel be exP   3 Pl they/them-and-me tell Ag

ges-v^3 j-oji-yo^{4}hli   d-og-a̲tvs-i^{23}di^{32}s-v   na^3
be exP   Pl they-and-I child   Pl they-and-I grow begin exP   that

yvwi
person

j-u-n-sdi^3 ji̲-d-a-nose^{23}h-v   hla-hno^3 vsgwu^3 yi-ni̲-g-a^{3}lsdi^{3}h-a-gwu
Pl 3 Pl little   Rel Pl 3 call exP   not and   even   nonF Spec 3 happen Pres just

ki̲lo
someone

j-u-ni-goh-v^{4}hi   ji̲-ge^{3}s-e^3 vsgina^3 yvwi
Pl 3 Pl see exP   Rel be repP   that   person

j-u-n-sdi   eli^{23}sgi̲ni
Pl 3 Pl little   although

i̲lvs^{4}gi   n-a-n-i^{3}ʔ-v^3
a few   Neg 3 Pl see exP

ki̱lo^3 ga̱-ji-yo^{23}ligi u-n-a̱delohos-v^{4}hi ges-v^3 gohu^{4}sdi ase^{4}gi ges-v^3

someone I/them know 3 Pl know exP be exP something peculiar be exP

ni̱-g-alsta̱nv^3?v̱s-g-v^3 a̱le y-i̱^{3}gi u-n-a̱tv-gan-v^{23}hi ges-v^3

Spec 3 happen Prog exP and nonF be 3 Pl hear exP be exP

kilo^3 a-ni-wo^{3}nis-g-v^3 ase^{3}sgi̱^{3}ni

someone 3 Pl speak Prog exP but

kilo^3 ni̱-d-a̱-ni^3-gowhtis-g-v^{23}-na vsgi-hno^3

someone Neg Pl 3 Pl see Prog exP Neg that and

i̱yu^{3}lsta̱nidolv^{23}hi y-i̱^{3}gi yvwi

happening nonF be person

j-u-n-sdi^3?i d-a-ni-hlose^{23}h-v^3?i hla̱-hno^3 vsgwo^3 di-sga^3?i̱s-di yi-ge^{3}s-e^3

Pl 3 Pl Pl 3 Pl blame exP not and and Pl fear Inf nonF be
little repP

a-n-a̱dis-g-o^3 yi̱-d-u-ni^3-hno-he^{23}hl-a u-n-a̱danhti̱^{23}h-e-hno

3 Pl say Prog Hab nonF Pl 3 Pl talked-about RecP 3 Pl friendly repP and

a̱le^3 o^{23}sda ges-v^3 iy-u̱^{3}-lsdahn-e^{2}h-di^3

and good be exP Inf 3 happen Dat Inf

yvwi iyu^{3}hno ni̱-d-a̱so^{3}dl̲veheh-v^{23}na

person if Neg Pl dare Neg

y-i̱^{3}gi a-n-a̱di^{23}s-g-o^3?i a̱le^3 y-i̱^{3}gi gvw-an-a̱dasde^{23}lh-di ges-v^3

nonF be 3 Pl say Prog Hab and nonF be 3 Pl help Inf be exP

gohu^{4}sdi ga^{3}na̱yegi yi̱-ni̱-j-u^{23}sdi^{3}da̱n-a wv^{23}ktv i̱di^{3}dla uhlo^{3}yi̱-gwu

something dangerous nonF Pl Pst be recP ahead toward same just

une^{23}la̱^{3}nvhi yi̱-d-v^{3}n-el-h^{4}di di-ni-ka̱nowa̱dido^{4}h-i ji̱-d-e^{23}kdih-a yvwi

god nonF Pl Pl Pl keep-eye-on Ag Rel Pl use person
have-faith Inf Pres

d-a-sdeli^{23}s-g-v · a^{3}hani · elo^{23}hi · ges-v^3 · nasgi-ya^3 · y-a-dv^{4}hn-a
Pl 3 help Prog exP · here · on-earth · be exP · that same · nonF 3 say Pres

vsgina^3 · yvwi · j-u-n-sdi^{4}ʔi
that · person · Pl 3 Pl little

ji-d-a-n-ose^{23}h-v^{4}ʔi · gohu^{4}sdi · y-v^{23}-gal^{3}stani^{23}d-a · ges-o^3 · iyu^{3}daliha^3
Rel Pl 3 Pl say exP · something · nonF 3 happen Pres · be Hab · once-in-a while

yi-n-v^{23}gaga^{3}lsd-a^3-gwu · g-aye^{23}lisi-di · vsgi-hno^3 · yi-n-u-l^{23}stanido^{4}l-a
nonF Pl not-possible recP just · 3 think Inf · that and · nonF Spec 3 happen Pres

a-n-adasdelis-g-o · yvwi · j-u-n-asdi
3 Pl help Prog Hab · people · Pl 3 Pl little

a-n-adi^{4}s-g-i · ges-v^3
3 Pl say Prog Ag · be exP

di-gigayv^{23}li^{3}g^3 · jiy-es-v^{4}ʔi
Pl parent · Rel be exP

sagwu^4-hno · iyu^{3}wa^{4}kdi · e-li^{3}si · e-dudu-hno^3 · usv^3
one and · time · 1Pos grandmother · 1Pos grandfather and · night

i^{3}ʔ-a-n-a^{3}ʔis-e^3 · j-u-ne^{3}nvsv^3 · idi^{3}dla · j-u-ni-lawiʔis-di^3
Rep 3 Pl walk repP · Pl 3 home · toward · Pl 3 Pl worship Inf

u-n-edol-v^{4}hi · usdi^4-hno · ganvhnv^3
3 Pl be exP · little and · road

i-a-n-a^{3}ʔis-e^3 · eli^3 · ilv^{4}sgi · iyuwa^{4}kdi · u-n-ilosidol-v^3
Rep 3 Pl walk repP · quite · few · time · 3 Pl go-through exP

ale^3 · u-ni-ki^{23}sad-a · ale^3 · gvne^{23}lagi-gwu · y-a-dv^{4}hn-a
and · 3 Pl accustomed-to Pres · and · memory just · nonF 3 say Pres

u-n-anht-e^3 d-ade^{23}yo^{32}le-g-v^3 usdi^3 ganvhnv^3 ase^{3}hno
3 Pl know repP   Pl curve Prog exP   little   road   but

ase^{4}gi   n-u-lstan-e^3
strange   Spec 3 happen repP

a-n-adi^{23}s-g-o^3 nahiyu^3 a-n-a^{3}ʔis-v^{4}ʔi   hla-hno^3 ajv^{23}ʔasdodi
3 Pl say Prog Hab   at-that -time   3 Pl walk exP   not and   light

y-a-n-i^{3}hyeh-e^3
nonF 3 Pl have repP

ase^{3}sgi^{3}ni   u-ni-ki^{23}sad-a   ges-e^3 d-ade^{23}yo^{32}le-g-v^3
but   3 Pl accustomed-to recP   be repP   Pl curve Prog exP

kohi-sgi^{3}ni^3 ges-v^{32}
but this time   be exP

d-u-wa^{3}ʔihlv^3 wi-d-u^{23}-ni^{3}nolh^{32}ji^{23}hl-e^3 jwu^{3}hno^3 u-n-adey^{23}s-di
Pl 3bush   Tr Pl 3 bump-into repP   when and   3 Pl go-around Inf

u-n-anelh^{3}tan-a   si^{23}gwu
3 Pl try recP   again

d-uwa^{3}ʔihlv^3 wi-d-u^3-ni^{3}nolh^{32}ji^{23}hl-e^{3}i   ilv^{23}sgi-hno^3 n-u-n-a^{3}nelhta^{3}n-e^3
Pl bush   Tr Pl 3 bump-into repP   few and   Spec 3 Pl try repP

u-n-adey^{23}s-di   d-uwa^{3}ʔihlv^3 a^{23}se^{3}hno   si^{23}gwu   uhna^3-gwu
3 Pl go-around Inf   Pl bush   but   again   there just

wi-d-a^3-   ale^3 u-n-ade^{3}yohn-e^3 ni-g-vwsd-e^3 a-n-adi^{23}s-g-o^{3}ʔi
ninolh^{32}ji^{23}hi^{3}h-e^3
Tr Pl 3 bump-into repP   and   3 Pl circle repP   Spec 3 seem   3 Pl say Prog
                                                    repP   Hab

nogwu^3-hno^3 w-u-ni^3-hwahtv^{4}h-a   udlanv^{4}dv   u-ni-ktv^{3}les-e^3 ale^3
now and   Tr 3 Pl find Pres   opening   3 Pl go-through repP   and

u-n-a^{23}hni̲^{3}gis-e^{3}	usdi	wi̲-g-a̲nv^{3}hn-v^{4}ʔi	ge^{3}-hno	i̲yv^{4}da	u-n-a^{23}hni̲^{3}gi^{4}d-a
3 Pl start-walking repP	little	Tr 3 road exP	over-there and	distance	3 Pl walk Pres

u-n-a̲delohos-e^{3}	j-u-ni^{3}-los-v^{3}	i̲di^{3}dla	wi̲^{3}-ʔa̲-n-a^{3}ʔis-e^{3}ʔi
3 Pl notice repP	Dst 3 Pl come-from exP	toward	Tr 3 Pl walk repP

i̲^{3}ʔ-u-n-a̲jv^{3}s-a̲-hno
Rep 3 Pl turn recP and

no^{23}gwu	o^{23}sda̲-gwu	w-u̲^{3}-ni-los-e^{3}	i̲lv^{3}hdlv^{3}ʔi̲-gwu
then	good just	Tr 3 Pl go-again repP	without-somewhere just

wi-ni-i̲d-u-^{23}ni-^{3}nolhji^{23}hl-v^{4}na
Tr Neg Pl 3 Pl bump-into recP Neg

Syllabary

ᎦᏅᏓᏗᏍᎪ ᏗᎩᎦᏴᎵᎨ ᏥᎨᏒ ᏃᏊᎴ ᎡᏚᏚ ᎡᎵᏏᏃ ᏥᎨᏒ ᎪᎩᏃᎯᏎᎯ ᎨᏒ ᏦᏥᏲᏟ ᏙᎦᏛᏏᏗᏒ Ꮎ ᏴᏫ ᏧᎾᏍᏗ ᏥᏓᏃᏎᎲ ᏞᏃ ᎥᏍᏊ ᏖᏂᎦᎵᏍᏗᎭᏊ ᎩᎶ ᏧᏂᎪᎲᎯ ᏖᎨᏎ ᎥᏍᎩᎾ ᏴᏫ ᏧᎾᏍᏗ ᎡᎵᏍᎩᏂ ᎢᎸᏍᎩ ᎾᏂᎥ ᎩᎶ ᎦᏥᏲᎵᎩ ᎤᎾᏕᎶᎰᏒᎯ ᎨᏒ ᎪᎱᏍᏗ ᎠᏎᎩ ᎨᏒ ᏂᎦᎵᏍᏔᏅᎥᏍᎬ ᎠᎴ ᏖᎩ ᎤᎾᏛᎦᏅᎯ ᎨᏒ ᎩᎶ ᎠᏂᏬᏂᏍᎬ ᎠᏎᏍᎩᏂ ᎩᎶ ᏂᏓᏂᎪᏩᏘᏍᎬᎾ ᎥᏍᎩᏃ ᎢᏳᎵᏍᏔᏂᏙᎸᎯ ᏖᎩ ᏴᏫ ᏧᎾᏍᏗᎢ ᏓᏂᏌᏎᎲᎢ ᏞᏃ ᎥᏍᏉ ᏗᏍᎦᎢᏍᏗ ᏖᎨᏎ ᎠᎾᏗᏍᎪ ᏖᏚᏂᏃᎮᏞ ᎤᎾᏓᏅᏘᎮᏃ ᎠᎴ ᎣᏍᏓ ᎨᏒ ᎢᏳᎵᏍᏓᏁᏗ ᏴᏫ ᎢᏳᏃ ᏂᏓᎭᏢᏙᎲᎾ ᏖᎩ ᎠᎾᏗᏍᎪᎢ ᎠᎴ ᏖᎩ ᎬᏩᎾᏓᏍᏕᎸᏗ ᎨᏒ ᎪᎱᏍᏗ ᎦᎾᏰᎩ ᏖᏂᏧᏍᏗᏓᎾ ᏮᎦᏛ ᎢᏗᏜ ᎤᏌᏖᏊ ᎤᏁᎳᏅᎯ ᏖᏛᏁᎵᏗ ᏗᏂᎧᏃᏩᏗᏙᎯ ᏥᎦᎬᏗᎭ ᏴᏫ ᏓᏍᏕᎵᏍᎬ ᎠᎭᏂ ᎡᎶᎯ ᎨᏒ ᎾᏍᎩᏯ ᏊᏛᏏ ᎥᏍᎩᎾ ᏴᏫ ᏧᎾᏍᏗᎢ ᏥᏓᏃᏎᎲᎢ ᎪᎱᏍᏗ ᏴᎦᎵᏍᏔᏂᏓ ᎨᎭ ᎢᏳᏓᎵᎭ ᏖᏅᎦᏕᎵᏍᏓᏊ ᎦᏰᎵᏍᏗ ᎥᏍᎩᏃ ᏖᏄᎵᏍᏔᏂᏙᏔ ᎠᎾᏓᏍᏕᎵᏍᎪ ᏴᏫ ᏧᎾᏍᏗ ᎠᎾᏂᏍᎩ ᎨᏒ ᏗᎩᎦᏴᎵᎨ ᏥᎨᏒᎢ ᏌᏊᏃ ᎢᏳᏩᎪᏗ ᎡᎵᏏ ᎡᏚᏚᏃ ᎤᏒ ᎢᎠᎾᎢᏎ ᏧᏁᏅᏒ ᎢᏗᏜ ᏧᏂᎳᏫᎢᏍᏗ ᎤᏁᏙᎸᎯ ᎤᏍᏗᏃ ᎦᏅᏅ ᎠᎾᎢᏎ ᎡᎵ ᎢᎸᏍᎩ ᎢᏳᏩᎪᏗ ᎤᏂᎶᏏᏙᎸ ᎠᎴ ᎤᏂᎩᏌᏓ ᎠᎴ ᎬᏁᎳᎩᏊ ᏊᏛᏏ ᎤᎾᏅᏓ ᏓᎦᏲᎴᎬ ᎤᏍᏗ ᎦᏅᏅ ᎠᏎᏃ ᎠᏎᎩ ᏄᎵᏍᏔᏁ ᎠᎾᏗᏍᎪ ᎾᎯᏳ ᎠᎾᎢᏒᎢ ᏞᏃ ᎠᏨᎢᏍᏁᏗ ᏯᏂᏰᎮ ᎠᏎᏍᎩᏂ ᎤᏂᎩᏌᏓ ᎨᏎ ᏓᎦᏲᎴᎬ ᎪᎯᏍᎩᎢ ᎨᏒ ᏚᏩᎢᏢ ᏫᏚᏂᏃᏥᏝ ᎢᎸᏍᎩᏃ ᏄᎾᏁᎵᏔᏁ ᎤᎾᎦᏯᏍᏗ ᏚᏩᎢᏢ ᎠᏎᏃ ᏏᏊ ᎤᏏᏊ ᏫᏓᏂᏃᎸᏥᎯᎮ ᎠᎴ ᎤᎾᎦᏲᏁ ᏂᎬᏩᏍᎦ ᎠᎾᏗᏍᎪ ᏃᏊᏃ ᏭᏂᏩᏛᎭ ᎤᏜᏅᏛ ᎤᏂᎦᏛᎴᏎ ᎠᎴ ᎤᎾᏂᎩᏎ ᎤᏍᏗ ᏫᎦᏅᏅᎢ ᎨᏃ ᎢᏴᏓ ᎤᎾᏂᎩᏓ ᎤᎾᏕᎶᎰᏎ ᏧᏂᎶᏒ ᎢᏗᏜ ᏫᎠᎾᎢᏎᎢ ᎢᎤᎾᏨᏌᏃ ᏃᏊ ᎣᏍᏓᏊ ᏭᏂᎶᏎ ᎢᎸᏢᎢᏊ ᏫᏂᏚᏂᏃᎵᏥᏢᎾ

English

I remember that my parents, my grandfather, and my grandmother would tell us, when we were children, about the Little People. Not just anyone had seen the Little People, but there were a few people that I know who had experienced some unusual happenings and had heard someone talking but had not seen them. When something like that had happened, they would say it was the Little People. The Little People were not to be feared, they would say when they talked about them, because they were friendly, and those who came into contact with them were to meet good fortune if they welcomed them. Also they would help in a time of need or if you were headed toward danger. Just as one would have faith in God and his angels, so were the Little People there to help. Once in a while something might happen that would seem extraordinary, and if it did, the Little People are there to help, my parents would say.

One night my grandmother and grandfather were walking home from church through a path they had been quite familiar with, familiar enough with it that they had no light with them. They knew every bend, every curve, but suddenly they walked into bushes. They tried to sidestep them and go around, but each attempt only caused them to walk into more bushes. They seemed to make a complete circle trying to go around the bushes. And just as suddenly as they had encountered the bushes, the obstacles were gone. They began to walk along the path again, and when they had gone a little way, they realized that they were headed in the direction that they had come from. They faced about and started toward their home and reached their destination with no problem.

Origin of Evil Magic

Homer Snell

Origin myths are legends explaining how some aspect of the natural world or of human behavior came to exist. "Origin of Evil Magic" is an origin myth that describes how magic came to be used to do harm to others.

RSS	ᏥᎨᏒ	ᎠᏃᎮᏍᎪ	ᎢᏍᎩᏃ	ᎤᏃᎮᏓ	ᎤᎵᏏ
edudu	jigesv	kanohesgo	vsgino	unoheda	ulisi
my grandfather	who was	he tells	and that	told by	his grandmother

ᏥᎨᏒ	ᎾᎲᎩ
jigesv	nahiyu
who was	then

ᏗᎪᎸᎬ	Ꮛ	ᏥᏗᏁᎮ		ᏗᏂᏣᎳᎩ	Ꮩ	ᎡᏘᏴ
dikalvgv	asi	jidinehe		anijalagi	do	etiyv
to the east	yet	when they lived there		Cherokees	really	long ago

ᏥᎨᏒ	ᎤᏁᎳᏬᎯ
jigesv	unelanvhi
then	God

ᏚᏁᎴ	ᎡᎵᏍᏗ	ᎾᏗ	ᎠᏃᎮᏍᎬ		Ꮎ
duhnele	elisdi	nadi	kanohesgv		na
he gave them	it seems	that is	he was talking about		that

ᏓᎾᏓᏁᏎ	ᏣᎾᏗ	ᎫᏍᏗ
danadanese	janadi	gusdi
they conjure each other	which they say	something

ᏣᎾᏓᏛᏁ	ᎾᏍᎩ	ᎠᏎᏃ	Ꮭ	ᎥᏍᎩ
janadadvne	nasgi	asehno	hla	vsgi
they do to you	that	but	not	that

ᎢᏳᏅᏙᏗ	ᏱᎩᎨᏥᏁᎴ
iyunvdodi	yigejinele
in order to use it	if it was given to them

ᎤᎾᎵᏍᏓᏴᏗ	ᎤᏂᏩᏛᏙᏗ	ᎨᏥᏁᎴ	ᎫᏍᏗ
unalisdayvdi	uniwadvdodi	gejinele	gusdi
their food	for them to find with	it was given to them	something

ᎤᏂᎯᏍᏙᏗ	ᎪᎱᏍᏗ
unihisdodi	gohusdi
for them to kill it with	something

ᎠᏃᏢᏍᎨ	ᎡᎵᏊ	Ꭸ	ᎢᏴ	ᎬᎴ	ᎡᎵ
anodlvsge	eligwu	ge	iyv	gvle	eli
they made it	it was possible	over there	from there	position	it was possible

ᎪᎱᏍᏗ	ᎬᏩᏂᎯᏍᏗ	ᎠᏫ
gohusdi	gvwanihisdi	awi
something	for them to kill	deer

ᏱᎩ	ᎠᎴ	ᎪᎱᏍᏗ	ᎢᎾᎨ	ᎡᎯ	ᏍᎩᏃ
yigi	ale	gohusdi	inage	ehi	sgino
for example	and	something	wild game	dweller	and that

ᎠᏁᎮ	ᎠᏂᏃᎭᎵᏙ	ᎠᏂᏔᎵ
anehe	aninohalido	anitali
there were	hunters	two of them

ᎠᏗᏍᎪ	ᎠᏂᏃᎭᎵᏙᎲ	ᏌᏊᏃ	ᏧᎾᏔᎾ	ᏓᎯᎮ
adisgo	aninohalidohv	sagwuno	junatana	dahihe
he says	while they were hunting	and one	big ones	he would kill

ᏐᎢᏃ	ᎤᏠᎨ	ᎤᏔᏂᏓ	ᏧᎾᏍᏗ	ᏓᎯᎮ
so?ino	udloge	utanida	junasdi	dahihe
and the other	he couldn't find	a bigger one	small ones	he would kill

ᏣᏗᎲ	ᎤᏩᏳᏤ	ᏣᏗᎲ
jadihv	uwayuje	jadihv
he was saying	he became jealous	he was saying

Ꮎ	ᏧᎾᏍᏗ	ᏗᎯᎯ	ᎠᏫ	ᏗᎯᏍᏙᏗ	ᏓᏥᏴᏓᏁᎵ
na	junasdi	dihihi	awi	dihisdodi	dajiyvdaneli
the	small ones	killer	deer	to kill with	I am going to use on him

ᏓᏥᎵ	Ꮎ	ᎠᏫ
dajili	na	awi
I am going to kill him	that	deer

ᏧᎾᏔᎾ	ᏥᏓᎯᎭ	ᎤᏛᏁ	ᏣᏗᎲ	ᏍᎩᎾ	ᎤᏫᏔᏁ
junatana	jidahiha	udvne	jadihv	sgina	uwvtane
big ones	the one who is killing them	he said	he was saying	that	he used

ᏧᏍᏓᏲᏓᏃ	ᎠᏗᎰ	Ꮎ	ᎸᏢ	ᎠᏴᏓᏆᎶᏍᎩ
jusdayodano	adiho	na	lvdlv	ayvdagwalosgi
tree struck by lightning	he says	that	somewhere	thunder

ᎤᏩᏂᎸ	ᏥᏂᏚᏍᏙ
uwanilv	jinidusdo
which was struck by	that exists

Ꮎ	ᏧᎵᏍᏡᏴ	ᎥᏍᎩᏃ	ᎢᏳᏍᏗ
na	julisdluyv	vsgino	iyusdi
that	that were split	and that	like it

ᏓᏃᏢᏗᎮ	ᏣᏗᎲ	ᏧᏂᏲᏍᏙᏗ
danodlvdihe	jadihv	juniyosdodi
they made out of them	he was saying	to shoot them with

ᏝᏅ	ᏯᏆᏅᏔ	ᎪᏁᏍᏗ	ᏯᎾᏗ
tlanv	yagwanvta	gojusdi	yanadi
and not	I don't know	something	if they say

ᏗᎪᏍᏓᏱᏍᎩᏂ	ᏂᏓᏅᏁᎮ
digosdayisgini	nidanvnehe
sharp ones however	they made them

ᏃᏊᏅ	Ꮎ	ᎠᏥᎸᎯ	ᏗᎪᏰᎲ	ᏂᏓᏅᏁᎮ	ᏃᏊᏅ	ᎯᎠ
nogwunv	na	ajilvhi	digoyehv	nidanvnehe	nogwunv	hi?a
and then	that	in the fire	heated	they would do	and then	this

ᏄᏍᏛ	ᏓᏂᏝᏗᏍᎨ	ᏓᎾᏍᎪᎵᏰᏍᎨ	ᎠᏗ
nusdv	danitladisge	danasgoliyesge	adi
place	they would lay them on	they would rub them	I guess

ᎫᏍᏗ	ᎠᏎ	ᎠᎾᏗᏍᎨ
gusdi	ase	anadisge
something	I guess	they would say

ᏱᏭᏂᎪ	ᎪᏁᏍᏗ	ᎢᏳᏍᏗ	ᎤᎾᏚᎵᏍᎬ
yiwunigo	gohusdi	iyusdi	unadulisgv
when they saw it at a distance	something	like	the one they wanted

ᏃᏇᏅ	ᎤᏁ	ᎢᏗᏢ
nogwenv	uhna	ididlv
and then	there	toward

ᏳᏂᎧᏔᏓ	ᏳᎾᏦᏔᎭᏊ	ᎠᏝᏫᏗᏍᎨ
yunikatada	yunajotahagwu	atlawidisge
when they would point	and when they just blow on it	it would fly

ᎤᏠᏱᏊ	ᎦᏂ
udloyigwu	gani
same as	a bullet

SⱤⱤZ	ᎪᎣ	OⴱⵔZ	DᏰC	SGⱤ
ganageno	gohusdi	unawino	ayehli	galosge
and it would fall	something	in the heart	in the middle	it would go through

ZⱤⴱⱰ	D
nogwulenv	a
and then also	this

ⴱⱰS	OⱤZᏰh	DⱤOⱰ	P
nanvga	unoyeni	agwunv	dlv
when they did	their hand	close by	somewhere

VⱰSGⱤ	ᏞᏜᏗᏗᏢ
dodigalosge	datladijihihe
they would come from	they would land

ᏞhⱤᏧᎥhⱰᏧᏢ	ZⱤⴱ	iⱤⱯZ	ⴱᎬⱰⴱ	DⱰᏱ	ⴱ
dinisgwanigodihe	nogwule	vsgino	nagvnele	adihv	na
they would put them away	and then	and that	was done to him	he said	that

ᏧⴱᎳⴱ	DⴱO	ᏧᏗ	ᏧⴱⱤᏧ	ⴱ	DⴱO	ᏧᏗ
junatana	awi	dihi	junasdi	na	awi	dihi
big ones	deer	killer	small ones	that	deer	killer

OⱤGᏀGᏟ	Ᏺ	TB	EⴱO
uwayujv	ge	iyv	gvle
as a jealous person	there	from	position

DⴱO	ᏱhᏱᏰᏧᎸ	iⱤⱯ	hᏞᏱᏰᏧᏢ	OⱤᏴᏧ
awi	jinijiyvneho	vsgi	nidajiyvneli	udvne
deer	that which I do to it	that	I will do to him	he said

VᏗGOⱰ	iⱤⱤ	ⱤⱯ
dohiyunv	vsgwu	sgi
and for sure	also	that

ꙨᎬᏁᏙ	ᏣᏗᎲ	ᏁᎯᏴ	ᎤᏂᏲᏤᏙ	ᎠᏗᎲ	ᎤᎾᎵᏍᏕᎸᏙᏗ
nagvnele	jadihv	nahiyu	uniyochele	adihv	unalisdelvdodi
it was done to him	he said	then	it was ruined	he said	their aid

ᎨᎲ	ᎢᏍᏓᏁᎳᏁᎸ		ᏠᎾᏓᎮᏙᏗᏏ
gehv	gegadanelanelv		junadahisdodigwu
that was	that was provided them		just something for them to kill each other with

ᏠᎾᏗᏤᏬᎥᏁ	ᎤᎾ	ᏚᏓᎴᏅᎮ	ᏗᎾᏓᏁᏎᏍᎩ
wunadanedliyvstane	uhna	judalenvhe	dinadanesesgi
it turned into	there	it began	conjurers of each other

ᏄᎵᏍᏔᏁ	ᎠᏗᏍᎬ	ᎧᏃᎮᏍᎩ
nulistane	adisgv	kanohesgi
it happened	he said	the one who tells it

Morpheme by Morpheme

e-dudu	ji-ges-v	ka-nohe²³s-g-o	vsgi-hno³	u-n-ohe⁴d-a
1Pos grandfather	Rel be exP	3 tell Prog Hab	that and	3 Pl tell Pres

u-li³si	ji-ges-v	nahiyu
3Pos grandmother	Rel be exP	then

dikalv³²gv	asi³	ji-di²³-n-e³h-e	a-ni-jalagi	do³
in-east	yet	Rel Pl Pl live repP	3 Pl cherokee	really

e⁴ti³²yv³	ji-ge³s-v	une²³hla³nvhi	d-u-n-e²³l-e
long-ago	Rel be exP	god	Pl 3 Pl give repP

e³li³si	na³	ka-n-ohe²³s-g-v	na³	d-a-n-ada-nes-e³
seem	that	3 Pl talk Prog exP	that	Pl 3 Pl Refl conjure repP

j-a-n-adi	gu²³sdi
Rel 3 Pl say	something

j-a-n-ada-dv^{3}n-e   nasgi   ase^{3}hno   hla^{3} vsgi
Pl 3 Pl Refl do repP   that   but   not   that

iyunv^{23}dodi   yi-g-e^{23}ji^{32}-n-el-e
for-that-purpose   nonF 3Pl Pas give Dat repP

u^{23}-n-alisdayv-di   u-ni^{23}-wadvdo-di   g-eji-ne^{23}l-e
3 Pl feed Inf   3 Pl find Inf   3 Pl Pas give Dat repP

gu^{23}sdi   u-ni^{23}-hisdo-di   gohu^{23}sdi
something   3 Pl kill Inf   something

a-n-ohlvs-g-e   eli^{4}-gwu   ge^{3} iyv^{3} gvle^{3} eli
3 Pl make Prog repP   possible just   over there   from   position   possible

gohu^{23}sdi   gv-wa-ni^{23}-his-di   awi
something   3pl kill Inf   deer

y-i^{4}gi   ale^{3} gohu^{23}sdi   ina^{3}ge   e^{23}h-i   sgi-no^{3}
nonF be   and   something   forest   dwell Ag   that and

a-n-eh-e   a-ni-nohalido   a-ni^{23}-tali
3 Pl live repP   3 Pl hunt   3 Pl two

a-di^{23}s-g-o   a-ni-nohali^{23}do^{32}h-v   sagwu^{4}-no   j-u^{23}-n-atana
3 say Prog Hab   3 Pl hunt exP   one and   Pl 3 Pl big

ahwi   d-a-hih-e   j-a-di^{23}h-v
deer   3 Pl kill repP   Pst 3 say exP

so?i-no^{3} u-dlo^{3}-g-e   utan-i^{4}da   j-u-n-asdi
other and   3 search-in-vain Prog repP   big more   Pl 3 Pl small

d-a-hih-e^{3} j-a-di^{23}h-v
Pl 3 kill repP   Pst 3 say exP

uw-ayuj-e   j-a-dih-v   na^{3} j-u-n-asdi   di-hih-i
3 get-angry repP   Pst 3 say exP   that   Pl 3 Pl small   Pl kill Ag

a̱wi   di-hi̱s-dodi   da̱-jiy-vdan-el-i   da-j-i̱l-i   na^3 awi
deer   Pl kill Inf   Fut 1 use-on Dat Fut   Fut 1 kill Fut that   deer

j-u-n-a̱tana   ji-d-a-hi̱h-a   u-dvn-e   j-a-di̱^{23}h-v   sgi̱na   uw-ta̱n-e^3
Pl 3 Pl big   Rel Pl 3 kill Pres 3 say repP Pst 3 say exP   that   3 use repP

j-u-sda̱yod-a̱^{3}-no^3 a-di̱^{23}h-o   na^3 lvdlv
Rel 3 struck-by-lightning recP and   3 say Hab   that   somewhere

a-yvdagwa̱los-g-i   u-wani̱^{3}l-v   ji̱-ni̱-du^{3}sd-o
3 thunder Prog Ag 3 strike exP   Rel Pl exist Hab

na^3 j-u-lisdlu̱^{3}y-v   vsgi̱-no^3 iyu^{4}sdi   d-a-n-odlvdi̱^{3}h-e
that   Pst 3 split exP   that and   like-that   Pl 3 Pl make-out-of-them repP

j-a-di̱^{23}h-v^3 j-u-ni-yo^{23}s-do̱di
Pst 3 say exP   Pl 3 Pl shoot Ins

hla̱-nv^3 y-a̱gw-onv̱^{3}t-a   gohu^{4}sdi   y-a-n-a̱di
not and   nonF 1 know Pres   something   nonF 3 Pl say

di̱-go^{23}sda̱yi̱-sgi^{3}ni   ni̱-d-a-n-v^{3}neh-e
Pl sharp but   Spec Pl 3 Pl make repP

nogwu^3-nv^3 na^3 a̱jilv^4-hi   di̱-goye^{23}hv
then and   that   fire in   Pl heated

ni̱-d-a-n-v^{3}neh-e   nogwu^3-nv   hi̱ʔa
Spec Pl 3 Pl do repP   then and   this

nusdv   d-a-ni-nla̱di^{32}s-g-e   d-a-n-a̱sgoli^{23}ye^{32}s-g-e   a̱^{3}di^3 gu^{4}sdi^3
place   Pl 3 Pl lay-on Prog repP   Pl 3 Pl rub Prog repP   possibly   something

a^{23}se   a-n-a̱di^{23}s-g-e
perhaps   3 Pl say Prog repP

yi̱-w-u^{23}-ni^3-go   gohu^{4}sdi   iyu^{3}sdi   u-n-a̱duli^{3}s-g-v
nonF Tr 3 Pl see   something   like   3 Pl want Prog exP

no^{23}gwu^3-nv   u^{3}hna   i̱di^{3}dlv
then and   there   toward

y-u^{23}-ni^4-ka̱ta̱d-a   y-u-n-a̱jo^{3}tah-a̱^{3}-gwu
nonF 3 Pl point Pres   nonF 3 Pl blow-on Pres just

a-tla̱widi^{23}s-g-e   udlo^{3}yi̱-gwu   ga̱^{3}ʔni
3 fly Prog repP   same just   bullet

g-a̱nv^{3}ge^{3}n-o   gohu^{4}sdi   hearti^4-no   a̱ye^{4}hli   g-alos-g-e
3 fall Hab   something   heart-in and   in-the-middle   3 go-through Prog
                                                           repP

nogwu̱^{3}-le^3-nv^3 a^3 n-a-n-v^{32}-g-a   j-u-n-oye^{4}ni   agwu-nv   dlv^3
then also and   this   Spec 3 Pl do   Pl 3 Pl hand   close-by and   somewhere
                                   Prog Pres

do-di-^{23}ga^{4}los-g-e   d-a-tla̱di^{32}ji-hi̱h-e
Dst Pl go-past Prog repP   Pl 3 land come repP

d-a^3-ni-sgwa̱nigo^{32} nogwu̱^{3}-le   vsgi-no^3 n-agv^3-nel-e   a-dih-v^3 na^3
dih-e^3
Pl 3 Pl save repP   then and   that and   Spec 3Pas do   3 say exP   that
                                                             repP

j-u^{23}-n-a̱ta̱na   a̱wi   d-i^{23}h-i   j-u-n-a̱sdi^3 na   a̱wi
Pl 3 Pl big   deer   Pl kill Ag   Pl 3 Pl small   that   deer

d-i^{23}h-i   uw-ayu^{3}j-v^3 ge   iyv^3 gvle^3 a̱wi   ji-ni̱-ji-yv^{3}neh-o
Pl kill Ag   3 get-jealous exP   there   from   position   deer   Rel Spec 1 do
                                                              Hab

vsgi   ni-da̱-ji^3-yv^{3}n-el-i   u-dvn-e   dohiyu^4-nv   vsgwu^3 sgi^3
that   Spec Fut 1 do Dat Fut   3 say repP   certainly and   also   that

n-agv^3-n-el-e   j-a-di̱h-v   nahi̱yu
Spec I/him do Dat repP   Pst 3 say exP   then

u-ni-yo^{3}chel-e	a-dih-v	u-n-alisdelv^{23}do-di	geh-v
3 Pl ruin repP	3 say exP	3 Pl aid Inf	be exP

geg-ada-ne^{3}la^{23}n-el-v	j-u-n-ada-h^{23}isd-odi^{3}-gwu
they/them conjure Dat exP	Rel 3 Pl Refl kill Inst just

w-u^{23}n-a^{3}danedliyvs-tan-e^{3}	uhna^{3}	j-u^{23}-da^{3}lenvh-e^{3}	di-n-adanese^{4}s-g-i
Tr Pl turn-into Caus repP	there	Pl 3 begin repP	Pl Pl conjure Prog Ag

n-u-listan-e^{3}	a-di^{23}s-g-v^{3}	ka-nohe^{4}s-g-i
Spec 3 happen repP	3 say Prog exP	3 tell Prog Ag

Syllabary

ᎡᏚᏚ ᏥᎨᏒ ᎧᏃᎮᏍᎪ ᎥᏍᎩᏃ ᎤᏃᎮᏓ ᎤᎵᏏ ᏥᎨᏒ ᎾᎯᏳ ᏗᎧᎸᎬ ᎠᏏ ᏥᏗᏁᎮ ᎠᏂᏣᎳᎩ Ꮩ ᎡᏆᏴ ᏥᎨᏒ ᎤᏁᎳᏅᎯ ᏚᏁᏚ ᎡᎵᏍᏗ ᎾᏗ ᎧᏃᎮᏍᎬ Ꮎ ᏓᎾᏓᏁᏎ ᏣᎾᏗ ᎫᏍᏗ ᏣᎾᏓᏛᏁ ᎾᏍᎩ ᎠᏎᏃ Ꮭ ᎥᏍᎩ ᎢᏳᏅᏙᏗ ᏑᎨᏥᏁᎴ ᎤᎾᎵᏍᏓᏴᏗ ᎤᏂᏩᏛᏙᏗ ᎨᏥᏁᎴ ᎫᏍᏗ ᎤᏂᎯᏍᏙᏗ ᎪᎱᏍᏗ ᎠᏃᏢᏍᎨ ᎡᎵᏊ Ꭸ ᎢᏴ ᎬᎴ ᎡᎵ ᎪᎱᏍᏗ ᎬᏩᏂᎯᏍᏗ ᎠᏫ ᏑᎩ ᎠᎴ ᎪᎱᏍᏗ ᎢᎾᎨ ᎡᎯ ᏍᎩᏃ ᎠᏁᎮ ᎠᏂᏃᏘᎵᏙ ᎠᏂᏔᎵ ᎠᏗᏍᎪ ᎠᏂᏃᏘᎵᏙᎲ ᏌᏊᏃ ᏧᎾᏔᎾ ᏓᎯᎮ ᏘᎢᏃ ᎤᏌᎨ ᎤᎳᏂᏓ ᏧᎾᏍᏗ ᏓᎯᎮ ᏣᏗᎲ ᎤᏩᏳᏤ ᏣᏗᎲ Ꮎ ᏧᎾᏍᏗ ᏗᎯᎯ ᎠᏫ ᏗᎯᏍᏙᏗ ᏓᏥᏴᏓᏁᎵ ᏓᏥᎵ Ꮎ ᎠᏫ ᏧᎾᏔᎾ ᏥᏓᎯᏘ ᎤᏛᏁ ᏣᏗᎲ ᏍᎩᎾ ᎤᏮᏔᏁ ᏧᏍᏓᏲᏓᏃ ᎠᏗᎰ Ꮎ ᎸᏢ ᎠᏴᏓᏆᎶᏍᎩ ᎤᏩᏂᎸ ᏥᏂᏚᏍᏙ Ꮎ ᏧᎵᏍᏯᏴ ᎥᏍᎩᏃ ᎢᏳᏍᏗ ᏓᏃᏢᏗᎮ ᏣᏗᎲ ᏧᏂᏲᏍᏙᏗ ᏝᏅ ᏊᏆᏅᏔ ᎪᎱᏍᏗ ᏊᎾᏗ ᏗᎪᏍᏓᏑᏍᎩᏂ ᏂᏓᏅᏁᎮ ᏃᏊᎧᏅ Ꮎ ᎠᏥᎸᎯ ᏗᎪᏰᎲ ᏂᏓᏅᏁᎮ ᏃᏊᎧᏅ ᎯᎠ ᏄᏍᏛ ᏓᏂᏝᏗᏍᎨ ᏓᎾᏍᎪᎵᏰᏍᎨ ᎠᏗ ᎫᏍᏗ ᎠᏎ ᎠᎾᏗᏍᎨ ᏑᏭᏂᎪ ᎪᎱᏍᏗ ᎢᏳᏍᏗ ᎤᎾᏚᎵᏍᎬ ᏃᏉᏅ ᎤᎿ ᎢᏗᎮ ᏳᏂᎧᏔᏓ ᏳᎾᏦᏔᏘᏊ ᎠᏝᏫᏗᏍᎨ ᎤᏌᏑᏊ ᏕᏂ ᏕᏅᎨᏃ ᎪᎱᏍᏗ ᎤᎾᏫᏃ ᎠᏰᏟ ᏕᎶᏍᎨ ᏃᏊᎴᏅ Ꭰ ᎾᏅᏕ ᎤᏃᏰᏂ ᎠᏊᎧᏅ Ꮲ ᏙᏗᏕᎶᏍᎨ ᏓᏝᏗᏥᎯᏢ ᏓᏂᏍᏆᏂᎪᏗᏢ ᏃᏊᎧᎴ ᎥᏍᎩᏃ ᎾᎬᏁᎴ ᎠᏗᎲ Ꮎ ᏧᎾᏔᎾ ᎠᏫ ᏗᎯ ᏧᎾᏍᏗ Ꮎ ᎠᏫ ᏗᎯ ᎤᏩᏳᏨ Ꭸ ᎢᏴ ᎬᎴ ᎠᏫ ᏥᏂᏥᏴᏁᎰ ᎥᏍᎩ ᏂᏓᏥᏴᏁᎵ ᎤᏛᏁ ᏙᎯᏳᏅ ᎥᏍᏊ ᏍᎩ ᎾᎬᏁᎴ ᏣᏗᎲ ᎾᎯᏳ ᎤᏂᏲᏤᎴ ᎠᏗᎲ ᎤᎾᎵᏍᏕᎸᏙᏗ ᎨᎲ ᎨᏕᏓᏁᎳᏁᎸ ᏧᎾᏓᎯᏍᏙᏗᏊ ᏭᎾᏓᏁᏟᏴᏍᏔᏁ ᎤᎿ ᏧᏓᎴᏅᎮ ᏗᎾᏓᏁᏎᏍᎩ ᏄᎵᏍᏔᏁ ᎠᏗᏍᎬ ᎧᏃᎮᏍᎩ

English

My grandfather tells me a story told by his grandmother when the Cherokees were still living in the east quite a long time ago. The Creator, it seems, gave them a gift. He was talking about that which they call conjuring, when they do things to one another. But that was not the purpose of the gift. It was given to them for the purpose of getting food by killing something. They made something that they could kill a deer with from a distance or other animals. And there were two hunters, they say. As they hunted, one of them would kill large deer, he said. And the other one couldn't find a big one, he just killed small ones, he said. The one that was killing small ones got jealous. He said, "I'm going to use the thing to kill deer with on him and kill him," he said. He used that, he says, where there's a tree struck by lightning and there are slivers, that's what they used, he said, to shoot them with. I don't know if they would say anything, but they would make them real sharp, and then they would burn the tips and put them right here, and they would rub them together, and I guess they would say something. And when they would see something that they wanted, they would point the sliver in that direction and blow on it, and it would fly just like a bullet. And the thing would fall to the ground as it passed through the heart. And when they would go like this with their hand, they would come from somewhere nearby and land on the hand, and they would save them. That's what was done to the one who killed big deer, he said, when the one who killed the small deer got jealous. "I'll do to him what I do to kill a deer from a distance," he said. It was then that the gift that was provided for them was ruined. It just turned to something to kill each other with. That's where the conjuring started, he said, telling his story.

Spearfinger

Annie Jessan

Beliefs about witches are a fundamental component of the traditional Cherokee belief system. Witches are considered to be inherently evil: they frequently do harm to people and even commit murder using evil magic. "Spearfinger" relates how a particularly evil witch was overcome. Annie Jessan of Cherokee, North Carolina, related this myth.

ᏚᏣBᏃ	ᎠᎭᎫᏃ	ᏙᎭG	ᎡᎫB
hetiyvno	gohidino	dohiyu	etiyv
and long ago	too long	really	long time

ᎬᏛᏗ	ᏙᎭG	Ꭿ	ᏥᏓᏥᏃᏒᏟᏓ
gvdvdi	dohiyu	hi	jidajinohetli
you can say	really	this	I am going to tell

ᏴᎩᎢᎤᏩᏍᎩ	ᏚᏙᎡ	ᎡᎯ	Ꮧ	ᏍᎩᏃ	ᏅᎩ	ᎢᏯᏂ
yvgi?uwasgi	dudo?e	ehe	age	sgino	nvgi	iyani
Spearfinger	her name was	she lived	woman	that	four	of them

ᎠᏂᏃᎭᎵᏙ
aninohalido
hunters

ᎤᎾᏂᎩᏎ	ᏧᎾᏓᎵ	ᏚᎾᏗᏅᏎ	ᏍᎩᏃ	ᎦᏚᏏ	ᎤᎾᏅᏓᏕ
unanigise	junadali	dunatinvse	sgino	gadusi	unanvdade
they left	their spouses	they took with them	and that	on a hill	they remembered

ᎤᏏ	ᎤᏂᎷᏤ	ᎤᏂᏃᎭᎵᏓᏍᏗ	Ꮓ	ᏐᏭ
uhna	uniluje	uninohalidasdi	no	sowu
there	they arrived	their place of hunting	then	one

ᏣᏥᏯᏅᎮ	ᎨᏴ	ᏗᎦᏙᎨ	ᏍᎩᎾ	ᏴᎩᎤᏩᏍᎩ
jajiyanvhe	geyv	digadoge	sgina	yvgiʔuwasgi
she was called	over there	she was standing	that	Spearfinger

ᎠᎴ	ᎤᏩᏰᏑᎦᏢ	ᎠᏃᏎᎰ	ᏍᎩᎾ	ᎨᎾ	ᏘᎾ	ᏗᎬᎢᏏ
ale	uwayesugatlv	anoseho	sgina	kena	tina	digvʔisi
and	one with a finger	they called	that	come	lice	let me kill them for you

ᎤᏬᎮᎴᎢᏅ	ᎠᎨ	ᏃᎴ	ᎤᏪᏅᏎ	ᎮᎾ	ᎤᏃᎮᎴᏅ	ᏭᎷᏣᏃ
uwoheleinv	age	nole	uwenvse	hena	unohelenv	wulujano
and told her	woman	and	she went	go	they told her	and when she arrived there

ᎤᏙᏳᏃ	ᏘᎾ	ᏥᏓᏲᏎᎰ	ᎢᏳᏍᏗ	ᏄᏩ
udoyuno	tina	jidayoseho	iyusdi	nuwa
and really	lice	as though she was looking for	like	[false start]

ᏄᏛᏁᎴ	ᎠᏎᏃ
nudvnele	aseno
she did	however

ᏓᎯᎮᏊᏃ	ᎠᏂᎨ	ᎥᏍᎩ	ᎠᎴ	ᏔᎵᏁ
dahihegwuno	anige	vsgi	ale	taline
but she was killing them	women	that	again	second

ᎤᎾᏂᎩᏌ	ᏍᏊ	ᏍᎩᏊ
unanigisa	sgwu	sgigwu
when they left	also	just that

ᎢᏯᏂ	ᏅᎩ	ᏃᏊ	ᏦᏊ	ᏚᎾᏘᏅᏎ
iyani	nvgi	nogwu	jogwu	dunatinvse
of them	four	then	three	they took them

ᏚᎾᏓᎵ	Ꮎ	ᏍᎩᏅᏫ	ᏍᎩ
junadali	na	sginv	sgi
their spouses	that	and that	that

ᎾᏣᏪᎮᎴ	ᎤᏦᏱᏍᏩ	ᎨᎾ	ᎠᎪᎮᎴ
najiwehele	ujoyigwu	kena	agohele
she was told	just the same	come	she was told

ᏃᏍᏩ	Ꮠ	ᎠᏂᎩᏍᎨ	Ꮎ
nogwu	so	ahnigisge	na
and then	other	she would go	that

ᏯᏂ	ᎠᏂᎨ	ᏚᏂᏲᎱᏎᎴ	ᏐᏩ
yani	anige	duniyohusele	sogwu
of them	women	they lost	one

ᏳᏳᎷᏣ	ᏍᎩᏃ	ᎠᏥᎢᎮᏊᏃ	ᎫᏥ
yuwuluja	sgino	aji?ihegwuno	jo?i
as she arrived	and that	they would just kill her	three

ᏌᏛᏗ	ᏥᏓᏗᏍᎪ	ᎢᏳᏍᏗ	ᎠᏥᏌᏛᏁᏃ	ᏍᎩᎾ	ᎤᏩᏍᎩ	Ꮎ
sadvdi	jidadisgo	iyusdi	ajisadvneno	sgina	uwasgi	nahna
trap	as we say	like	and she was trapped	that	Spearfinger	there

ᎯᎠᏗ	ᏂᎾᏛᏁᎸ	ᎠᎪᎮᎴ	ᎠᎨᏲᏁ	ᏍᎩᎾ	ᎠᎨ	ᏍᎩᎾ
hi?adi	hnadvnelv	agohele	ageyone	sgina	age	sgina
and this	you do	she was told	she was taught	that	women	that

Ꮓ	ᎠᏴᏃ	ᎣᏥᏍᎦᏯ	ᏓᏲᏣᏛᏅᎢᏍᏔᏂ	Ꮎ
no	ayvno	ojisgaya	dayojadvnv?istani	na
and	and I	we men	we will prepare	that

ᎣᏥᏂᏴᏗ	ᎨᎮᏍᏗ
ojiniyvdi	gehesdi
for us to grab her	it will be

ᎤᏛᏁ	ᏙᏃ	ᎤᏂᏂᏴᎮ	ᏧᏬᏰᏂ	ᏚᎾᏢᎴ	ᏍᎩᎾ
udvne	dono	uniniyvhe	juwoyeni	dunatlvle	sgina
he said	and truly	they caught her	her hands	they tied them up	that

ᎠᎨ	ᏴᎩᎤᏩᏍᎩ	ᎾᏃ	ᏃᏊ	ᎠᏂᏲᎯᎲᎮᏃ	ᎦᎶᏇ
age	yvgiʔuwasgi	nano	nogwu	aniyohihvheno	galogwe
woman	Spearfinger	and also	then	they were shooting her	gun

ᎬᏅᏗ	Ꮎ	ᎦᏂ	ᏕᎬᏩᏂᎲ	ᏙᏌ	ᎤᏂᏣᏔ	ᎠᏗᏍᎨᎢᏊᏃ
gvnvdi	na	gani	degvwanihv	dosa	unijata	adisgeʔigwuno
with	the	bullets	as they hit her	mosquito	they are many	she was just saying

ᏕᎬᏂᎮ	ᏓᎨᎯᏙᎮ	ᏙᏌ	ᎠᏗᏍᎬ
degvnihe	dakehidohe	dosa	adisgv
she was hitting them	she was chasing them away	mosquito	she said

ᎦᏂ	ᎬᏩᏂᎲ	ᎾᏃ	ᏅᏯ
gani	gvwanihv	nano	nvya
bullets hitting her	and the	and that	rock

ᎤᏄᏩ	ᎠᏃᏎᎰ	ᎢᎦᏓ	ᏙᏛ
unuwa	anoseho	igada	dodv
she had on	they called her	some	what

ᎤᏍᏗ	ᏚᏙᎡ	ᎤᎬᏫᏳᎮ	ᏍᎩᏃ	Ꮩ
usdi	dudoʔe	ugvwiyuhe	sgino	do
like	her name	instead	that	really

ᏍᎩᏃ	ᎤᏂᏂᏴᎮ	ᎤᏙᎯᏳ	ᏍᎩᎾ
sgino	uniniyvhe	udohiyu	sgina
and that	they caught her	really	that

ᎠᎨ	ᏄᏩᏂᏌᏁ	ᏍᎩᏃ	i
age	nuwanisane	sgino	v
woman	she caused it	and that	uh

ᏍᎩᎾ	ᏥᎦᏗ	ᎦᏂ	ᎬᏩᏂᎲ	ᏙᏌ
sgina	jigadi	gani	gvwanihv	dosa
that	which I say	bullets	they were hitting her	mosquito

ᎤᏂᏣᏔ	ᏳᏛᎿ
unijata	yudvhna
they are many	when she would say

ᎾᏗᏃ	ᎤᏂᎷᏤ	ᎠᏂᏍᎦᏯ	ᏃᏭ	ᏦᎢ	ᏯᏂ	ᎤᎾᏍᎪᏎ	ᎤᎧᏲᏓ
nadino	uniluje	anisgaya	nowu	jo?i	yani	unasgose	ukayoda
and that	they came	men	then	three	of them	they dug	dry

ᎠᏓ	ᎤᏂᎳᏕ	ᏍᎩᏃ	ᏂᎦᏓ	ᎤᎾᏛᏅᎢᏍᏓᏁ
ada	unilade	sgino	nigada	unadvnv?istane
wood	they placed it into	and that	all	they prepared

ᏍᎩᎾ	ᏔᎵᏅ
sgina	talinv
that	and two

ᎧᎶᏇᎩᏗ	ᏧᏂᎸᏓᎸᏓ	ᏍᎩᎾ	ᎠᏓ	ᏧᏂᏍᏓᎷᎢᏍᏗ	ᎢᏳ	ᏍᎩᎾ
kalogwegidi	junilvdalvda	sgina	ada	junisdalu?isdi	iyu	sgina
locust	splinters	that	wood	for them to split	then	that

ᏂᏚᏅᏁᎴ	ᏃᏊᎴ	ᏍᏆᎸᏂᏍᏗ
nidunvnele	nogwule	sgwalvnisdi
they did	and also	to hit on the head with (an instrument)

ᏄᏅᏁᎴ	ᏍᎩᎾ	ᏃᏊ	ᏍᎩ
nunvnele	sgina	nogwu	sgi
they did	that	then	that

ᏱᏁᏛᏁᎳ	ᏰᏗᎷᎦ	Ꮩ	ᏥᏈᏯ
yinedvnela	yediluga	do	jigwiya
if we do to her	we can kill her	really	too many

ᏓᏛᏗ	ᎠᏂᎨ	ᎤᏛᏁ	ᏌᏊ
datvdi	anige	udvne	sagwu
she is doing away with	women	he said	one

ᎠᏍᎦᏯ	ᎥᏃ	ᎤᏪᎯᏍᏓᏁᎮ	ᎤᏓᎵᎢ
asgaya	vno	uwehisdanehe	udali?i
man	very much	she was hurting	his spouse

ᎠᏥᎡᎸ	ᏍᎩᏃ	ᏂᎦᏗ
aji?elv	sgino	nigadi
being killed	and that	all

ᎤᏂᏅᏁ	ᎠᎨ	ᏍᎩᏅ	ᏅᏯ	ᎤᏄᏩ	ᎤᏏ	ᎣᏂ
uninvne	age	sginv	nvya	unuwa	uhna	oni
they laid her down	woman	that	stone	coat	there	behind

ᏧᏂᎭᏔᏁ	ᏍᎩᎾ
junihatane	sgina
they drove it	that

ᏗᏍᏓᎷᏍᏙᏗ	ᎠᏓ	ᏍᎩᎾ	ᏚᎾᎬᎩᏎ	ᏍᎩᎾ
disdalusdodi	ada	sgina	dunakvgise	sgina
to splinter with (an instrument)	wood	that	they unraveled it	that

ᏅᏯ	ᎤᏏᏭ	Ᏻ	ᎠᏥᎸᏰᏃ	ᏱᎪᏔᎾ	ᏥᎪᏯ
nvya	uhnawu	no	ajilvyeno	yigotana	jigoya
stone	coat	and	and in the fire	when you build a fire	bug

ᏣᏔᏍᎩᏍᎪ	ᏥᎢᎢᎢ
jatasgisgo	jiiiiiiiiiii
as it explodes	psssssssssss

ᏣᏗᏍᎪ	ᏍᎩᏃ	ᏄᏪᏎ	ᎠᎨ	Ꮎ	ᎠᎪᏬᏍᎬ	ᎤᏏᎮᏅ
jadisgo	sgino	nuwese	age	na	agohvsgv	uhnahenv
as it sounds	and that	it sounded like	woman	the	as it burned	and there

ᏉᏂᎴᏁ   ᎦᏚᏃ   ᏅᏚ   ᎤᏂᎳᏪᏚ
wunilvne   gaduno   ada   widunilade
they placed her and on top wood   they placed them

ᏉᏂᎴᏅ   ᏅᎨ   ᎠᎪᎲᏍᎬ
wunilvna   age   agohvsgv
when they placed her woman as she burned

ᏔᏣᏙᎵᏆ   ᏍᎩᏅ   ᏔᏣᏙᎵᏍᎨᏍᏗ   ᏗᏓᏅᎺ   ᏓᏨᏁᏟ
ijadolegwa   sginv   ijadolegwasgesdi didanvwo   dajvnejeli
you all learn that   for you to learn   medicine   I am going to tell you

ᏅᎺᏗ   ᏥᏄᏓᎴᏍᏉ   ᏂᎦᏛ   Ꭿ   ᏓᏨᏁᏟ
nvwodi   jinudalesgwu   nigad   hi   dajvnejeli
medicine   all kinds   all   this   I am going to tell you

ᎤᏪᏗ   ᏚᏬᎮᎵ
uweti   duwohele
old   she told them

ᏍᎩᏃᏃ   ᏱᏄᎵᏍᏔᏅ   ᏗᏟᎸ   ᏔᏣᏅᏓᏗ꞉Ꭰ   ᎤᏛᏁ
sgino   yinulistana   ajilv   ijanvdadi?a   udvne
and that   when it happens   fire   you all remember   she said

Morpheme by Morpheme

he³tiyv⁴-no   gohi⁴di-no   dohiyu
long-ago and   long and   really

dohiyu   e³tiyv   g-v²³-dv-di   dohiyu   hi
really   long time   3 can-say Inf   really   this

ji-da̲-ji³²-nohelh²³
Rel Fut 1 tell

yv³gi̲   u̲-wa⁴sgi
spear   3 finger

d-u-do^3?-e^3 h-e^3
Pl 3 named repP   live repP

age^3 sgi-no^3
woman   that and

nv^{3}gi   iyani   a-ni-nohalido
four   number   3 Pl hunt

u^4-n-a^{4}ni^{4}gis-e^3 j-u^3-n-a^{3}da^{3}li   d-u-n-atinv^{3}s-e^3
3 Pl leave repP   Pl 3 Pl spouse   Pl 3 Pl take-along repP

sgi^3-no   gadu^{4}si   u-n-anvda^{3}d-e^3
that and   hill-on   3 Pl remember repP

uhna^3 w-u^3-n-i^{4}luj-e   u^3-ni^3-no^{3}ha^{3}li^{3}da^{4}s-di
there   Tr 3 Pl arrive repP   3 Pl hunt Inf

no^3 sowu
then   one

j-aji^{32}y-anvh-e   ge^{3}yv   di-g-ado^{32}-g-e^3 sgina^3
Pl 3Pas be-called exP   over-there   Dst 3 stand Prog repP   that

yvgi   u-wa^{4}sgih^3
spear   3 finger

ale^3 uw-aye^{23}sugadlv   a^3-n-oseh-o^{32}
and   3 fingernail   3 Pl call Hab

sgina^3 k-e^{3}n-a
that   2 come Imp

tina   di-gv^3-is-i
louse   Pl I/them kill Imp

uw-ohe^{23}l-e^3?i^3-no^3 age^3 nole^3 uw-env^{3}s-e^3
3 tell repP and   woman   and   3 go repP

h-en-a
2 go Imp

u-n-ohe^{23}l-e^{3}n-v^3 w-u^3-luj-a̲-no^{23}
3 Pl tell Dat exP   Tr 3 arrive Pres and

udoyu^4-no   tina
really and   lice

ji-da-yo̲s-e^{3}h-o   iyusd^3 n-u-dv^{3}nel-e^3 ase^{3}no^3
as Pl look-for Dat Hab   like   Spec 3 do repP   however

d-a-hi̲h-e^3-gwu̲^{3}-no^3 a̲-ni-ge^3 vsgi^3 a̲le^3
Pl 3 kill repP just and   3 Pl woman   that   and

tali-ne^3 u-n-a^{23}ni^{3}gis   sgwu^3 sgi-gwu
two Ord   3 Pl leave   one   that just

iya^{3}ni   nvgi   no^{23}gwu   jo-gwu^3
in-number   four   then   3 just

d-u-n-atinv^{3}s-^{3}e   j-u-n-adali   na^3 sgi-nv   sgi^3
Pl 3 Pl take repP   Pl 3 Pl spouse   that   that and   that

n-aji̲-wehe^{23}l-e^3 ujo^{3}yi̲-gwu   k-e^{3}n-a   a̲-g-ohe^{23}l-e^3
Spec 3Pas tell repP   same just   2 come Imp   3Pas tell repP

nogwu   so^3 a-ni^3-gisg-e^3 na^3
then   other   3 Pl go repP   that

y-u̲w-u^{3}luj-a   sgi̲-no^3 aji̲-h-e^3-gwu^3-no^3 jo̲ʔi^3
nonF 3 arrive Pres   that and   3Pas kill repP just and   three

ya̲^{3}ni   a̲-ni-ge^3 d-u-ni-yohu^{23}se^{3}l-e^3 sogwu^3
in-number   3 Pl woman   Pl 3 Pl lose repP   one

sadvdi   ji-d-a-di^{3}s-g-o
trap   Rel Pl 3 say Prog Hab

iyu^{4}sdi   aji-sadv^{32}n-e^3-no^3
like   3Pas trap repP and

sgina^3 uw-a^{3}s-g-i   nahna^3
that   3 spear Prog Ag   there

do^{3}no-no-u- hiʔa-di^3 h-n-adv^{3}nel-v ag-ohe^{23}l-e^3
[false start]   this and   2 Spec do exP   3Pas tell repP

ag-eyo^{23}n-e^3 sgina^3 age^3 sgina^3
3Pas teach repP   that   woman   that

no^3 ayv-no^3 uji-sgaya   day-o^{23}j-a^{3}dvnvista^{3}n-iy
and   I and   1 man   Fut they-and-I prepare Fut

na^3 oji-niyv^4-di   geh-e^{3}sdi
that   they-and-I trap Inf   be Fut Prog

u-dvn-e^3 do^4-no   u-ni-ni^{3}yvh-e^3
3 say repP   truly and   3 Pl catch repP

duju-du
false start

j-uw-oye^{4}ni   d-u-n-adlv^{3}l-e^3 sgina^3
Pl 3 hand   Pl 3 Pl tie-up repP   that

age^3 yvgi-uw-a^{4}s-gi   na-no^3
woman   NonF 3 spear Prog Ag   also and

nogwu   a-ni-yohih-v^{23}-heno^3 galogwe^3
then   3 Pl shoot exP and   gun

gvnv^{4}di   na^3 ga^{3}ni   de-g-v^{3}wani^{3}h-v
with   the   bullet   Pl they hit exP

dosa
mosquito

u-ni-ja^{3}ta   a̱-dis-g-e^3?i̱^{3}-gwu^3-no^3
3 Pl many   3 say Prog repP just and

de-g-v^{3}ni̱^{3}h-e^3 d-a-gehi^{3}doh-e^3
Pl 3 hit repP   Pl 3 chase repP

dosa   a-di^{23}s-g-v
mosquito   3 say Prog exP

gani   gv-wani^{3}h-v   na^3-no   nvya
bullets   they hit exP   that and   rock

u^4-nu̱w-a   a^3-n-ose^{3}h-o   iga^{3}a   dodv^3
3 wear Pres   3 Pl call Hab   some   what

usdi
like

d-u-do^{3}h-e^3 ugvwi̱yu^{3}he^3 sgi-no^3
Pl 3 name repP   instead   that and

do   sgi-no^3 u-ni-ni^{3}yvh-e^3 udohiyu
really   that and   3 Pl catch repP   really

sgi̱na^3 a̱ge^3 n-uw-a^{3}nisa̱n-e^3
that   woman   Spec 3 cause repP

sgi-no^3 v
that and   uh

sgina   ji-g-adi   gani   gv-wani^{3}h-v
that   Rel 1 say   bullet   they hit exP

dosa   u-ni-ja^{3}ta   y-u-dv^{4}hn-a
mosquito   3 Pl many   nonF 3 say Pres

na^{3}di^3-no^3 u-ni-lu^{3}j-e^3
that and   3 Pl arrive repP

a-ni-sgaya   no   jo?i
3 Pl man   then   three

ya$_a^3$ni   u-n-asgo^{23}s-e^3
in- number   3 Pl dig repP

ukayoda
dry

ada
wood

j-uni^3-lad-e^3 sgino^3 niga^{4}da   u-n-advnv^{3}istan-e^3 sgina^3 ta^{3}li^3-nv^3
Pl 3 put-into repP   that   all   3 Pl prepare repP   that   two and

kalogwe^{23}gidi   j-u-ni-lvdalv^{4}d-a   sgina^3
locust   Pl 3 Pl splinter Pres   that

ada   j-u-ni-sdalu^{3}is-di   iyu^3 sgina^3
wood   Pl 3 Pl splinter Inf   then   that

ni-d-u-n-v^{3}nel-e^3 nogwu^3-le^3 sgwalv^{23}n-isd^{32}
Spec Pl 3 Pl do repP   also and   long-object Inst

n-u-nv^{3}nel-e^3 sgina^3
Spec 3 Pl do repP   that

nogwu   sgi
then   that

yi-n-e^{23}dv^{32}n-e^{4}l-a   y-e^{3}d-ilu^{32}g-a
nonF 1Pl do Dat Pres   nonF 1Pl kill Pres

do   jigwiya
really   too-many

d-a-tv^{3}di
Pl 3 do-away

a̲-ni-ge^3 u-dvn-e^3 sagwu^3 a̲sga̲ya
3 Pl woman   3 say repP   one   man

v^4-no^3 uw-ehisda^{32}neh-e^3 u-dali?i
quite-a-lot   3 hurt repP   3Pos spouse

a-ji̲?e^{23}l-v   sgi̲-no^3 ni̲ga^{4}di   sgi̲-no^3
3 kill exP   that and   all   that and

u-ni-nv^{3}n-e^3 a̲ge^3 sgi̲nv^3 nvya-u^{4}nu̲wa
3 Pl lay-down repP   woman   that   stone-coat

u-hn-a^3 oni
3 wear Pres   behind

j-u-ni^3-ha̲ta̲n-e^3 sgi̲na^3
Pl 3 Pl stick repP   that

di^3-sd-alusdo-di   ada
Pl 3 splinter Inf   wood

sgi̲na^3 d-u-ni-likaduna̲gv^{23}gis-e^3 sgi̲na^3
that   Pl 3 Pl unravel repP   that

nvya-uhna^{3}wu   no^3 ajilv̲ye^{23}-no
stone-coated   and   fire and

yi-g-otan-a
nonF 3 build-fire Pres

ji̲go^{23}ya   j-a-ta̲sgi^{3}s-g-o
bug   Rel 3 explode Prog Hab

j-a-di^{23}s-g-o   sgi̲-no^3 n-u-wes-e^3 a̲ge^3
Rel 3 sound-like Prog Hab   that and   Spec 3 sound-like repP   woman

na^3 a-go^{3}hvs-g-v^4-hv   u̲hna^3-he^{23}nv
the   3 burn Prog exP but   there and

w-u-ni^{3}-lvn-e^{3}	gadu^{4}-no
Tr 3 Pl place repP	on-top and

ada	wi-d-u^{23}-ni^{3}lad-e^{3}
wood	Tr Pl 3 place repP

w-u-ni^{3}-lv^{4}n-a	age^{3}	a-go^{3}hv-s-g-v
Tr 3 Pl place Pres	woman	3 burn Prog exP

ij-adole^{3}gw-a	sginv^{3}	ij-adolegwa^{23}s-ge^{3}sdi
2Pl learn-from Imp	that	you-all learn-from Imp Fut Pres

didanvwo	da-j-v^{3}-ne^{3}jel-i
medicine	Fut you give Fut

nvwo^{32}ti	jin-u-dale^{4}s-gwu	niga^{4}da	hi?
medicine	Pl Spec kind just	all	this

da-jv^{3}-ne^{3}j-el-i	nvwo^{32}ti	d-uw-ohe^{23}l-e^{3}
Fut I-you tell Dat Fut	medicine	Pl 3 tell repP

sgi-no	yi-n-u^{23}l-istan-a	ajilv
that and	nonF Spec 3 happen imP	fire

wi-j-anv^{23}da^{3}dis-ge^{3}sdi	u-dvne^{3}n-v
Tr you-all remember Fut-Prog	3 say exP

Syllabary

ᎮᏘᏴᏃ ᎪᎯᏗᏃ ᏙᎯᏳ ᎡᏘᏴ ᎬᏛᏗ ᏙᎯᏳ Ꭿ ᏥᏓᏥᏃᎮᏟ ᏴᎩᎤᏩᏍᎩ ᎦᏙᎡ ᎡᎮ ᎠᎨ ᏍᎩᏃ ᎤᎩ ᎢᏇᏂ ᎠᏂᏃᎲᎵᏙ ᎤᎾᏂᎩᏎ ᏧᎾᏓᎵ ᎦᎾᏘᎤᏎ ᏍᎩᏃ ᏚᎦᏏ ᎤᎾᎤᏓᏚ ᎤᏖ ᎤᏂᎷᏤ ᎤᏂᏃᎲᎵᏓᏍᏗ Ꮓ ᎲᏊ ᏨᏥᏇᎤᎮ ᎨᏴ ᏗᏚᏙᎨ ᏍᎩᎾ ᏴᎩᎤᏩᏍᎩ ᎠᎴ ᎤᏩᏰᏑᏚᎵ ᎠᏃᏎᎰ ᏍᎩᎾ ᎨᎾ ᏘᎾ ᏗᎬᎢᏏ ᎤᏌᎮᎴᎢᎤ ᎠᎨ ᏃᎴ ᎤᏪᎤᏎ ᎮᎾ ᎤᏃᎮᎴᎤ ᏊᎷᏟᏃ ᎤᏙᏳᏃ ᏘᎾ ᏥᏓᏅᏎᎰ ᎢᏳᏍᏗ ᏅᏩ ᏅᏛᏁᎴ ᎠᏎᏃ ᏓᎯᎮᏯᏃ ᎠᏂᎨ ᎥᏍᎩ ᎠᎴ ᏔᎵᏁ ᎤᎾᏂᎩᏌ ᏍᏯ ᏍᎩᏯ ᎢᏇᏂ ᎤᎩ ᏃᏯ ᏦᏯ ᎦᎾᏘᎤᏎ ᏧᎾᏓᎵ Ꮎ ᏍᎩᎤ ᏍᎩ ᎾᏥᏪᎮᎴ ᎤᏦᎼᏯ ᎨᎾ ᎠᎪᎮᎴ ᏃᏯ Ꮂ ᎠᏂᎩᏍᎨ Ꮎ ᏇᏂ ᎠᏂᎨ ᎦᏂᏅᎱᏎᎴ ᎲᏯ ᏳᏊᎷᏟ ᏍᎩᏃ ᎠᏥᎢᎮᏯᏃ ᏦᎢ ᏌᏛᏗ ᏥᏓᏗᏍᎪ ᎢᏳᏍᏗ ᎠᏥᏌᏛᏁᏃ ᏍᎩᎾ ᎤᏩᏍᎩ ᎾᏖ ᎯᎠᏗ ᏖᏛᏁᏅ ᎠᎪᎮᎴ ᎠᎨᏅᏁ ᏍᎩᎾ ᎠᎨ ᏍᎩᎾ Ꮓ ᎠᏴᏃ ᎼᏥᏍᏚᏯ ᏓᏅᏟᏛᎤᎢᏍᏔᏂ Ꮎ ᎼᏥᏂᏴᏗ ᎨᎮᏍᏗ ᎤᏛᏁ ᏙᏃ

ᎤᏪᏂᏴᏒ ᏚᏛᏇᏂ ᏎᏪᏍᏛ ᏫᏯᎾ ᏗᏞ ᏴᏲᏍᎦᏫᏯᏱ ᎾᏃ ᏃᏫ ᎠᏂᎯᎫᏗᏴᏃ ᏍᎦᏫ ᎤᏒᏗ Ꮎ
ᏍᎯ ᏎᎦᎯᏇ ᎤᏄ ᎤᏂᏣᎳ ᎠᏬᎤᏢᏔᎧᏃ ᏎᎯᎢ ᎴᎢᏛᏫᎢ ᎤᏄ ᎠᏬᎤᎬ ᏍᎯ ᎬᎦᏂᏇ ᎾᏃ
ᎤᏓ ᎤᏣᎦ ᏍᏃᏔᏓ ᎢᏑ Ꮴ° ᎤᎾᏗ ᏍᏙᎢ ᎤᎬᏲᎢᏬ ᏪᏯᏃ Ꮙ ᎠᏴᏃ ᎤᎯᎯᏇᎢ
ᎤᏙᏝᎨ ᎠᏯᎾ ᏗᏞ ᏋᎦᎯᎥᎠ ᎠᏴᏃ Ꭲ ᎠᏯᎾ ᏆᏍᏗ ᏍᎯ ᎬᎦᏂᏇ ᎤᏄ ᎤᏂᏣᎳ ᎬᎾᎬ
ᎾᎷᏃ ᎤᎯᎷᏫ ᏗᎠᏬᏎᎠ ᏃᏛ ᏓᏔ ᎠᎯ ᎤᎾᏯᎠ4 ᎤᎠᏆᎵ ᏛᎵ ᎤᎯᏪᏍ ᎠᏴᏃ ᎯᏍᎵ
ᎤᎾᎤᎤᎢᏔᎤᏫᎠ ᎠᏴᏃ ᏪᏒᎤ ᎠᎬᏲᎠᎢ ᏓᎯᎦᎢᎦᎵ ᎠᏴᏃ ᏛᎵ ᏓᎯᎠᎤᎷᎺᏔᎠᎠ ᏔᎬ ᎠᏴᏃ
ᎯᏍᎤᎢᎯᎤ ᏃᎠᎤ ᎠᏔᏆᎯᎠᎠ ᏆᎤᎢᎯᎤ ᎠᏴᏃ ᎾᏃ ᎠᏴ ᏍᎯᎶᎢᎳ ᏴᎯᎷᏎ Ꮙ ᏆᏉᎠ
ᎶᎷᏗ ᏗᎯᏞ ᎤᎤᎢᎤ ᎯᎠ ᏓᎤᏍᎠ ᎢᏃ ᎤᎠᏯᎤᏬᎵᎠᏞ ᎤᎵᏇᏔ ᏗᎯᏒᎦ ᎠᏴᏃ ᎯᏏᎵ ᎤᎯᎤᎤᎢᎤ
ᏗᏞ ᎠᏴᎤ ᎤᏄ ᎤᏣᎦ ᎤᎤᏉ ᏎᎯ ᏓᎯᏫᏩᎵᎢ ᎠᏴᏃ ᏝᎠᎷᎺᎠᎤᏛ ᏛᎵ ᎠᏴᏃ ᏎᎤᎬᎤ4
ᎠᏴᏃ ᎤᏄ ᎤᏉᎤ Ꮓ ᏗᎯᏆᎢᎠᏃ ᏓᎠᏪᎤ ᎴᎠᎤ ᏨᏫᎠᏯᎤᎠ ᎴᎢᎢᎢᎢ ᏟᎠᏬᎠ ᎠᏴᏃ
ᏋᎤ94 ᏗᏞ Ꮎ ᏓᎠᎸᎠᎬ ᎤᏠᏬᎤ ᏦᎯᎨᎵ ᏎᏎᎾ ᏛᎵ ᎤᎯᎯᏪᏍ ᏦᎯᎨᎤ ᏗᏞ ᏓᎠᎸᎬᎬ ᏔᎬᎤᎤᏐᎢ
ᎠᏴᎤ ᏔᎬᎤᎤᏐᎢᎠᏬᎢᎤᎠᎵ ᏝᎶᎤᏰ ᎶᎬᏔᎤᏇ ᎤᎤᏔ ᎴᎦᎶᎤᎠᎤ ᎯᏍᎵ Ꮽ ᎶᎬᏔᎤᏇ
ᎤᎠᏯᏔ ᏎᎤᏇᏛ ᎠᏴᏃ ᏝᎤᎵᎠᏬᎤ ᏗᎯᎦ ᏔᎬᎤᎴᎠᏛ ᎤᎤᏔ

English

This story that I'm going to tell happened many years ago, a very long time ago.
There was a woman called "Spearfinger." Four hunters took their wives hunting
with them one day, and when they reached the rocky mountain where they
thought their hunting place was, they saw a woman standing off at a distance.
She called to one of the wives to come to her: "Let me check you for lice," she told
the wife. She went because the others told her to go. When she reached the place
where "Spearfinger" was, sure enough, she acted like she was checking her for
lice. But she killed her instead. The next time the four hunters went hunting, one
of them was without a wife, but the others had theirs. Again "Spearfinger" called
out to one of the wives and killed her, too. They lost three women that way, and
finally they set a trap for "Spearfinger." One woman was instructed on what to do,
and "we men will capture her," one man said. Sure enough, they captured
"Spearfinger" and bound her hands. And they were shooting at her with a gun,
but she would just say, "There are a lot of mosquitoes," and she would try to bat
them away. Some people would call her "rock wearer," and I wonder what she
really was. But they did capture "Spearfinger" with the help of the woman. And
the men dug a hole to bury her in. In the deepest part of the hole, they put dry
wood and prepared everything. They took slivers of locust wood to make clubs
with. "Maybe if we do that, we would be able to kill her. She is just killing too
many women," said one man. He was very hurt because his wife had been killed.
And so they laid the "rock wearer" down there. They stuck a hewing axe in her

back and penetrated the rock she was wearing. And then just as a bug makes a whistling noise when you throw it into a fire, "Spearfinger" made that same kind of noise. They piled wood on top of her as she burned.

"Learn from this the powers. I shall show you varieties of medicine, and when you see this happening with fire, you are to remember what has happened here."

Transformation

Durbin Feeling

"Transformation" is a story about the transformation of a woman into something else. The something she became was known to pass by the house, and the dogs would pursue it.

ᎡᏙᏓᏛ	ᏥᎨᎲ	ᎡᏥ	ᏥᎨᎲ	ᎢᏧᎳᏆ	ᎠᏂᏃᎮᏍᎪ
edodadv	jigehv	eji	jigehv	ijulagw	anihnohesgo
yes my father	who was	my mother	who was	both of them	they would tell

ᎨᏅ	ᎣᎬᏏ	ᎾᎥ	ᎡᎮ	ᎠᎦᏴᎵᎨ	ᎤᎵᏍᎦᏍᏛ
gehnv	oaksi	na?v	ehe	agayvlige	ulsgasd
and there	town of Oaks	near	she lived	an old woman	Ulsgasd

ᏧᏙᎢᏓ	ᎤᏩᏍ	ᎦᏁᎵ	ᎨᎮ	ᎡᏥ	ᏥᎨᎲ
judo?ida	uwas	ganel	gehe	eji	jigehv
was named	she alone	one who lived	was	my mother	who was

Ꮎ	ᏧᎾᏓᏂᏱᏓ	ᏧᎾᏛᏒ	ᎨᎮ	ᎠᏗᎰ	ᏗᏂᏲᏟ
na	jundaniyida	juntvsv	gehe	adiho	diniyohli
they	orphans	ones who had grown up	was	she says	children

ᎨᎲ	ᎤᏲᎱᏒ	ᎨᎮ	ᎤᏂᏥ	ᎤᏂᏙᏓᏂᏅ	ᏧᏛᎯᏍᏔᏅ
gehv	uyohusv	gehe	uniji	unidodahnv	jutvhistanv
as for them	dead	was	their mother	and their father	he raised them

Ᏺ4 ᏫᎮᏝᏫᏗ Ᏽ& ᎠᏗᎭᏫ ᎤᎩᎸᏗ ᎡᏙᎲ
gese wogedasdi gehv adihv ukilvdi edohv
was we would go there was she said on horseback he would travel

ᎠᏗᎭᏫ ᏝᏇᎲᎵ ᏚᎨᎵ ᎤᎾᎭᎵꞋᎥ ᎠᏗᎭᏫ ᎠᏗᏗᎵᎪ
adihv dalonige sogwil unahla?v adihv aktinego
she said yellow horse he owned she said she would take me along

ᏣᏗᎭᏫ ᏚᏫᎴᎥᏍᎥ ᏔꞋᎵᎭ ᏚᏍᎲᏗ ᏔꞋᎵᎭ ᎢᏳᏍᎥ
jadihv juwenvsv ta?liha jusvhid ta?liha iyusv
she said to his home two nights in two days

ᎢᎥ ᎢᏥᏯᏗᎲᏃᎸ ᏳᏛᎾ ᎠᎦᎵᏍᎪᎸᏓᏁᎰ
iyv ijiyatihnohlv yudvhna agalisgolvdaneho
then I will bring him/her back when he said she would be given permission

ᎡᏙᏗ ᏥᎨᎲ
edod jigehv
my father who was

ᎣᏍᏕᎪ ᏣᏗᎭᏫ ᎣᏂᎥ ᎦᏓᏅᏖᎰ ᏣᏗᎭᏫ ᎠᎬᎥᏌᎲᎥ
osdego jadihv ohniyv gadanvteho jadihv agwvsahnv
we would go she said later on I would think about it she said I alone

ᎠᏏᎢᎮ ᎨᎵᎰ ᏣᏗᎭᏫ ᎥᎾᎥ ᎠᏥᏍᎩᎵ ᎨᎮ
aksvhihe geliho jadihv vhnv atsisgil gehe
I would spend the night I think she said and very ghostly she was

ᏣᏗᎭᏫ Ꮎ ᎠᎦᏴᎵᎨ ᏃᎫᎲᎥ ᎤᏔᎥ ᏃᎫ
jadihv na agayvlige nogwuhnv utan nogwu
she said the old woman and then adult then

ᏂᎨᏎ ᏃᎫ ᎡᏥ ᏥᎨᎲ ᎾᏂᏁᎴ ᏃᎫ
nigese nogwu eji jigehv naninele nogwu
he was then my mother who was they were already married then

RVᏝ	ΘZ	ᏂGAᏗ	DᏯ	blackfox	hollow
edod	nahno	jiyukdi	agwu	blackfox	hollow
my mother	and that	straight	here	Blackfox	Hollow

CΘᏗᎮ	ᏂᎱᏓᏝᏈB	ᏗᏗ	ᏂᏂZᏞ		JVTᏝ	ᏗᏗ
janadiho	jiwukedaliy	ned	dvninol		judo?id	ned
as they say	through the ravine	Ned	Sneaking Up On Him		named	Ned

JᏗWᏐ	DΘᏗᎮ	ᏗᏗ	Ꮺ	D4	ᏂᏁᏚ
juneldv	andiho	ned	dv	ase	jigehv
where he had lived	they say	Ned	yes	probably	who was

OᏬᏝ	D4	ᏗSᏗᏄ	SΘ	ᏁOᏬ	SVR
udod	ase	diganelv	dew	hehnv	dudo?e
his father	maybe	he lived	Dave	because	he was named

SΘ	ᏂhZᏞ		SVR	OᏝ	ᎩG	OᏞᎩ
dew	dvninol		dudo?e	uhna	kilo	udlvgi
Dave	Sneaking Up On Him		he was named	there	someone	sick person

SOᏂ	DWᏅG	DᏗᎮ	AᏠᏝ	iᏯᏯ	OᏞᏂVᏐ
ganhge	atanuj	adiho	gohida	vsgwu	udlvjidole
was lying	young girl	he says	a long time	also	she was sick

ΘᏬ	ᏂSᏗᏯ	JᏇᏯ	ΘΘᏞᏯᏗᏯ	BΘ	ᎩG
nahnv	jigadihv	tsgwiya	nanalsdihv	yvwi	kilo
and that	which I said	many	happen to them	people	someone

GPG	ᏂSᏗᏯ	ᏯᎩZ	VᏄ	TB	OᏃᏝ
yudlvja	jigadihv	sgihno	doyi	iyv	unote
when he/she would get sick	which I said	and that	outside	there	they had a fire going

OᏝ	OhSΘᏬᏯᎮ		DhΘΘ	TGᏯᏗᏘ
uhna	uniganawosge		aniwina	iyusdiha
there	they were warming themselves		young men	just (men)

ᎤᎾᏓᏡᎨ	ᎩᏟᏅ
unadalhge	gitlihnv
they were in a group	and dogs

ᏂᎪᎸ	ᏧᎵᏏᏅᏛ	ᎤᎾᏕᏯᏙᏗᎮ	ᎫᏍᏗ
nigolv	julsihnvd	unadeytohdihe	gusd
all the time	nightly	it bothered them	something

ᎠᏂᎨᎮᎨ	ᎠᏂᏕᏯᏍᏔᏂᎯᎮ
anikehege	anideystanihihe
they would run after it	around the house

ᎦᎵᏦᏕ	ᎠᏊᏅ	Ᏼ	ᏫᎦᏅᏅ	ᏫᎧᎾᎷᏛ	ᎤᏅᏓᏟ
galjode	agwunh	yv	wiganvhnv	wikanalhdv	unvdahli
house	and here	nearby	down the road	up the incline	on the ridge

ᎢᏳᏍᏗ	ᎢᎦᏅᎿ	ᏍᎩᎾ	ᎠᎦᏴᎵᎨ	ᏧᏪᏅᏒ	ᎢᏗᏜ
iyusd	iganvhna	sgina	agayvlige	juwenvsv	ididla
likeness	there is a road	that	old woman	her home	toward

ᏥᏥᏃᎮ	ᎤᏅᏅ	ᏃᏊ	ᎠᏂᎷᎨ	ᏞᎦᏅ
jijinohe	uhnvhnv	nogwu	aniluhge	hleghnv
the one I am talking about	road	now	they were arriving	for a while

ᎠᏎ	ᎠᎾᏂᏢᏍᎨ	ᎩᏟ	ᏃᏊᎴ	ᎠᏁᎷᎲᏍᎪ	ᏣᏗᎲ
ase	ananhdlvsge	gitli	nogwule	anehluhvsgo	jadihv
maybe	they would lie down	dogs	and then	they would bark	she said

ᎠᎾᏁᎷᎩᏍᎪ	ᎦᎵᏦᏕ	ᏭᏂᏕᏯᏍᏗᎮ	ᎩᏟ	ᎤᎿᏅ	ᏚᏃᎸ
ananelugisgo	galjode	wunideysdihe	gitli	uhnahnv	dunohlv
they would race after	house	they would run around	dogs	and there	they sat

ᏴᏫ	ᎠᏊᏅ	ᎢᏴ	ᎠᎾᏝᎥᏍᏗᎮ	ᎩᏟ	ᏝᏃ
yvwi	agwuhnv	iyv	anatlavsdihe	gitli	hlahno
people	and nearby	toward	they would come running by	dogs	and not

ᎪᏍᏓ	ᏯᏂᎪᏩᏘᎮ	ᏣᏗᎲ	ᎩᏟᏊᏅ	ᎢᎦ	ᏓᏂᎪᏩᏘᎮ
gosd	yanigowhtihe	jadihv	gitligwuhnv	iga	danigowhtihe
something	they did not see	she said	just dogs	that is all	they would see

ᎤᎾ	ᏳᏂᎿᎷᏔᎾ	ᏫᎧᎾᎷᏛ	ᏅᏃ	ᏃᏊ	ᎠᏂᏫᏄᏣ
uhna	yunihnalhtana	wikanalhdv	nvno	nogwu	aniwinuja
there	as they chased it	up the hill	up the road	now	young men

ᏦᎢᎭ	ᎢᏯᏂ	ᏗᏗᏍᏕᎳ	ᎩᏟ	ᏗᏗᏅᏫᏍᏓ	ᎤᎾᏛᏁ
jo?iha	iyani	didisdel	gitli	didinvhwisda	unadvhne
three	of them	let us help them	dogs	let us sic them on	they said

ᏗᎦᏍᏆᏄᏗ	ᎣᏂ	ᏭᎾᏝᎥᏍᏔᏁ	ᏙᏅ	ᏭᏂᏑᎵᎪᏣ	ᎩᏟ
disgwaldi	ohni	wunatla?vstane	dohnv	wunisuligoj	gitli
at a run	behind	they ran after	sure enough	when they stopped	dogs

ᏃᏊᎴ	ᏫᏚᏂᏅᏫᏍᏔᏁ	ᏃᏊᎴ	ᏩᎾᏁᎷᎩᏍᎨ	ᎠᏊᏛ	ᎢᏴ
nogwule	widuninvhwistane	nogwule	wananelugisge	agwudv	iyv
then again	they sicced them again	and then	they ran after again	nearby	distance

ᏃᏊᎴ	ᏫᎬᏩᎨᎲᏎ	ᎨᏊᏅ	ᎥᏍᏊ	ᎢᏴ	ᎬᏩᎨᎲᏎ
nogwule	wigvwhkehvse	gegwnv	vsgwu	iyv	gvwhkehvse
and then	they ran after it	and just there	also	that far	they ran after it

ᏃᏊ	ᏫᎬᏩᏢᏔᎮ	ᏃᏊ	ᎬᏂ	ᏪᏌᏅ	ᎤᏪᎷᏁ
nogwu	wigvwadlvtahe	nogwu	kvhni	wesahnv	uwehluhne
now	they caught up with it	now	it was apparent	and cat	meowed loudly

ᏪᏍ	ᏯᏂᏗᏒᏂ	ᎩᏟ	ᏧᏪᎷᎪ	ᏍᎩ	ᏂᎦᏪᏍᎨ
wes	yanidisvhni	gitli	juwehluhgo	sgi	nigawesge
cat	when they mauled it	dogs	as it meows loudly	that	it was meowing

Ɵiꙥꙩ Ꭰꙥ ᎢᏴ ᎢᏀꙥᏋ ᎤᏂᎷᏫ ᏃꙥᏬ
na?vgwuhnv agwu iyv iyusd unilule nogwule
and nearby here that far like they lacked and then

ᎤᎠᏗᏗᎡᎪᏬ Ꮢ Ꭰꙥ ꙥᏚꙩ ᏗᏚ ᏡᏂᎴꙢᏫ
unaliti?ele si agwu wiganvhnv didla wunikehvse
it got away from them yet nearby down the road toward they ran
                     after it

Ꭸꙥ ᎢᏴ ᎤᏂᎨᎲᏓ ᏃꙥᏬ ꙥᏯᏛᎸᏔᎮ ᏏꙥᏃ
gegwu iyv unikehvda nogwule wunadlvtahe sigwuhno
just there that far they had then they caught up and again
        chased it again with it

ᏪᏎ ᏂᏍꙥᏎᎨᏏ ᎠᏂᎡᏔ?ᎢᏎ ƟiᎮᏟᏔꙥᎫ ᏩᎠᏟᏔ?ᎢᏎ Ꮓꙥ
wes nigawesge anatla?ise na?vhnige?isdi wanatla?ise nogwu
cat it was they were closer still they ran after it then
  meowing running

ᎤᎾᏕᎶᏎ Ꮓꙥ ᏄᏓᎴ ᏂᏍꙥᏎᎬ ᏰᏪ Ꮓꙥ
unadelose nogwu nudale nigawesgv yvwi nogwu
they realized then different it was making sounds person now

ᏂᏍꙥᏎᎨ ᎤᎾᏛᎦᏁ Ꮓꙥ ᎩᏟ
nigawesge unatvgane nogwu gitli
it was making a sound they heard it then dogs

ᏓꙥᎦᎨ Ꮲ
dasgage he
it was getting on to them [the sound made in getting after the dogs]

ᎠᏗᎮ ᏓꙥᎦᎨ ᎩᏟ ᎤᎾ Ꮓꙥ ꙥᎾᎴᎿꙥᏫᏟ
adihe dasgage gitli uhna nogwu wunalehnawstane
it said it was getting on to them dogs there now they came to a stop

Ɵ ᎠᎾᎳꙥᏕᎵꙥᎩ ꙥᏗᏂꙥᎫᎥ Ꮓꙥ ᎩᏟ iꙥᎩᎲ
na analsdelisgi widunisgajv nogwu gitli vsgihnv
the the helpers they called off now dogs and that

ᎠᏂ	ᏧᏙᎢᏓ	ᏍᏊ	ᎤᏜᏩᏍᏛ	ᎠᏂ	ᏍᏊ
an	judoʔid	sgwu	udlawsdv	ann	sgwu
Ann	named	also	who she stayed with	Ann	also

ᏚᏙᎥ	ᎠᎩᏥ	ᏥᎨᏒ	ᎠᏂ	ᎤᎧᏲᏓ	ᏧᏙᎢᏓ
dudoʔv	agiji	jigesv	ann	ukahyod	judoʔid
her name was	my mother	who was	Ann	Dry	named

ᎤᏜᏩᏍᏛ	ᎠᏗᎲ	ᏍᎩᏃ	ᎣᏍᏗᎦᏘᏴ	ᎠᏗᎲ	ᎤᏲᎱᏍ
udlawsdv	adihv	sgihno	osdigatiyv	adihv	uyohus
who stayed with her	she said	and that	we were caring for her	she said	when she died

Ꮎ	ᎠᎦᏴᎵᎨ	ᏃᏊᏅ	ᎡᏙᏓ	ᏥᎨᏒ	ᏃᏊ
na	agayvlige	nogwuhnv	edod	jigesv	nogwu
that	old woman	and then	my father	who was	then

ᎤᎴᏩᏓᏃ	ᏧᏙᎢᏓ	ᎡᎲ	ᎤᏗᏗᏜ	ᎠᏐᏳᎶᏗ	ᏧᏍᎪ
ulehwadahno	judoʔid	ehv	udididla	anayulhdi	jusgo
Ulehwadahno	named	lived	farther	by the shore	at Oaks

ᏦᎩ	ᏗᏜ	ᎦᏁᏌ	ᏗᎪᏢᏍᎩ	ᏥᏓᏃᏢᏍᎬᏊᏅ	ᎦᏁᏌ
jogi	didla	ganesa	digohlvsgi	jidanohlvsgvgwuhnv	ganesa
upstream	toward	casket	maker	because they made them themselves	casket

ᎾᎯᏳ	ᏥᎨᎲ	ᎥᏍᎩᎾ	ᎤᏂᏅᏎ	ᎤᏬᏢᏅᏗ
nahiyu	jigehv	vsgina	uninvse	uwohlvndi
then	which was	that	they sent him	for him to make

ᎾᎥᏊᏅ	ᏒᏆᏞᏍᎩ	ᎤᏬᏢᏒ	Ꮻ	ᎦᏍᎩᎶ	ᏧᏙᎢᏓ
naʔvgwuhnv	svgwalosgi	uwohlvsv	wil	gasgilo	judoʔida
and just nearby	sawmill	he had	Will	Chair	named

ᎡᎵᏊ	ᏒᎯᏰᏱ	ᏗᏜ	Ꮲ	ᏔᎵ	ᎢᏴ
eligwu	svhiyeyi	didla	dlv	taʔli	iyv
possible	evening	toward	somewhere	two	then

ᎡᎵᏊ	ᏲᏥᏃᎦ	ᎦᏁᏌ	ᏍᎩᏊ	ᎢᏴ	ᏢᏢ
eligwu	yojinog	ganesa	sgigwu	iyv	dlvdlv
possible	we will bring it	casket	just that	that time frame	sometime

ᎤᏍᏆᏕᏍᏗ	ᎤᏓᎷᎸᏊ	ᎡᏍᏓᏬᎥ	ᎡᏗᎸᏗᏊᏅ
usgwadesd	udalulvgwu	esdawo?v	edilvdigwuhnv
he will be finished	just before	bathe her	for us to just place her into

ᎢᎦ	ᏱᎩ
iga	yigi
that is all	it would be

ᎦᏁᏌ	ᏲᎩᏃᎳ	ᎣᎩᏃᏎᎸ	ᎠᏗᎲ	ᎡᏙᏓ
ganesa	yoginohla	oginoselv	adihv	edod
casket	when we bring it	he told us	she said	my father

ᏥᎨᏒ	ᎤᏂᎩᏍ	ᎡᎵ	ᏏᎾᎴᎢ	ᎤᏂᎩᏒ	ᏙᏅ
jigesv	uhnigis	eli	sinale?i	uhnigisv	dohnv
who was	when he left	possible	in the morning	he left	and also

ᎢᎦ	ᎣᎩᎾᎵᏍᏓᏴᏅ	ᎠᏗᎲ	Ꮭ	ᎩᎶ	ᏱᎦᎾᏄᎪᎪ
iga	oginalsdayvhnv	adihv	hla	kilo	yigananugogo
noontime	when we had just eaten	she said	not	someone	was not coming around

ᏣᏗᎲ	ᎣᎩᎾᎵᏍᏓᏴᏃᎿ
jadihv	oginalsdayvhnohna
she said	when we had finished eating

ᎤᎵᏍᏓ	ᏃᎩᎾᏛᏁᎵᏙᎸ	ᏣᏗᎲ	ᏃᏊ
uhlisd	noginadvnelidolv	jadihv	nogwu
quickly	we worked	she said	then

ᎤᎾᎴᏅᎮ	ᏣᏗᎲ	ᏯᏖᏃᎯᏊᏅ	ᎯᎠ	ᏄᏍᏛ	ᏥᏓᏂᎸᎥᏍᎬ
unalenvhe	jadihv	hyatenohigwuhnv	hi?a	nusdv	jidanihlv?vsgv
they began	she said	just on the floor	this	which was	they would lay them

ᏳᏲᎤᏍ	ᎩᎶ	ᎠᏓᏱᎩ	ᎪᏍᏗ	ᏥᏓᏂᏗᏍᎬ	ᏯᏖᏃ
yuyohus	kilo	adayig	gosd	jidanidisgv	hyahten
when he died	someone	maybe wood	or something	they would lay down	board

ᏓᏂᏝᏗᏍᎬ	ᏍᎩᏃ	ᏄᏅᏅ	ᎤᎾᎴᏅᎲ	ᏣᏗᎲ	ᏃᏊ
danihladisgv	sgihno	nunvhnv	unalenvhv	jadihv	nogwu
they laid them on	and that	how they did	they started	she said	then

ᎠᎾᏬᏍᎬ	ᏙᏯ	ᎤᏲᎢ	ᏂᏚᏍᏛ	ᏣᏗᎲ	ᏗᎦᏅᏍᎨᏂ
anawosgv	doya	uyoʔi	nidusdv	jadihv	diganvsgen
they bathe it	very	bad	they were	she said	her legs

ᎩᏟ	ᏕᎬᏩᏍᎦᎶᏨ	ᏝᏍᎩᏂ	ᎬᏕᎶᎰᎯᏍᏗ	ᏱᎨᎮ	ᏣᏗᎲ
gilh	degvwsgalhjv	hlasgin	gvdelohohisd	yigehe	jadihv
dogs	where they had bitten her	but not	to tell	you could not	she said

Ꮎ	Ꮟ	ᎬᏅᏊ	ᎤᏲᎱᏒ	ᏂᎨᏒᎾ	ᏚᎵᏍᏚᎢᏎ
na	si	gvhnvgw	uyohusv	nigesvna	dulsduʔise
the	yet	while she was alive	when dead	she was not	they opened up

ᏣᏗᎲ	ᏂᎬᏅ	ᏧᎵᏔᎸᎢᏓ	ᎨᎮ	ᏕᎦᏬᎬ	ᏣᏗᎲ
jadihv	nikvhnv	jultalvʔida	gehe	degawogv	jadihv
she said	and all over	there were punctures	it was	they were running sores	she said

Morpheme by Morpheme

e-doda^{3}-dv^{3}	ji-geh-v	e-ji^{3}
1Pos father indeed	Rel be exP	1Pos mother

ji-geh-v	iju^{3}la^{3}-gw	a-ni-hnohe^{23}s-g-o
Rel be exP	both just	3 Pl tell Prog Hab

ge-hnv	oaks-i	naʔv
there and	oaks Loc	near

e-h-e³   a̲-ga̲yv²³li³ge   ulsgasd³
3 live repP   3 old-woman   ulsgasd

j-u-do²³ʔi̲d-a   u̲-was²³   ga̲-nel²³
Rel 3 name recP   3 alone   3 live

geh-e³   e-ji³   ji-geh-v
be repP 1Pos mother Rel be exP

na³   j-u-n-dani²³yid-a   j-u-n-tvs-v
them   Pl 3 Pl orphan recP   Pst 3 Pl grow-up exP

geh-e³   a-di̲²³h-o   di-ni-yo²³hli
be repP 3 say Hab   Pl Pl child

geh-v   u-yohus-v   geh-e
be exP   3 die exP   be repP

u-ni-ji³   u-ni-doda̲³-hnv   j-u̲-tvhi̲sta̲³n-v
3 Pl mother   3 Pl father and   Pl 3 rear exP

ges-e³   w-og-edas-di   geh-v³
be repP Tr they-and-I go-there Inf be exP

a-di̲²³h-v³   ukilvdi   e-do³h-v³
3 say exP   on-horseback   3 travel exP

a-di̲²³h-v³   da̲lo²³ni̲³ge   so²³gwil³   u-n-a³²hla̲ʔ-v
3 say exP   yellow   horse   3 Pl have exP

a-di̲²³h-v³   ak-ti̲ne³g-o³
3 say exP   he/me take-along Hab

j-a-di̲²³h-v   j-uwe³nvsv   ta̲ʔli-ha
3 say exP   3 home   two exactly

jusv²³hid   ta̲ʔli-ha   iyu³sv   iyv
night   two exactly   day   then

i-ji-^{3}yajahni^{23}hl-v^3 y-u-^{23}dvhn-a   a^3-g-alisgolvda^{32}neh-o
Rep 1 come-back exP   nonF 3 say recP   Pass 3 given-permission Hab

e-dod   ji-geh-v   o^3-sd-e^3-g-o^3
1Pos father   Rel be exP   they-and-I go Prog Hab

j-a-di^{23}h-v^3 ohni^{32}-yv^3 g-adanv-te^{23}h-o   j-a-di^{23}h-v^3 agw-v^{4}sa-hnv^{32}
Pst 3 say exP   later-on   1 think Prog Hab   Pst 3 say exP   1 myself and

ak-svhih-e^3 g-eli^{32}h-o^3 j-a-di^{23}h-v^3 v^4-hnv
1 spend-night repP   1 think Hab   Pst 3 say exP   very and

adsgil   geh-e^3
ghostly   be repP

j-a-di^{23}h- v^3 na^3 a-gayv^{23}li^{3}ge   nogwu^3-hnv^3
Pst 3 say exP   the   3 old-woman   then and

utan   nogwu
big   then

ni-ge^{3}s-e   nogwu
Spec be repP   then

e-ji^3 ji-geh-v   n-a-ni^3-nel-e   nogwu
1Pos mother   Rel be exP   Spec 3 Pl marry repP   then

e-dod   na^3-hno^3 jiyukdi   a^{3}gwu   blackfox   hollow
1Pos father   that and   straight   here   blackfox   hollow

j-a-n-adi^{23}h-o   ji-w-u^{23}ke^{3}daliy^{34} ned^{23} dvni^{3}nol   u-do^3?id   ned^{23}
Rel 3 Pl call Hab   Rel Tr ravine   ned   dvninol   3 named   ned

j-u-nel^{3}dv   a-n-di^{23}h-o^3 ned^{23}
Pst 3 be-married   3 Pl say Hab   ned

dv^3 ase^3 ji-geh-v
yes   probably   Rel be exP

u-dod   ase^3
3Pos father   maybe

de-g-a^{3}ne^{23}l-v^3 dew^{23} he^{3}hnv^3 d-u-do^{3}ʔ-e^3
Pl 3 live exP   dave   because   Pl 3 be-named repP

dew^{23} dvni^{3}nol   d-u-do^{3}ʔ-e^3 uhna^3
dave   dvninol   Pl 3 named repP   there

kilo   u-dlv^4-g-i
someone   3 sick Prog Ag

g-anh-g-e^3 a-t<u>a</u>nuj^{23} a-d<u>i</u>^{23}h-o   gohid^{23} vsgwu^3 u-dlv^{3}jido^{3}l-e^3
3 lie Prog repP   3 young-   3 say Hab   a-long-time   also   3 sick repP
                        girl

na^{3}hnv^3 ji-g-<u>a</u>di^{3}h-v   tsgwiya^3 n-a-n-alsd<u>i</u>^{23}h-v^3
that and   Rel 1 say Pst   too many   Spec 3 Pl begin-to-be exP

yvwi   kilo
people   someone

y-u-dlv^{4}j-a   ji-g-<u>a</u>di^{3}h-v   sgi-hno^3 do^{23}yi   <u>i</u>yv   u-n-o^{23}t-e
nonF 3 get-sick recP   Rel 1 say   that and   outside   there   3 Pl tend-fire
        exP   repP

uhna^3 u-ni-gan<u>a</u>wos-g-e^3 <u>a</u>-ni-wi^{4}na   iyu^{3}sdi-ha   u-n-<u>a</u>dalh^3-g-e^3
there   3 Pl warm Prog   3 Pl young-man   same exactly   3 Pl group Prog
        repP   repP

gitli^3-hnv^3
dog and

n<u>i</u>go^{23}lv   juls<u>i</u>^{3}hnvd^{34} u-n-<u>a</u>deytohd<u>i</u>^{3}h-e   gusd^{23}
always   nightly   3 Pl bothered repP   something

a-ni-ke^{23}he^{32}-g-e^3 a-ni-dey^{23}st<u>a</u>nih<u>i</u>h-e^3
3 Pl run-after Prog repP   3 Pl around-corner-of-house repP

galjo^{23}de^3 a^{3}gwu-nh^3 yv
house   here and   nearby

wi̱-g-a̱nv^{3}hn-v   wi̱-k-a̱nal^{3}hd-v   unv^{23}dahli
Tr 3 down-the-road exP   Tr 3 ascend-incline exP   rocky

iyusd^{23} i-ga̱nv^{3}hn-a   sgina^3 a̱-gayv^{23}li̱^{3}ge   j-u̱-we^{3}nvsv   i̱di^{3}dla
likeness   Dst road Pres   that   3 old-woman   Pl 3 house   toward

ji̱-ji-noh-e^3 una^{3}hnv^3
Rel 1 talk-about repP   road

nogwu   a-ni-luhg-e   hleg-hnv
now   3 Pl arrive repP   while and

ase   a^3-n-a^{3}nhdlvs-g-e   gitli
maybe   3 Pl lie-down Prog repP   dog

nogwu̱^{3}-le^3 a̱^{3}-n-ehlu̱hv^{3}s-g-o^3 j-a-di̱h-v^3
then and   3 Pl bark Prog Hab   Pst 3 say exP

a̱^{3}-n-a^{3}nelu^{23}gi^{32}s-g-o^3 galjo^{23}de^3 w-u-ni^3-deysdih-e^3 gitli
3 Pl run-after Prog Hab   house   Tr 3 Pl run-around repP   dog

uhna^3-hnv   d-u-n-o^{23}hl-v
there and   Pl 3 Pl sit exP

yvwi   a^{3}gwu^3-hnv^3 iyv   a-n-atla^{3}ʔisdih-e^3
people   nearby and   toward   3 Pl run-by repP

gitli
dogs

hla̱-hno^3 gosd^{23} y-a̱-ni^3-gowhtih-e^3
not and   something   nonF 3 Pl see repP

j-a-di̱^{23}h-v^3 gitli-gwu^3-hnv^3 i^{23}ga   d-a-ni-gowhti̱^{3}h-e
Pst 3 say exP   dog just and   all   Pl 3 Pl see repP

uhna^3 y-u-ni^3-hnalht<u>a</u>n-a   wi-k<u>a</u>nalh^{3}dv   nvno^{23} no^{23}gwu
there   Tr 3Pl chase recP   Tr up-hill   up-road   now

<u>a</u>-ni-winu^{4}ja   j<u>o</u>ʔi-ha   iy<u>a</u>^{3}ni
3 Pl young-man   three Ord   of-them

d-idi^{23}-sdel^3 gitli
Pl you Pl-and-I help   dog

di-d-i^{23}n-v^{3}hw<u>i</u>sde   u-n-<u>a</u>dvhn-e^3
Pl Pl you/I make   3 Pl say repP

di^{23}sgwaldi   ohni
at-a-run   behind

w-u^{23}-n-<u>a</u>^{3}tl<u>a</u>ʔvst<u>a</u>n-e^3 do^{23}-hnv
Tr 3 Pl run-after repP   indeed

w-u-n<u>i</u>^{3}-suligoj^3
Tr 3 Pl stop

gitli
dog

nogw<u>u</u>^{3}-le^3 w<u>i</u>-d-<u>u</u>^{3}-ni-nvhw<u>i</u>st<u>a</u>^{3}n-e   nogw<u>u</u>^{3}-le^3
then and   Tr Pl 3 Pl sick repP   then and

w-<u>u</u>^{3}-n-a^{3}nelu^{23}gi^{32}s-e^3 a^{3}gw<u>u</u>^{3}-dv^3 iyv   nogw<u>u</u>^{3}-le^3
Tr 3 Pl run-after repP   nearby indeed   that-far   then and

wigvwh^{3}ke^{23}hv^{32}se^3 ge^3-gw-nv   vsgwu^3 iyv^3 gv-whke^{23}hv^{32}-se^3
Tr 3 Pl run-after   there just and   also   that-far   they/him run-after
                                                                          repP

no^{23}gwu   wi-gv^3-w<u>a</u>dlvt<u>a</u>h-e^3
now   Tr 3Pl catch-up repP

nogwu   kv^{4}hni
now   apparently

we^{23}sa^3-hnv^3 u-wehlu̱hn-e^3 wes^{23} y-a̱-ni^3-disv^{23}hni
cat and   3 meow-loudly repP   cat   when 3 Pl maul

gitli   j-u-wehluh-g-o
dog   Pl 3 meow-loudly Prog Hab

sgi^3 ni̱-g-a̱wes-g-e^3
that   Lat 3 meow Prog repP

na?v^3-gwu-hnv   agwu   iyv^3
nearby just and   here   that far

iyusd^{23} u-ni-lu^{3}l-e^3 no^{23}gwu̱^{3}-le^3
like   3 Pl lack repP   then-and

u^3-n-a̱liti^3?el-e^3 si^3 a^{3}gwu^3 wi̱-ganv^{3}hnv   di^{3}dla   w-u^3-ni-ke^{23}hv^{32}s-e^3
3 Pl get-away   yet   nearby   Tr road   toward   Tr 3 Pl run-after repP
  repP

ge^{23}gwu   iyv^3 u-ni-ke^{23}hv^{4}d-a   no^{23}gwu̱^{3}-le^3
there just   that-far   3 Pl chase recP   then-and

w-u̱^{3}-n-adlvta̱h-e^3 sigwu^3-hno^3 wes^{23} ni̱-g-a̱wes-g-e^3
Tr 3 Pl catch-up-with repP   again and   cat   Spec 3 meow Prog repP

a-n-a̱tla̱^{3}?is-e^3 na?v^{23}-hni̱^{3}ge^4?-i̱sdi   w-a̱-n-a̱^{3}tla̱?is-e^3 no^{23}gwu
3 Pl run repP   close Inf   Tr 3 Pl run repP   then

u-n-a̱delos-e^3 no^{23}gwu   nu^{3}da̱le   ni̱-g-a̱wes-g-v^3
3 Pl realize repP   then   different   Lat 3 utter Prog exP

yvwi   no^{23}gwu   ni-g-awes-g-v^3
person   now   Lat 3 utter Prog exP

u-n-a̲tvga^{32}n-e^3 nogwu^3
3 Pl hear repP   then

gitli   d-a-sga^{32}-g-e^3 he^{43}
dog   Pl 3 Prog repP   dog-call

a-di̲^{23}h-e   d-a-sga^{32}-g-e^3
3 say repP   Pl 3 get-on-to-them Prog repP

gitli   uhna^3
dog   there

no^{23}gwu   w-u^{23}-n-a̲^{3}lehna̲wsta̲n-e^{32}
now   Tr 3 Pl come-to-stop repP

na^3 a̲-n-alsdeli^{4}s-g-i   wi̲-d-u-ni^3-sgaj-e^3 no^{23}gwu
the   3 Pl help Prog Ag   Tr Pl 3 Pl call-off repP   now

gitli   vsgi-hnv^3
dog   that and

an^{23} j-u-do^{3}ʔid   sgwu^3 u-dlaw^{32}sd-v^3 an^{23} sgwu^3
ann   Rel 3 be-named   also   3 stay-with exP   ann   also

d-u-do^{3}ʔ-v^3 a̲gi-ji^3
Pl 3 be-named exP   1Pos mother

ji-ges-v   an^{23} ukahyod^{23} j-u-do^{3}ʔid
Rel be exP   ann   ukahyod   Rel 3 be-named

u-dlaw^{32}sd-v^3 a-di̲h-v^3 sgi̲h-no^3
3 stay-with exP   3 say exP   that and

osdi-gati^{23}y-v^3 a-di̲^{23}h-v^3 u-yohus^{23}
they-two-and-I care-for exP   3 say exP   3 die

na^3 a̲-ga̲yv^{23}li̲^{3}ge   nogwu^3-hnv^3
that   3 old-woman   then and

e-dod   ji-ges-v   no^{23}gwu
1Pos father   Rel be exP   then

ulehwa^{3}da^3-hno   j-u-do^3?id   eh-v^3
ulehwadahno and   Rel 3 be-named   live exP

udli^{3}di^{3}dla   ama-yulh^{4}di   jusg-o   jogi   di^{3}dla
farther toward   water-by   oaks at   upstream   toward

ganesa   di-g-ohlv^4-ssickg-i
casket   Pl 3 make Prog Ag

ji-d-a-n-ohlvs-g-v^{23}-gwu^3-hnv^3
then Pl 3 Pl make Prog Exp just and

ganesa
casket

nahiyu^3 ji-geh-v^3 vsgina^3 u-ni-nv^{23}s-e
then   Rel be exP   that   3 Pl send repP

u-wohlvn-di   na?v^{23}
3 make Inf   nearby

gwu-hnv   svgwalosgi^3
here and   sawmill

uw-ohlv^{3}s-v^3 wil^{23} gasgilo^3 j-u-do^{23}?id-a
3 have exP   will   chair   Rel 3 be-named recP

eli^{23}gwu   suhiye^{23}yi   di^{3}dla   dlv^3 ta^3?li   iyv^3
possible   evening   toward   somewhere   two   then

eli^{23}gwu   y-oji-nog^{23} ganesa^3 sgi-gwu^3 iyv^3 dlvhdlv^3
possible   nonF they-and-I   casket   that just   that-time- frame   sometime
bring

u-sgwa̲^{3}d-esd^3 udalu^{3}lv^4-gwu   e-sda̲wo^{3}ʔv
3 finish Fut Prog   before just   Imp bathe

edi-lvdi^{23}-gwu-hnv   i^{23}ga
Imp place-flexible-position just and   all

y-igi
nonF be

ga̲nesa^3 y-ogi^3-no^{4}hl-a   ogi̲-nose^{23}l-v^3
casket   nonF-they-and-I bring recP   he/them-and-me tell exP

a-di̲^{23}h-v^3 na^3
3 say exP   that-one

e-dod
1Pos father

ji-ges-v   u^{23}-hni̲^{3}gis
Rel be exP   3 leave

eli^3 si̲nale̲ʔi^3 u^{23}-hni̲^{3}gis-v   do^{23}-hnv
possible   in-the-morning   3 leave exP   also and

i^{23}ga   ogi̲n-alsda^{32}y-v-hnv^3 a-di̲^{23}h-v^3
at-noon   he-and-I eat exP and   3 say exP

hla^3 ki̲lo^3 yi̲-g-a̲na^{3}nugo-g-o^3
not   someone   nonF 3 come-around Prog Hab

j-a-di̲^{23}h-v^3 ogi̲n-alsda^{32}y-v^{23}-hno̲hna
Pst 3 say exP   he-and-I eat Comp and

uhlisd^{23} n-ogi̲-n-a̲dv^{3}ne-li^{23}do^{32}l-v^3 j-a-di̲^{23}h-v^3 nogwu
quickly   Spec they-and-I Pl work around exP   Pst 3 say exP   then

u-n-alenvh-e^3 j-a-di̲^{23}h-v^3 hyahteno^{23}-hi̲-gwu^3-hnv^3
3 Pl begin repP   Pst 3 say exP   floor-on just and

hi?a   nusdv³
this   was

j̲i-d-a-ni-hlv³?v̲s-g-v³   y-u²³-yo³hus³⁴
Rel Pl 3 Pl make Prog exP   nonF 3 die

kilo   adayig³
someone   board

gosd²³   j̲i-d-a-ni-di³²s-g-v³   hyahten²³
something   Rel Pl 3 Pl lie-down Prog exP   board

d-a-ni-hl̲adi³²s-g-v³   sg̲i-hno³
Pl 3 Pl lay-on Prog exP   that and

n-u-nvhn-v
Spec 3 do exP

u-n-a̲lenvh-v³   j-a-d̲i²³h-v³   no²³gwu   a-n-a̲wo³s-g-v
3 Pl start exP   Pst 3 say exP   then   3 Pl bathe Prog exP

do³ya   u-yo̲?i³   ni̲dusdv³   j-a-d̲i²³h-v³   di-g-a̲nvsgen²³
very   3 bad   were   Pst 3 say exP   Pl 3 leg

gilh   de-gvw³sgalh-j-v³   hl̲a-sgin³   g-vdeloho²³h-isd
dog   3 Pl Pas bite Exp   not but   3 tell Inf

yi̲-ge³h-e³   j-a-d̲i²³h-v³   na³   si³
nonF be repP   Pst 3 say exP   she   still

g-vhn-v-gw²³   u-yohus-v³   ni̲-ge³s-e   d-u-lsdu³?i̲s-e³
3 alive Exp just   3 die exP   already be repP   Pl 3 open-up repP

j-a-d̲i²³h-v³   ni̲kv²³-hnv   j-u-lt̲alv³?id-a
Pst 3 say exP   all-over and   Pl 3 puncture recP

geh-e³   de-g-a³wos-g-v³   j-a-d̲i²³h-v
be exP   Pl 3 ooze Prog exP   Pst 3 say exP

Syllabary

ᎡᏙᏓᏛ ᏥᎨᏯ ᎡᏥ ᏥᎨᏯ ᎢᏧᎳᏊ ᎠᏂᏃᎮᏍᎪ ᎨᏅ ᎣᎬᏏ ᎾᎥ ᎡᎮ ᎠᎦᏴᎵᎨ ᎤᎵᏍᎦᏍᏛ ᏧᏙᎢᏓ ᎤᏩᏍ ᎦᏁᎵ ᎨᎮ ᎡᏥ ᏥᎨᏯ Ꮎ ᏧᎾᏓᏂᏜᏓ ᏧᎾᏛᏒ ᎨᎮ ᎠᏗᎨ ᏗᏂᏲᏟ ᎨᏯ ᎤᏲᎱᏒ ᎨᎮ ᎤᏂᏥ ᎤᏂᏙᏓᏂᏅ ᏧᏛᎯᏍᏔᏅ ᎨᏎ ᏑᎨᏓᏍᏗ ᎨᏯ ᎠᏗᏯ ᎤᎩᏄᏗ ᎡᏙᏯ ᎠᏗᏯ ᏓᏩᏂᎨ ᏐᏇᎵ ᎤᎾᏝᎥ ᎠᏗᏯ ᎠᏆᏘᏁᎪ ᏣᏗᏯ ᏧᏬᏅᏒ ᎳᎵᏐ ᏧᏒᎯᏓ ᎳᎵᏐ ᎢᏳᏒ ᎢᏴ ᎢᏥᏇᏘᏃᏄ ᏳᏛᎾ ᎠᎦᎵᏍᎪᏄᏓᏁᎨ ᎡᏙᏓ ᏥᎨᏯ ᎣᏍᎦᎪ ᏣᏗᏯ ᎣᏂᏴ ᎦᏓᏅᏞᎨ ᏣᏗᏯ ᎠᏋᏌᏅ ᎠᎦᏒᎯᎮ ᎨᎵᎨ ᏣᏗᏯ ᎥᏅ ᎠᏥᏍᎩᎵ ᎨᎮ ᏣᏗᏯ Ꮎ ᎠᎦᏴᎵᎨ ᏃᏊᎧᏅ ᎤᏔᏅ ᏃᏊ ᏂᎨᏎ ᏃᏊ ᎡᏥ ᏥᎨᏯ ᎾᏂᏁᏨ ᏃᏊ ᎡᏙᏓ ᎾᏃ ᏥᏳᎪᏗ ᎠᏊ blackfox hollow ᏣᎾᏗᎨ ᏥᏘᎨᏓᎵᏴ ᏁᏗ ᏛᏂᏃᎵ ᏧᏙᎢᏓ ᏁᏗ ᏧᏁᎳᏛ ᎠᎾᏗᎨ ᏁᏗ Ꮫ ᎠᏎ ᏥᎨᏯ ᎤᏙᏓ ᎠᏎ ᏗᎦᏁᏄ ᎦᎾ ᎮᏅ ᏕᏙᏒ ᎦᎾ ᏛᏂᏃᎵ ᏕᏙᏒ ᎤᏖ ᎩᎶ ᎤᎵᎩ ᎦᏅᎨ ᎠᎳᏄᏟ ᎠᏗᎨ ᎪᎯᏓ ᎥᏍᏊ ᎤᎵᏥᏙᏨ ᎾᏅ ᏥᎦᏗᏯ ᏧᏇᏇ ᎾᎾᎵᏍᏗᏯ ᏴᏫ ᎩᎶ ᏳᎵᏩ ᏥᎦᏗᏯ ᏍᎩᏃ ᏙᏜ ᎢᏴ ᎤᏃᏞ ᎤᏖ ᎤᏂᎦᎾᏑᏍᎨ ᎠᏂᏫᎾ ᎢᏳᏍᏗᏐ ᎤᎾᏓᏇᎨ ᎩᏟᏅ ᏂᎪᏄ ᏧᎵᏏᏅᏛ ᎤᎾᎦᏇᏙᏗᎮ ᏗᏍᏗ ᎠᏂᎨᎮᎨ ᎠᏂᎦᏇᏍᏔᏂᎯᎮ ᎦᎵᏦᎦ ᎠᏊᎧᏅ Ᏼ ᏫᎦᏅᏅ ᏫᎧᎾᎷᏛ ᎤᏅᏓᏟ ᎢᏳᏍᏗ ᎢᎦᏅᏖ ᏍᎩᎾ ᎠᎦᏴᎵᎨ ᏧᏬᏅᏒ ᎢᏗᏜ ᏥᏥᏃᎮ ᎤᏅᏅ ᏃᏊ ᎠᏂᎷᎨ ᏓᎦᏅ ᎠᏎ ᎠᎾᏂᎵᏍᎨ ᎩᏟ ᏃᏊᎧᏨ ᎠᏁᎷᏯᏍᎪ ᏣᏗᏯ ᎠᎾᏁᎷᎩᏍᎪ ᎦᎵᏦᎦ ᏘᏂᎦᏇᏍᏗᎮ ᎩᏟ ᎤᏖᏅ ᏕᏃᏄ ᏴᏫ ᎠᏊᎧᏅ ᎢᏴ ᎠᎾᏝᎥᏍᏘᎮ ᎩᏟ ᏝᏃ ᎪᏍᏓ ᏇᏂᎪᏩᏘᎮ ᏣᏗᏯ ᎩᏟᏊᎧᏅ ᎢᎦ ᏓᏂᎪᏩᏘᎮ ᎤᎾ ᏩᏂᏖᎷᎳᎾ ᏫᎧᎾᎷᏛ ᎤᏃ ᏃᏊ ᎠᏂᏫᏄᏟ ᏦᎢᏐ ᎢᏇᏂ ᏗᏗᏍᎦᎳ ᎩᏟ ᏗᏗᏅᏫᏍᏓ ᎤᎾᏛᏁ ᏗᎦᏍᏆᏄᏗ ᎣᏂ ᏘᎾᏝᎥᏍᎳᏁ ᏙᏅ ᏘᏂᏇᎵᎪᏟ ᎩᏟ ᏃᏊᏨ ᏫᏕᏂᏅᏫᏍᎳᏁ ᏃᏊᏨ ᏳᎾᏁᎷᎩᏍᎨ ᎠᏊᏛ ᎢᏴ ᏃᏊᏨ ᏫᎬᏳᎨᏯᏎ ᎨᏊᎧᏅ ᎥᏍᏊ ᎢᏴ ᎬᏳᎨᏯᏎ ᏃᏊ ᏫᎬᏳᎵᎳᎮ ᏃᏊ ᎬᏂ ᏬᏌᏅ ᎤᏬᎷᏁ ᏬᏍ ᏇᏂᏗᏒᏂ ᎩᏟ ᏧᏬᎷᎪ ᏍᎩ ᎲᎦᏬᏍᎨ ᎾᎥᏊᎧᏅ ᎠᏊ ᎢᏴ ᎢᏳᏍᏛ ᎤᏂᎷᏨ ᏃᏊᎧᏨ ᎤᎾᎵᏘᏒᏨ Ꮟ ᎠᏊ ᏫᎦᏅᏅ ᏗᏜ ᏘᏂᎨᏯᏎ ᎨᏊ ᎢᏴ ᎤᏂᎨᏯᏓ ᏃᏊᎧᏨ ᏘᎾᎵᎳᎮ ᏏᏊᏃ ᏬᏌ ᎲᎦᏬᏍᎨ ᎠᎾᏝᎢᏎ ᎾᎥᏂᎨᎢᏍᏗ ᏳᎾᏝᎢᏎ ᏃᏊ ᎤᎾᎦᎶᏎ ᏃᏊ ᏄᏓᏨ ᎲᎦᏬᏍᎬ ᏴᏫ ᏃᏊ ᎲᎦᏬᏍᎨ ᎤᎾᏛᎦᏁ ᏃᏊ ᎩᏟ ᏓᏍᎦᎨ Ꭾ ᎠᏗᎮ ᏓᏍᎦᎨ ᎩᏟ ᎤᎾ ᏃᏊ ᏘᎾᏨᏖᏫᏍᎳᏁ Ꮎ ᎠᎾᎵᏍᎦᎵᏍᎩ ᏫᏕᏂᏍᎦᏧ ᏃᏊ ᎩᏟ ᎥᏍᎩᏅ ᎠᏂ ᏧᏙᎢᏓ ᏍᏊ ᎤᏜᏩᏍᏛ ᎠᏂ ᏍᏊ ᏕᏙᎥ ᎠᎩᏥ ᏥᎨᏒ ᎠᏂ ᎤᎧᏲᏓ ᏧᏙᎢᏓ ᎤᏜᏩᏍᏛ ᎠᏗᏯ ᏍᎩᏃ ᎣᏍᏗᎦᏘᏴ ᎠᏗᏯ ᎤᏲᎱᏍ Ꮎ ᎠᎦᏴᎵᎨ ᏃᏊᎧᏅ ᎡᏙᏓ ᏥᎨᏒ ᏃᏊ ᎤᏨᏩᏓᏃ ᏧᏙᎢᏓ ᎡᏯ ᎤᏗᏗᏜ ᎠᏡᏳᎶᏗ ᏧᏍᎪ ᏦᎩ ᏗᏜ ᎦᏁᏌ ᏗᎪᎵᏍᎩ ᏥᏓᏃᎵᏍᎬᏊᎧᏅ ᎦᏁᏌ ᎾᎯᏳ ᏥᎨᏯ ᎥᏍᎩᎾ ᎤᏂᏅᏎ ᎤᏑᎵᏅᏗ ᎾᎥᏊᎧᏅ ᎡᏆᎶᏍᎩ ᎤᏑᎵᏒ Ꮻ ᎦᏍᎩᎶ ᏧᏙᎢᏓ ᎡᎵᏊ ᎡᎯᏴᏜ ᏗᏜ Ꮅ ᎳᎵ ᎢᏴ ᎡᎵᏊ ᏲᏥᏃᎦ ᎦᏁᏌ ᏍᎩᏊ ᎢᏴ ᎵᎵ ᎤᏍᏆᎦᏍᏗ ᎤᏓᎷᏄᏊ ᎡᏍᏓᏑᎥ ᎡᏗᏄᏗᏊᎧᏅ ᎢᎦ ᏜᎩ ᎦᏁᏌ ᏲᎩᏃᏝ ᎣᎩᏃᏎᏄ ᎠᏗᏯ ᎡᏙᏓ ᏥᎨᏒ ᎤᏂᎩᏍ ᎡᎵ ᏏᎾᏨᎢ ᎤᏂᎩᏒ ᏙᏅ ᎢᎦ ᎣᎩᎾᎵᏍᏓᏴᏅ ᎠᏗᏯ Ꮭ ᎩᎶ ᏜᎦᎾᏄᎪᎪ ᏣᏗᏯ ᎣᎩᎾᎵᏍᏓᏴᏃᏖ ᎤᎵᏍᏓ ᏃᎩᎾᏛᏁᎵᏙᏄ ᏣᏗᏯ ᏃᏊ ᎤᎾᏨᏅᎮ ᏣᏗᏯ ᏇᏞᏃᎯᏊᎧᏅ ᎯᎠ ᏄᏍᏛ ᏥᏓᏂᎵᎥᏍᎬ ᏩᏲᏅᏍ ᎩᎶ ᎠᏓᏜᎩ ᎪᏍᏗ ᏥᏓᏂᏗᏍᎬ ᏇᏞᏃ ᏓᏂᏝᏗᏍᎬ ᏍᎩᏃ ᏄᏅᏅ ᎤᎾᏨᏅᏯ ᏣᏗᏯ ᏃᏊ ᎠᎾᏑᏍᎬ ᏙᏇ ᎤᏲᎢ ᏂᏕᏍᏛ ᏣᏗᏯ ᏗᎦᏅᏍᎨᏂ ᎩᏟ ᎦᎬᏩᏍᎦᎶᏨ ᏝᏍᎩᏂ ᎬᎦᎶᎨᎯᏍᏗ ᏜᎨᎮ ᏣᏗᏯ Ꮎ Ꮟ ᎬᏅᏊ ᎤᏲᎱᏒ ᏂᎨᏒᏫ ᏕᎵᏍᏕᎢᏎ ᏣᏗᏯ ᎲᎬᏅ ᏧᎵᏔᏄᎢᏓ ᎨᎮ ᎦᏕᏑᎬ ᏣᏗᏯ

English

My father and my mother both would tell this story. Over there near Oaks, an old woman named Uskast lived alone. According to my mother, she and the other children had been raised by their father because their mother had died. We would go and visit her, she said, and the old woman would travel around on her yellow horse. She would take me home to her, she said, for about two days. She said she would tell my father that she would bring me home in a couple of days, and my father would let me go. Later on, she said, she thought about how spooky this old woman had been. After she had become an adult and had married my father, there was a trail through what they called Blackfox Hollow, where Ned Blackfox lived. There was a young girl out there who was sick for quite a while. There would be a lot of people who would come and sit up when someone got sick. They had built a fire outside where they would warm themselves, and most of them were young men. And every night their dogs would growl and bark at something, and they would chase it. The dogs would chase it around the house and then down the trail and up a small hill. The dogs would chase it up to the top of the hill, and then they would quit chasing it and they would return. The dogs would lie down for a while, and then suddenly they would start chasing it again, and the people couldn't see what they were chasing. Finally some of the young men decided to help the dogs and see what it was they were chasing. When the dogs quit chasing it at the top of the hill, the men sicced the dogs, and the dogs continued the chase. The dogs chased it a short distance and caught up with it, and they could hear a cat meowing fiercely. The cat seemed to get away from the dogs, but the dogs caught up with it again and started fighting it. This time when they heard it, they heard a person. The person would yell "Hey!" trying to call the dogs off. The men came to a halt and called the dogs back. And this lady named Ann—my mother's name was Ann, too, Ann Dry—stayed with her. She and I were setting up with this lady when she died, she said. And then my father and a man named Ulehwat, a casket maker, back then they made their own caskets, so they sent for him to make a casket. There was a sawmill close by operated by someone named Will Chair. They said that they could possibly have the casket ready by two that afternoon. They asked them to have the deceased ready, bathed and clothed, by then so all they would have to do would be to put her in the casket. So after lunch they hurried and prepared the place on the floor and made a platform. When they started bathing her, she said, they found puncture wounds all over her legs that hadn't healed but were running with sores as if they had been caused from dog bites.

Two Dogs in One

Durbin Feeling

In this story, Durbin Feeling relates an unusual incident: the family dog apparently spent an evening in two different places with different family members. The reason for this phenomenon is unknown.

TᎾᏍᏯ	ᎾᏍᎫᎠ	ᏥᎨᏒ	ᏥᏧᏣᎬᎤ	Ꮢ	ᏥᎨᏒ	ᎣᎩᎸᎬᎤᏗ	ᎨᏒ
ilvsgi	nadetiya	jigesv	jichujagwu	si	jigesv	ogilvgwodi	gesv
a few	years	when it was	I just a boy	yet	when it was	we liked	it was

ᎠᏓᏴᎳᏨᏍᎩ	ᎣᎦᎦᏙᏍᏙᏗ	ᎭᏍᏂ	iᎠᎤ	ᎣᎬᏌ	ᎢᏲᎯ
adayvlatvsgi	ogagatosdodi	hlano	vsgwu	ogvsa	yogihe
television	for us to watch it	but not	also	we ourselves	we didn't have

ᎠᏓᏯᎳᏨᏍᎩ	ᎳᎤ	iᎠᎤ	ᎠᎾᏍᏆᎠᏯᎤ	ᏲᏂᏙᎬᏁ	ᎣᏥᏁᎸ
adayalatvsgi	tlale	vsgwu	angalisgigwu	yinidogvne	ojinelv
television	and not	also	electricity even	we didn't have	where we lived

ᏍᏈᏦ	Ꭰ4ᎠᏯᎢ	Ꮎi	ᎢᎧᏍᎶᏆ	ᎣᎭᏫ	ᎠᏓᏴᎳᏨᏍᎩ	ᎳᎤ
galijode	asesgini	na?v	ijogadali	unihv	adayvlatvsgi	hlano
house	however	near	we apart	they had	television	and not

iᎠᎤ	ᎤᏫᎦᎬ	Ꮎi	ᏲᏂᏙᎦᏓᎴ		Ꮲ	Ꭰ4
vsgwu	udohiyu	na?v	yinidogadale		dlv	ase
also	really	near	not close to each other		somewhere	I suppose

ᏑᏟᎶᏓ	ᎢᏴ
sudliloda	iyv
one mile	distance

ᏛᏂᏁᎸ	ᎠᏎᏃ	ᎣᏤᎪ	ᏙᏣᎦᏙᏍᏔᏁᎪ
dvninelv	aseno	ojego	dojagatostanego
they lived at a distance	however	we would go	for us to watch

ᎠᏓᏴᎳᏛᏍᎩ	Ꮲ
adayvlatvsgi	dlv
television	approximately

ᏍᎪᎯ	ᎠᏰᏟ	ᎠᏟᎢᎵᏒ	ᎢᎪᎯᏓ	ᏬᏤᏙᎰ	ᎧᏃᎮᏓ
sgohi	ayehli	atli?ilisv	igohida	wojedoho	kanoheda
ten	half	time	until	we would go there and return	news

ᎤᏂᏃᎮᏠᏅ	ᎢᎪᎯᏓ	ᎥᏍᎩᏃ	ᎢᏲᎨᎵᏒᎯ	ᎨᏒ	ᏌᏊ
uninohetlonv	igohida	vsgino	iyogelisvhi	gesv	sagwu
after the telling of	until	and that	what we had thought	it was	one

ᎢᏳᏩᎪᏗ	ᎣᎨᏅᏒ	ᎡᏙᏓ	ᎡᏥ	ᏦᏍᏓᏓᏅᏟ	ᎠᏴᏃ	ᎥᎩᏙᏃ
iyuwagodi	ogenvsv	edoda	eji	josdadanvdli	ayvno	vgidono
time	we went	father	mother	brother	and I	and my sister

ᎨᏒ	Ꮟ	ᏩᏥᎾ	ᏥᏚᏂᎩᏍᏗᏗᏒ	ᏧᎾᏕᎶᏆᏍᏗ	ᎥᏍᎩ	ᏄᏍᏛ
gesv	si	wajina	jidunigisdidisv	junadelogwasdi	vsgi	nusdv
who is	yet	Washington	operation	schools	that	place

ᏪᎲ	ᎥᏍᎩᏃ	ᎢᏳᏍᏗ	Ꮭ	ᏲᎨᎳᏗᏙᎮ
wehv	vsgino	iyusdi	tla	yokeladidohe
she lived there	and that	reason	not	she was not with us

ᎩᏟᏃ	ᎥᏍᏊ	ᎤᏬᏗᎨ
gitlino	vsgwu	uwodige
and dog	also	brown

ᎣᎩᎧᎲ	ᎣᏍᏓ	ᎦᏃᎭᎵᏙᎯ	ᎠᎴ	ᎥᏍᏊ	ᎦᎵᏦᏕ	ᎤᎦᏎᏍᏗ	ᎠᎴ
ogikahv	osda	ganohalidohi	ale	vsgwu	galijode	ugasesdi	ale
we had	good	hunter	and	also	house	watcher	and

ᎤᏬᎯᏳᎯᏍᏓ	ᎯᏅᏙᎮᏍᏗ	ᏱᎪᏎᎳ	ᎠᏅᏙᎲᏍᎬ	ᎠᎴ	ᎥᏍᏊ
uwohiyuhisda	hinvtohesdi	yigosela	anvtohvsgv	ale	vsgwu
obedient	stay	when you tell him	he would stay	and	also

ᏲᏣᏘᏁᎦ	ᎤᏪᏅᏍᏗᏊ	ᎨᏒ	ᎥᏍᎩᏃ
yojatinega	uwenvsdigwu	gesv	vsgino
if we took him with us	he would go	it was	and that

ᎩᏟ	ᎣᎩᏍᏓᏩᏛᏒ	ᎣᎨᎾ	ᏬᎩᎷᏣᏃ	ᎤᎾ	ᏧᏁᏅᏒ
gitli	ogisdawadvsv	ogena	wogilujano	uhna	junenvsv
dog	he followed us	when we went	and when we arrived	there	at their home

ᎤᎾᏊ	ᏙᏱ	ᏗᏢ	ᎠᏲᏓᏝᎲ	ᎤᏅᏏᏅ	ᎣᎩᎦᏘᏛ
uhnagwu	doyi	didlv	ayodatlahv	unvsinv	ogigatidv
and just there	outside	toward	on the porch	he lay down	he waited for us

ᏗᎣᏣᏂᎩᏍᎬ	ᎢᎪᎯᏓ	ᎾᎯᏳᏅ	ᏃᏊ	ᎣᎦᏛᏅᎢᏍᏔᎾ
di?ojanigisgv	igohida	nahiyunv	nogwu	ogadvnv?istana
as we returned	until	and at that time	then	as we got ready to

ᏂᏛᎣᎦᏂᎩᏍᏗ	ᏙᎦᎴᏅ	ᏂᎦᏓ	ᎠᎴ	ᎦᎶᎯᏍᏗ	ᎢᏗᏝ
nidv?oganigisdi	dogalenv	nigada	ale	galohisdi	ididla
upon our return	as we got up	all	and	door	toward

ᎣᏣᎢᏒ
oja?isv
as we walked

ᎤᎾᎴᏅᎲ	ᏓᎾᏟᏃᎮᏍᎬ	ᎡᏙᏓ	ᎡᏥ	ᎾᏃ	ᎠᏂᏐᎢ	ᎥᏍᎩᏃ
unalenvhv	danatlinohesgv	edoda	eji	nano	aniso?i	vsgino
they began again	to talk	father	mother	and	others	and that

ᏄᎾᏛᏁᎳ	ᏭᏅᎪᏨᏊ	ᏦᏍᏓᏓᏅᏟ	ᎠᎴᏃ	Ꮲ	ᏔᎵ
nunadvnela	wunvgojvgwu	josdadanvtli	aleno	dlv	tali
when they did	he just went on out	my brother	and	about	two

ᎢᏯᏔᏬᏍᏔᏅ	ᎢᏴ	ᎢᎬᏱ	ᏓᏳᎴᏅ	ᎠᏴᏃ	ᎨᏒ
iyatawostanv	iyv	igvyi	dayulenv	ayvno	gesv
minutes	about	ahead	he started out	and for ourselves	which was

ᎡᏙᏓ	ᎠᎴ	ᎡᏥ	ᎣᎦᎵᎪᎯ	ᏃᏊ	ᏦᎩᏄᎪᏣ	Ꮎ	ᎤᏬᏗᎨ	ᎩᏟ
edoda	ale	eji	ogaligohi	nogwu	joginugoja	na	uwodige	gitli
father	and	mother	together	then	as we came out	the	brown	dog

ᎣᎩᎧᎲ	ᏚᎴᏅ	ᏙᏱ	ᏗᏢ	ᎠᏲᏓᏝᎲ	ᎦᏅᎬᎢ	ᎥᏍᎩᏃ
ogikahv	dulenv	doyi	didlv	ayodatlahv	ganvgvʔi	vsgino
ours	he got up	outside	toward	porch	he was lying	and that

ᎩᏟ	ᎣᎨᎳᏛᏒ	ᏄᏓᏅᎯᏒ	ᏦᎨᏅᏒ	ᎢᏳᏓᏅᎯᏓ
gitli	okeladvsv	nudanvhisv	jogenvsv	iyudanvhida
dog	he joined us	the distance	to our home	as far as

ᏫᎣᎩᎷᏣᏃ	ᏦᎨᏅᏒ	ᏦᏍᏓᏓᏅᎵ	ᎦᏳᎳ	ᏭᏬᏈ
wiʔogilujano	jogenvsv	josdadanvhli	gayula	wuwohlv
and when we returned	to our home	my brother	already	he was home

ᎣᎩᏒᏍᏗᏃ	ᏃᏊ	ᎣᏣᏛᏅᏍᏗᏍᎬ	ᏙᏣᏟᏃᎮᏍᎬ
ogisvsdino	nogwu	ojadvnvʔisdisgv	dojatlinohesgv
and our bedtime	then	we were preparing	we were talking

ᎠᎩᏁᎢᏍᏔᏅ	Ꮎ	ᎩᏟ	ᏦᎩᏍᏓᏩᏛᏍᏔᏅ	ᏄᏓᏅᎯᏒ
akineʔistanv	na	gitli	jogisdawadvstanv	nudanvhisv
I mentioned	the	dog	him following us home	the distance

ᏦᏍᏓᏓᏅᏟᏃ	ᎡᏝᏪ	ᏄᎵᏍᏔᏅ
josdadanvtlino	etlawe	nulistanv
and my brother	silent	he became

LS	D4Z	ZⱭ	OᏌᏗG
tlega	aseno	nogwu	uneja
for a while	but then	when he	spoke up

ᎭD	ꙊᏍᎱR	SVⱭ	ᏉSᏢⱭVᏝ	DBZ
hiʔa	nuwesv	gadohv	yigalisdoda	ayvno
this	he said	how	can that be	me also

iⱭⱭ	ꙊᏝOᏗR	Ᏺ ...
vsgwu	nudanvhisv	jidvgisdawadvsda
also	the distance	he followed me

Morpheme by Morpheme

ilv^{4}sgi	nadeti^{23}ya	ji-ges-v^3	ji-chuja-gwu	si^3	ji-ges-v^3	ogi-lv^{23}gwodi	ges-v^3
few	year	Rel be exP	1 boy just	yet	Rel be exP	they-and-I like	be exP

a-dayv^{23}latvs-g-i	og-agato^{23}sdo^3-di	hla-no^3	vsgwu^3
3 in-view Prog Ag	they-and-I watch Inf	not and	also

og-v^{23}s-a	y-ogi-h-e
they-and-I have repP	nonF you-and-I have repP

a-dayv^{23}latvs-g-i	tla-le^3	vsgwu^3	a-n-gali^{23}s-g-i^3-gwu
3 in-view Prog Ag	not and	also	3 Pl flow Prog Ag just

yi-nido^{23}gv^{3}ne^3	oj-ine^{23}l-v^3
nonF 1 Pl have repP	they-and-I live exP

galhjo^{23}e	ase^{3}sgi^{3}ni	naʔv^3	ij-o^{3}gada^{4}li
house	however	near	they-and-I apart

u-ni-h-v^3	a-dayv^{23}latvs-g-i	hla-no^3
3 Pl have exP	3 in-view Prog Ag	not and

vsgwu³   udohiyu³   na?v³   y-ini-do²³ga³dal-e³
also   really   nearby   nonF you-and-I apart repP

dlv
somewhere

a²³se³   sudlilo⁴da   iyv³
probably   one-mile   distance

d-v-ni³-ne-lv³   ase³no   oj-e³-g-o³
Pl 3 Pl live exP   however   they-and-I go Prog Hab

d-oj-agado²³sta³ne-g-o³   a-dayv²³ladvs-g-i   dlv³
they-and-I watch Prog Hab   3 in-view Prog Ag   approximately

sgo²³hi   aye⁴hli   adli³?ili³sv   igo³hi⁴da   w-oj-e³doh-o³   kanohe²³da
ten   half   time   until   Tr they-and-I go-   news
                                                        around Hab

u-ni-nohe²³dlo³n-v   igo³hi⁴a   vsgi-no³   i-yo³g-elisv⁴h-i   ges-v³   sagwu³
3 Pl tell exP   until   that and   Rep they-and-I   be exP   one
                                                  think Ag

iyu³wa⁴gdi   og-env³s-v³   e-doda   e-ji³
time   they-and-I go exP   1Pos father   1Pos mother

j-osd-adanv⁴dli   ayv-no   vgi-do²³-no
Pl he-and-I brother   I and   1Pos sister and

ges-v³   sa³   wajina   ji-d-u²³-ni⁴-gisdi³dis-v
be exP   yet   washington   Rel Pl 3 Pl govern exP

j-u-n-adelogwas-di   vsgi   nusdv³
where 3 Pl learn Inf   that   place

w-eh-v
Tr attend exP

vsgi-no^3 iyu^{4}sdi tla^3 y-og-e^{3}ladidoh-e^3
that and   reason not   nonF he/them-and-I be-with repP

gidli-no^3 vsgwu uwo^{23}di^{3}ge
dog and   also   brown

ogi-kah-v^3 osda ga-nohelido^{4}h-i ale^3
they-and-I have exP good 3 hunt-around Ag and

vsgwu^3 galhjo^{23}de u^{23}-gas-esdi   ale^3
also   house   3 watch Fut-Prog and

uw-ohiyuhi^{4}sd-a hi-nv^{3}doh-e^{3}sdi y-ig-o^{32}s-e^{4}l-a
3 obey Pres   2 stay Fut-Prog   nonF they-and-I say Dat Pres

a-n-v^{3}dohvs-g-v^3 ale^3 vsgwu^3
3 Pl stay Prog exP and   also

y-oj-a^{32}tine^{4}g-a   uw-env^{3}sdi-gwu
nonF they-and-I take-away Pres 3 go Inf just

ges-v vsgi-no^3
be exP that and

gitli ogi-sda^{32}wadv^{3}s-v^3 og-e^{4}n-a
dog   he/them-and-I follow exP they-and-I go Pres

w-ogi^3-luj-a^3-no   uhna^3 j-u-n-e^{3}nvsv^3
Tr they-and-I arrive Pres and   there   Pl 3 Pl home

uhna^3-gwu do^{23}yi di^{3}dlv ay-oda^{32} u-n-vsin-v^3 ogi-gati^{3}d-v^3
                             tlah-v
there just outside toward 3 porch exP 3 Pl lie-down he/them-and-I
                                          exP   wait exP

di-ʔo^3-j-a^{23}ni^{3}gis-g-v^3 igo^{3}hi^{4}a nahiyu^4-nv no^{23}gwu og-advnv^{3}istan-a
Dst they-and-I return until   at-that-time then   they-and-I prepare
  Prog exP   and   Pres

ni-d-v^3-?og^{23}ani^{3}gi-sdi   d-og-alen-v^3 niga^{4}da   al^3 galohisdi^3 idi^{3}dla
1 Pl return Inf   Pl they-and-I   all   and   door   toward
                          get-up exP

oj-a^3?is-v
they-and-I walk exP

u^3-n-alenvh-v^3 d-a-n-adlinohe^{23}s-g-v   e-doda
3 Pl begin-again exP   Pl 3 Pl talk Prog exP   1Pos father

e-ji^3 na^{3}h-no   a-ni^{23}-so?i   vsgi-no^3
1Pos mother   that and   3 Pl other   that and

n-u-n-adv^{3}ne^{4}l-a   w-u-n-vgo^{3}j-v^{23}-gwu   j-osd-adanv^{4}dli   ale^{23}-no^3 dlv
Spec 3 Pl do Pres   Tr 3 Pl go-out exP just   Pl he-and-I   and and   about
                                             brother

ta^3?li
two

iy-a^3-tawostan-v^3 iyv^3 igv^{23}yi   d-a-y-u^{23}le^{3}n-v^3 ayv-no   ges-v^3
one-unit 3 hold-breath   about   ahead   Dst 3 start exP   I and   be exP
  Exp

e-doda   ale^3 e-ji^3 og-aligo^4-hi   no^{23}gwu
1Pos father   and   1Pos mother   they-and-I be-together Ag   then

j-ogi^3-nugo^{4}j-a   na^3 u-wo^{23}di^{3}ge   gitli
Pl they-and-I come-out Pres   the   3 brown   dog

ogi-kah-v   d-u-len-v^3 do^{23}yi   di^{3}dlv   ayoda^{32}tlahv   ga-nv-g-   vsgi-no^3
                                                              v^{23}-?i

they-and-I   Pl 3 get-up   outside   toward   porch   3 lie Prog   that and
  our exP   exP   exP

gitli   ok-eladv^{32}s-v^3 nudanvhi^{3}sv   j-og-e^{3}nvsv   iyu^{3}da?ehi^{4}da
dog   he/them-and-me   distance   Pl they-and-I home   as-far-as
        follow exP

wi^3-ʔogi^3-luj-a^3-no   j-og-e^{3}nvsv
Tr they-and-I return Pres and   Pl they-and-I home

j-o-sd-adanv^{4}hli   ga^{3}yula   w-o-wo^{23}hl-v^3
Pl he-and-I brother   already   Tr 3 be-home exP

ogi-svs-di^4-no   no^{23}gwu   oj-advnv^{3}isdi^{23}s-g-v   d-oj-adlinohe^{23}s-g-v
they-and-I be-bedtime   then   they-and-I prepare   Pl they-and-I talk
   Inf and   Prog exP   Prog exP

ak-ine^{3}ʔistan-v^3 na^3 gitli   j-ogi^3-sdawadvstan-v   nudanvhi^{3}sv
1 mention exP   the   dog   Pst they-and-I follow exP   distance

j-osd-adanv^{23}dli-no   ehlawe^3 n-u-listan-v^3
Pl he-and-I brother and   silent   Spec 3 become exP

hle^{4}ga   ase^{3}no   no^{23}gwu   u-n-e^{4}j-a
for-a-while   but   when   3 Pl speak-up Pres

hiʔa   n-u-wes-v   gadohv^3 yi-g-alisdo^{4}d-a   ayv-no^3
this   Spec 3 say exP   how   nonF 3 occur Pres   I and

vsgwu^3 nudanvhi^{3}sv   jidv^{23}-gisdawadv^{3}sd-a
also   distance   he-me follow Pres

Syllabary

ᏔᏬᎧᏯ ᎤᏏᎯᏬ ᏂᏯᎡ ᏂᏓᏣᏬ Ꮒ ᏂᏯᎡ ᏒᏯᏋᏫᏗ ᏝᎡ ᎠᏓᏆᏍᏬᏯ ᏒᏍᏍᏙᏬᎯᏗ ᏝᏃ
ᎢᏬᏬ ᏒᎡᎤ ᏃᏯᏈ ᎠᏓᏆᏍᏬᏯ ᏝᏙ ᎢᏬᏬ ᏗᎤᏍᏈᏯᏬ ᏎᏂᎥᎬ ᏒᏂᏒᏋ ᏒᏈᎩᏍ
ᏗᎴᏬᏯᏘ ᎤᎢ ᏔᎧᏍᏢᏈ ᎤᎲᏛ ᎠᏓᏆᏍᏬᏯ ᏝᎡ ᎢᏬᏬ ᎤᎾᏤᎦ ᎤᎢ ᏒᎯᏉᏍᏙ Ꭾ ᏗᎴ
ᎦᏟᎦᏢ ᏘᏰ ᎷᎯᏒᏋ ᏗᎴᎤ ᏒᎤᎠ ᎠᎦᏒᏬᎥᎳᎠ ᎠᏓᏆᏬᏯ Ꭾ ᏬᎠᎤ ᏗᏰᏟ ᏗᏟᏈᎴ
ᏔᎠᎤᏝ ᎤᏫᏫᎢ ᎥᏁᎵ ᎤᏂᏎᏈᏳ ᏔᎠᎤᏝ ᎢᏬᏯᏃ ᏔᏂᎵᏈᎴᎠ ᏂᎡ ᎤᏬ ᏔᎦᎦᎴ
ᏒᎢᎤᎡᎢᏒ ᎡᎥᏢ ᎡᎯᎡ ᎧᏬᎵᎵᎤᏟ ᏗᏴᎤᏃ ᎢᏴᎥᏃ ᏂᎡ Ꮟ ᎦᎳᎤ ᏂᏒᎯᏰᏬᏗᎴ ᏦᎤᏒᎦᏬᏗᎴ
ᎢᏬᏴ ᎲᏬᎶ ᎾᏫ ᎢᏬᏯᏃ ᏔᎦᏬᏗ Ꮃ ᎷᎾᏬᎠᏫᏈ ᏯᏟ ᎢᏬᏬ ᎤᏬᎸᎢ ᏒᏯᏬ ᏒᏬᎵ
ᏎᏃᏆᏈᎥᎤ ᏗᎦ ᎢᏬᏬ ᏒᏈᎩᏍ ᎤᏍᏞᏬᏗ ᏗᎦ ᎤᏬᏞᎦᏱᏬᎵ ᏬᎤᏙᏈᏬᏗ ᏒᎠᏞᏫ
ᏙᎤᏬᎸᎤᏬᎡ ᏗᎦ ᎢᏬᏬ ᎷᎦᏣᏂᏍ ᎤᏲᎤᎤᏬᎳᏬ ᏂᎡ ᎢᏬᏯᏃ ᏯᏟ ᏒᏯᏬᏟᎦᏬᎵᏒ ᏒᏂᎤ
ᎤᏯᎻᎬᏃ ᎤᎢ ᏗᏟᎤᎡ ᎤᏏᏬ ᏙᎤ ᎠᏁᎵᎵᏬ ᎤᎤᏉᎤ ᏒᏯᏎᏂᏊ ᏟᏂᏣᏂᏬᎡ
ᏔᎠᎤᏝ ᎤᎠᎦᎤᎤ ᏃᏬ ᏒᏍᏛᎤᎢᏔᏬᎤᎤ ᏂᏲᏒᏂᏯᏬᏗ ᏒᏍᏙᎤ ᏂᏍᎵ ᏗᎦ ᏒᏣᎠᏬᏗ

ᎢᏗᏜ ᎣᏣᎢᏒ ᎤᎾᏛᏅᎲ ᏓᎾᏟᏃᎮᏍᎬ ᎡᏙᏓ ᎡᏥ ᎾᏃ ᎠᏂᏐᎢ ᎥᏍᎩᏃ ᏄᎾᏑᏁᎳ ᏧᏅᎪᏨᏉ ᏦᏍᏓᏓᏅᏟ ᎠᏛᏃ Ꮲ ᎳᎵ ᎢᏫᎳᏌᏍᎳᏅ ᎢᏴ ᎢᎬᏱ ᏓᏳᏛᏅ ᎠᏴᏃ ᎨᏒ ᎡᏙᏓ ᎠᏛ ᎡᏥ ᎣᎦᎵᎪᎯ ᏃᏉ ᏦᎩᏄᎪᏣ Ꮎ ᎤᏌᏗᎨ ᎩᏟ ᎣᎩᏭᎲ ᏕᏛᏅ ᏙᏱ ᏗᏢ ᎠᏲᏓᏝᎲ ᎦᏅᎬᎢ ᎥᏍᎩᏃ ᎩᏟ ᎣᎨᎳᏑᏒ ᏄᏓᏅᎯᏒ ᏦᎨᏅᏒ ᎢᏳᏓᏅᎯᏓ ᏬᎣᎩᎷᏣᏃ ᏦᎨᏅᏒ ᏦᏍᏓᏓᏅᎵ ᎦᏳᎳ ᏧᏌᏄ ᎣᎩᏒᏍᏗᏃ ᏃᏉ ᎣᏣᏑᏅᏍᏗᏍᎬ ᏙᏣᏟᏃᎮᏍᎬ ᎠᎩᏁᎢᏍᎳᏅ Ꮎ ᎩᏟ ᏦᎩᏍᏓᏳᏑᏍᎳᏅ ᏄᏓᏅᎯᏒ ᏦᏍᏓᏓᏅᏟᏃ ᎡᏝᏪ ᏄᎵᏍᎳᏅ ᏓᎦ ᎠᏎᏃ ᏃᏉ ᎤᏁᏣ ᎯᎠ ᏄᏪᏒ ᎦᏙᎲ ᏱᎦᎵᏍᏙᏓ ᎠᏴᏃ ᎥᏍᏉ ᏄᏓᏅᎯᏒ ᏥᏑᎩᏍᏓᏳᏑᏍᏓ

English

A few years ago, when I was just a boy, we really enjoyed watching television. We did not have a television, and we did not even have electricity, but our neighbor had a television. We really did not live that close to them, either. It was about a mile to where they lived. We would go and watch television and stay until about ten thirty, after the evening news. That is what my father, my mother, my brother, and I did one time. My sister, though, was attending a government boarding school, and that is why she was not with us. We had a dog that was a good hunter and a watch dog and very obedient. If we told him to "stay," he would, and if we allowed him to go, he would. That dog went with us where we went. When we arrived at our neighbor's house, the dog just laid down on the porch and waited for us until we were ready to go. Then when we were ready to start home, we all stood up as we started toward the door. My parents and the others began to talk, and when they did that, my brother just walked on out and got about a two-minute head start. When my father, mother, and I came out the door, our dog got up from the porch, and that dog walked all the way home with us. When we got home, my brother was already there. As we were getting ready for bed and we were talking, I mentioned that our dog had followed us all the way home, and my brother became silent for a while—and when he spoke he said, "How could that happen? He was with me all this time."

Water Beast

Sam Hair

"Water Beast" is an account of a historical event that occurred shortly before the beginning of the Civil War. It was told by the late Sam Hair of Hulbert, Oklahoma. In the story, two men see a strange water creature, which they interpret as an omen of negative events about to occur. Their fears are soon realized with the outbreak of the Civil War, which had disastrous consequences for the Cherokee people.

ӨᏬᎩᏃ	ᎯᎠ	ᎠᎻᏔᏞ	ᎠᎻᏬᏚᏬ	ᎠᎻᏚᏬᎨᎯᏞ	
nasgihno	hiʔa	anitaʔli	anisgaya	anigawehihe	
and that	these	two	men	were paddling	

ᏮᏟ	ᎤᏬᏦ	ᎤᏄᏦᏚ			
jiyu	usdi	unajode			
canoe	small	they were in			

ᏦᎩ	ᎠᏚᏒ	ᎠᎻᏚᏬᎨᎯᏞ		ᏦᏄᎤᏬᏚᎾ	ᎤᏔᎾ
jog	akti	anigawehihe		jukanvsden	utan
upstream	toward	they were paddling		bull	big

ᏬᎩ	ᎤᏔᏆ	ᏟᎻᏚᏬᏬᎠ	ᏦᏄᎤᏬᏚᎾ	ᎦᏚ	ӨᏬᎩ
yig	uhnalv	jinigawesgo	jukanvsden	wahg	nasgi
maybe	mean	as it snorts	bull	cow	that

ᏔᎦᏬᏦ	ᎤᏄᏒᏚᏞ	ᏞᏃ	ᏬᏛᏆᎠᏦᏬᏢ		Ꮤ	Ꮶᏸ
iyusd	unhtvgane	hlahno	yidanukdisge		hna	didla
like	they heard	and not	they did not judge the direction		there	toward

ᏞᎡ	ᎠᏂᎪᎳᏦᏲᎲᎢᏎᏱᎭ	ᏇᏛ	ᎮᎠᎢ	ᎤᏩᎾ
gesv	anigowahtisge?isgin	nahna	hi?a	utana
which	they were seeing it	there	this	big

ᏇᏛ	ᎬᏩᏦᏎᎡ	ᎠᎹᏱᎲᎢ	ᎠᎾᏟᏈ	ᏏᏍ	ᎨᏎᏱ	Ꮎ
nahna	watalesv	amayihnv	ayehliyv	gese	nasgi	na
there	a hole	in the water	half of	was	that	that

ᎠᏩᏦᎡ	ᏇᏛᏃ	ᎾᏎᎥᏦᎾ	ᏇᏛ	ᏟᎤᎵᏍᏆᎷᏓᏗᏎ
atalesv	nahnahno	widunakahnan	nahna	di?ulsgwaludawdise
hole	and there	when they looked	there	head visible while in water

ᏧᎧᏅᏎᏛ	ᎡᎬ	ᎣᏍᏓᏃ	ᏧᏄᎪᎮᏃ	ᎾᏎᎩᎾ
jukanvsden	egw	osdahno	junugochon	nasgina
bull	large	and good	when it completely came out	that

ᏧᎧᏅᏎᏛ	ᏇᏛ	ᎬᏩᏦᎡ	ᎠᎹᏯ	ᏚᎤᏕᏗᏁ	Ꮓ
jukanvsden	nahna	watalesv	amay	i?udetine	now
bull	there	hole	in water	dived	then

ᎾᏚᎵᎬᏳᎮ	ᎤᏂᏍᎦᏍᏓᏁᎴ	Ꮓ	ᎾᏎᎩ	ᎮᏍ	ᎠᏂᏔᏟ
widuligvhye	unisgasdanele	now	nasgi	hi?	anita?li
submerged itself	they were frightened	then	that	these	two

ᎠᏂᏍᎦᏯ	ᏥᏳ	ᎤᎾᏝᎢ	ᎠᏂᎦᏪᎲᏢ	ᎭᏝᏎᏱᎲ	ᎾᏍᎦᎶᎯ
anisgay	jiyu	unaja?i	anigawehihv	hadlvsgini	wigalohi
men	canoe	occupants	as they paddled	I wonder where	it went

ᎤᏁᎵᏎ	ᎤᎾᏛᎥᏁᎬᎤᎴ	ᏲᏱ	ᏒᏬ	ᎤᎾᏕᎶᎰᏎᎭᏃ	ᏥᏳ
unelise	unadvnegwule	yig	sgwu	unadelohosahno	jiyu
they thought	or they said	or	also	and when they found out	canoe

ᏇᏛ	ᎮᏍ	ᎤᎾᏣᎥ	ᏇᏛ	ᏥᎬᎠᏗ	ᎭᏫᏂᏗᏗᎵ
nahna	hi?	unajav	nahna	jiyukd	hawinididl
there	this	they were	there	center	underneath

ᏂᏚᎥᏕᎲᏁ	ᏧᎧᏅᏎᏛ	ᏚᏟᏓᏍᏔᏫᏛᎮ	ᏗᎦᏅᎯᏓᎭᏃ	ᏍᎷᎬ
ni?udvhne	jukanvsden	i?udlistawidvhe	diganvhidahno	dulugv
it was	bull	it twisted its head	and long	horns

ᎾᏍᎩ
nasgi
that

ᏚᏔᏁ	ᏚᏟᏆᏗᏁᎴ	ᏧᏳ
duhtane	duhlihgwadinele	jiyu
it used	it turned over	canoe

ᏚᏂᎬᏤᏃ	ᎠᏂᏍᎦᏯ	ᏎᏃ	ᎤᎾᏳᎢᏅᏎ
dunigvjehno	anisgaya	sehno	unayu?invse
they fell into the water	men	but	they swam

ᏚᎾᎵᏘᏎ	ᎤᏣᏘᎾ	ᏗᏜ	ᎤᏕᎸ	ᏭᏢᏍᏔᏁ	ᏌᏊ
dunaltise	ujatin	didl	udelv	wutlvstane	sagwu
they ran away	another	direction	out of sight	he ran	one

ᏐᎢᏅ	ᎠᎭᏂ	ᏗᏜ	ᏚᎾᎦᎴᏅᎮ	ᎠᎯᏗᎨ	ᏧᎾᏓᎩᏯᏍᏗ
so?ihnv	ahan	didl	dunagalenvhe	ahidige	junadakiyasdi
and the other	here	direction	they separated	easier	to outrun

ᎤᏂᏰᎸᏁ	ᎢᏳᏅ	ᎤᎾᎵᎪᏒ	ᏱᎨᏎ	ᏚᎾᎵᏘᏏᏗᏒ	ᏌᏊᏅᎧ
uniyelvhne	iyuhnv	unaligosv	yigese	dunaltisidisv	sagwuhnvka
they thought	if	they together	if it was	as they ran away	as one

ᎢᏧᎳ	ᏳᏂᎨᎲᏎ	ᏃᏭᏅ	ᏚᎾᎦᎴᏅ	ᎾᏏ	Ꭿ
ijul	yunikehvse	nowuhnv	dunagalenv	nahna	hi?
both	it would have chased them	and so	when they separated	there	this

Ꮭ	ᏱᏚᏭᎪᏔᏁ	ᎢᏳᏍᏗ	ᎤᎨᎲᏍᏗ	ᏧᎧᏅᏍᏕᎾ	ᏫᏚᎵᎬᏰᏊ
hla	yiduwuktane	iyusd	ukehvsdi	jukanvsdena	widuligvhyegw
not	did not determine direction	which	to chase	bull	ducked under

ᎾᏏ	ᎤᏔᏅ	ᎠᏔᎴᏒ	ᎢᏗᏢ	ᏚᏭᎪᏔᏁ	ᎠᎹᏱ	ᎭᏫᏂᏅ
nahna	utan	atalesv	ididl	duwuktane	amay	hawinhnv
there	big	hole	toward	headed	in water	under and

ᏄᏛᏁᎴ	ᎣᏂ	ᎤᏂᎪ	ᏍᎩᎾ	ᏧᎧᏅᏍᏕᎾ	ᎤᏔᏅ
nudvnele	ohni	unigo	sgina	jukanvsdena	utan
it did	last	they saw it	that	bull	big

ᏗᏔᎴᏒ	ᎤᏍᏓᎦᎸ	ᎾᎿ	ᏗᏜ	ᏩᏴᏟᏙᎮ	ᏭᏂᎪᎮ
ditalesv	usdagalv	nahna	didla	wayvhlidohe	wunigohe
hole	cave	there	toward	it was entering	they saw

ᎠᏰᏟᏅ	Ᏼ	ᎨᏎ	ᎠᎹᏱ	ᎠᏰᏟ	ᎢᏴ
ayehlihnv	yv	gese	amay	ayelh	iyv
half of it	distance	was	in water	half	of it

ᎤᎧᏲᏛ	ᎾᏍᎩᎾ	ᎤᏔᏅ	ᏩᏔᎴᏒ	ᏰᎵᏇ	ᏧᎧᏅᏍᏕᎾ
ukahyodv	nasgina	utan	watalesv	yeligw	jukanvsdena
dry land	that	big	hole	enough	bull

ᎤᏔᏅ	ᎬᏩᏴᏍᏗ	ᎢᎩᏓ	ᎨᏎ	ᎠᏔᎴᏒ	ᎾᎿᏃ
utan	gvwayvsd	ikid	gese	atalesv	nahnahno
big	to enter	size	was	hole	and there

ᏭᏴᎴ	ᎣᏂ	ᎤᏂᎪᎲ	ᎾᏍᎩ	Ꭿ	ᏧᎧᏅᏍᏕᎾ
wuyvhle	ohni	unigohv	nasgi	hiʔ	jukanvsdena
it entered	last	they saw	that	this	bull

Morpheme by Morpheme

nasg$\underline{i}$-hno	h$\underline{i}$ʔa	$\underline{a}$-ni^{23}-t$\underline{a}^{3}$ʔli	$\underline{a}$-ni-sg$\underline{a}$ya	a-ni-g$\underline{a}$we^{23}h$\underline{i}^{3}$h-e
that and	this	3 Pl two	3 Pl man	3 Pl paddle repP

jiyu^{3}	usdi^{3}	u-n-$\underline{a}$jo^{32}d-e
canoe	small	3 Pl be-in repP

jog	$\underline{a}^{3}$kti	a-ni-g$\underline{a}$we^{23}hi^{3}h-e^{3}	wahg$\underline{a}$-hno	juk$\underline{a}$nvsde^{23}n	u^{3}tan
upstream	toward	3 Pl paddle repP	cow and	bull	big

y-i^{3}g	u-hnal-v^{23}	j$\underline{i}$-n$\underline{i}$-g-$\underline{a}$wes-g-o^{3}	juk$\underline{a}$nvsde^{23}n	wahg	nasgi
nonF be	3 mean exP	Rel Lat 3 snort Prog Hab	bull	cow	that

iyu^{23}sd   u-n-htvga^{32}n-e^3 hl<u>a</u>-hno^3 yi-d-<u>a</u>-n-u^{3}kdis-g-e^3 hna   didla
like   3 Pl hear repP   not and   nonF Pl 3 Pl direct   there   toward
Prog repP

ges-v   a-ni-gowahti^{23}s-g-e^3?i-sg<u>i</u>n^3 nahna^3 h<u>i</u>?a   u^{23}t<u>a</u>na
be exP   3 Pl see Prog repP but   there   this   big

nahna   <u>wata</u>^{3}lesv^3 <u>ama</u>^{23}-y<u>i</u>^{4}-hnv^3 <u>a</u>ye^{23}hli^{32}yv^3 ges-e   nalsgi   na^3
there   a hole   water in and   half   be repP   that   that

at<u>a</u>lesv^3 nahna^3-hno   w<u>i</u>-d-u^{23}-n-<u>akah</u>n-a-n   nahna
hole   there and   Tr Pl 3 Pl look recP and   there

di^3-?u-l-sgw<u>a</u>lu^{23}da^{32}wa^{2}d-<u>i</u>^{3}se   wahg
this-direction 3 Refl head-moving-in-water repP   cow

juk<u>a</u>nvsden   e^{23}gw   o^{23}sda-hno   j-u-nu^{3}gochon   nasg<u>i</u>na   wahg
bull   large   good and   Rel 3 come-out   that   cow

juk<u>a</u>nvsde^{23}n   nahna   w<u>a</u>^{3}t<u>a</u>^{3}lesv^3 <u>ama</u>^{23}-y   <u>i</u>^{3}?-u-det<u>i</u>n-e^3 now^{23}
bull   there   hole   water in   again 3 dive repP   then

w<u>i</u>-d-u^3-l<u>i</u>gv^{3}hy-e^3 u-ni-sga^{3}sdanel-e^3 now^{23} nasgi   h<u>i</u>?   <u>a</u>-ni^{23}-ta?l
Tr Pl 3 submerge repP   3 Pl fear repP   then   that   this   3 Pl two

<u>a</u>-ni-sg<u>a</u>y   jiyu^3 u^{23}-n-<u>aj-a</u>?i   a-ni-gawe^{2}h<u>i</u>^{3}h-v^3 h<u>a</u>dlv^{23}-sg<u>i</u>^{3}ni
3 Pl man   canoe   3 Pl occupy Pres   3 Pl paddle exP   where perhaps

u-n-eli^{32}s-e   u-n-advn-e^3-gwu^{3}le^3 y-<u>i</u>^{3}g   sgwu   u-n-adeloho^{23}s-a-hno
3 Pl think repP   3 Pl say repP or   nonF be   also   3 Pl discover imP and

jiyu
canoe

nahna   h<u>i</u>?   u-n-jo^{32}d-v   nahna   jiyu^{23}kd   h<u>a</u>wi^{3}n<u>a</u>-di^{3}dl
there   this   3 Pl be-there exP   there   center   beneath toward

ni^3?-u-dvhn-e^3 wahg
Spec 3 say repP   cow

jukanvsde^{23}n   i^3?-u-dli^{3}stawidvh-e^3
bull   Rep 3 twist-head repP

di-ga-n-vhi^{23}da-hno   d-ulugv
Pl 3 Pl long and   Pl horn

nasgi
that

d-u-htan-e   d-u-hlihgwadi^{3}nel-e^3 jiyu
Pl 3 use repP   Pl 3 turn-over repP   canoe

d-u-ni-gv^{3}j-e^3-hno   a-ni-sgay   ase^{3}hno   u-n-ayu^3?inv^{3}s-e
Pl 3 Pl fall-in repP and   3 Pl man   but   3 Pl swim repP

d-u-n-alti^{3}s-e   ujatin^{23} di^{3}dl   u-del-v^3
Pl 3 Pl run-away repP   another   direction   3 out-of-sight exP

w-u^{23}-tlvstan-e^3 sagwu
Tr 3 run repP   one

so?i-hnv   a^{3}han   di^{3}dl   d-u-n-aga^{1}envh-e   ahi^{23}di^{3}ge   j-u-n-adakiya^{32}s-di
other   there   direction   Pl 3 Pl separate   easier   Pst 3 Pl outrun
  and   repP   Inf

u-ni-yel-v-hne^3 iyuhnv   u-n-aligos-v
3 Pl think exP and   if   3 Pl together exP

yi-ge^{32}s-e   d-u-n-alti^{3}sidi^{3}s-v   sagwu^3-hnv-ka
nonF be repP   Pl 3 Pl run-away exP   one and as

ijul^3 y-u-ni^3-kehvs-e   nowu^3-hnv   d-u-n-agalen-v^3 nahna   hi?
both   nonF 3 Pl chase repP   so and   Pl 3 Pl separate exP   there   this

hla^{3}	y̲i-d-u̲-wu^{3}kta̲n-e	i̲yu^{23}sd	u-kehv^{32}s-di	wahg
not	nonF Pl 3 determine repP	which	3 chase Inf	cow

wi̲-d-u^{3}-li̲gv^{3}hy-e^{3}-gw
Tr Pl 3 submerge repP just

nahna	u^{23}tan	ata̲lesv	i̲di^{3}dl	d-u-wukta̲n-e	a̲ma-y	ha̲wi^{3}n-hnv
there	big	hole	toward	Pl 3 head-for repP	water in	under and

n-u-dv^{3}nel-e	ohni^{3}	u-ni-go^{3}	sgi̲na	wahg	u^{23}tan
Spec 3 do repP	last	3 Pl see	that	cow	big

dita̲^{3}lesv	usda^{32}ga̲lv	nahna	didlv	w-a̲^{3}-yvhli^{23}do^{32}h-e	w-u-ni^{3}-go-he
hole	cave	there	toward	Tr 3 enter repP	Tr 3 Pl see repP

a̲ye^{23}hli̲-hnv	yv^{3}	ges-e	a̲ma^{23}-y	a̲ye^{23}h	i̲yv
half-way	distance	be repP	water in	half	distance

uka̲hyodv	nasgi̲na	u^{23}tan	wa̲ta̲^{3}lesv	yeli^{23}gw	wahga
dry-land	that	big	hole	enough	cow

u^{23}tan	g-vwa̲yv^{23}-sd	i^{23}ki̲da	ges-e	ata̲lesv	nahna-hno
big	3 enter Inf	size	be repP	hole	there and

w-u-yv^{3}hl-e	ohni^{3}	u-ni-go^{3}h-v	nasgi	hi?	wahga
Tr 3 enter repP	last	3 Pl see exP	that	this	cow

Syllabary

ᎾᏍᎩᏃ ᎯᎠ ᎠᏂᏔᎵ ᎠᏂᏍᎦᏯ ᎠᏂᎦᏘᎯᏢ ᏥᏳ ᎤᏍᏗ ᎤᎾᏦᎦ ᏦᎩ ᎠᎦᏗ ᎠᏂᎦᏘᎯᏢ ᏧᎧᎤᏍᎦᎾ ᎤᏔᎾ ᏱᎩ ᎤᎿᏄ ᏥᏂᎦᏘᏍᎪ ᏧᎧᎤᏍᎦᎾ ᏩᎦ ᎾᏍᎩ ᎢᏳᏍᏗ ᎤᎾᏛᏚᏁ ᏝᏃ ᏱᏓᏄᎪᏗᏍᎨ Ꮏ ᏗᏜ ᎨᏒ ᎠᏂᎪᏩᏗᏍᎨᎢᏍᎩᏂ ᎾᎿ ᎯᎠ ᎤᏔᎾ ᎾᎿ ᏩᏔᎴᏍᏒ ᎠᎹᏱᎤ ᎠᏰᏟᏴ ᎨᏎ ᎾᏍᎩ Ꮎ ᎠᏔᎴᏒ ᎾᎿᏃ ᏫᏚᎾᎧᎿᎾ ᎾᎿ ᏗᎤᎵᏍᏆᎷᏓᏩᏗᏎ ᏧᎧᎤᏍᎦᎤ ᎡᏆ ᏅᏍᏓᏃ ᏧᏄᎪᏦᎾ ᎾᏍᎩᎾ ᏧᎧᎤᏍᎦᎤ ᎾᎿ ᏩᏔᎴᏒ ᎠᎹᏱ ᎢᎤᎦᏗᏁ Ꮓ ᏫᏚᎵᎬᏰ ᎤᏂᏍᎦᏍᏓᏁᎴ Ꮓ ᎾᏍᎩ Ꭿ ᎠᏂᏔᎵ ᎠᏂᏍᎦᏯ ᏥᏳ ᎤᎾᏨᎢ ᎠᏂᎦᏘᎯᏊ ᏈᏢᏍᎩᏂ ᏫᎦᎶᎯ ᎤᏁᎵᏎ ᎤᎾᏛᏁᏯᎧᎴ ᏱᎩ ᏍᏯ ᎤᎾᎦᎶᎨᏌᏃ ᏥᏳ ᎾᎿ Ꭿ ᎤᎾᏨᎥ ᎾᎿ ᏥᏳᎪᏗ ᏈᏫᏂᏗᏢ ᏂᎤᏛᏁ ᏧᎧᎤᏍᎦᎾ ᎢᎤᏟᏍᏔᏫᏛᏢ ᏗᎦᎤᎯᏓᏂᏃ ᏚᎷᎬ ᎾᏍᎩ ᏚᏔᏁ ᏚᏟᏆᏗᏁᎴ ᏧᏳ ᏚᏂᎬᏙᏃ ᎠᏂᏍᎦᏯ ᏎᏃ ᎤᎾᏳᎢᎤᏎ ᏚᎾᎵᏗᏎ ᎤᏨᏗᎾ ᏗᏜ ᎤᎦᏄ

ᎩᏆᏫᏒ ᎤᏬ ᏓᎢᎣᎤ ᎠᏢᎯ ᏗᏛ ᏎᎣᏍᏓᎣᏈ ᎠᏝᎵᎱ ᏓᎤᏯᏍᏍᏗ ᎤᎯᏴᎦᏒ ᎢᎪᏌᎤ ᎤᎡᏛᎯᎠ ᏌᏈᎴ ᏎᎣᏝᏰᏗᎡ ᎤᏬᎤᏍ ᏔᏛᏫ ᏣᎴᏈᏐᎴ ᏃᎫᎤ ᏎᎣᏍᏓᎤ ᎡᏝ Ꭿ Ꮭ ᏙᏎᎫᏱᏫᏒ ᎢᎪᏫᏗ ᎤᏈᏐᏫᏗ ᏚᏎᎤᏍᏎ ᎤᏎᏈᎬᏐ ᎡᏝ ᎤᎥᎣᎤ ᎠᎥᏓᎬ ᎢᎠᏈ ᏎᏁᏫᏒ ᎠᎿᏍ ᏤᎠᏂᎤ ᏛᏍᏆ ᏙᏂ ᎤᎯᎪ ᏍᏯᎬ ᏚᏎᎤᏍᏎ ᎤᎥᎣᎤ ᏛᏫᏓᎬ ᎤᏍᏬᏝᏍᏇ ᎡᏝ ᏙᎨ ᏣᎬᏟᏉ ᏍᎯᎠᏈ ᎠᏈᏟᎤ Ꮗ ᏢᏆ ᏓᎦᏅ ᏓᏈᏟ ᏔᏉ ᎤᎦᎮᏅ ᎡᏍᏯᏎ ᎤᎥᎣᎤ ᏣᏫᏓᎬ ᏰᏢᏐ ᏚᏎᎤᏍᏎ ᎤᎥᎣᎤ ᎡᏟᏈᏍᏗ ᏔᏴᎸ ᏢᏆ ᎠᏫᏓᎬ ᎡᏝᏃ ᏏᏰᎸ ᎠᎿ ᏤᎠᏂᏒ ᎡᏍᏯ Ꭿ ᏚᏎᎤᏍᏎ

English

Two men were paddling a canoe upstream when they heard a bull snorting, but they could not determine the direction from which it came. But up ahead, they could see a big cave that was partly in water and partly onshore. As they looked toward the opening of the cave, they saw a bull swimming downstream toward them. When the bull swam completely out of the cave, it went under. The men became frightened. "Where did it go?" they thought. The next thing they knew, the bull was directly beneath their canoe. The bull twisted its head, and with is long horns it turned the canoe over, and the men fell into the water. The men swam to shore with the bull right behind them. When they reached dry land, they split up and the bull stopped. Not knowing which one to chase, the bull went back into the water and headed toward the cave. The last they saw of the bull, it was going back into the cave.

Diary

Author Unknown

Written in 1927, "Diary" is an account written by a woman who has lost her two sons and their father. She is writing about how she feels about her loss. She believes that nobody cares how she feels. This story reflects the depression and despair experienced by those in mourning. This narrative was donated to Durbin Feeling and is part of his personal collection.

DhᏍᎾEᎫ	31Ꭿ	1927	ᏏᎪᏍᎩ
ansgvti	31ne	1927	hilvsgi
May	31st	1927	a few

TᏍᎠᏐ	ᏔᎪᏍᎳᏂ	AᏏ	TAᏏ
ikanejv	dagowelani	kohi	igohi
words	I will write	today	day

DIᏞᏂWᏉᏫᎬ	ᏏSᎫ	D4ᏉᎬᏉᎬ	ᏏhᏛᏍᏝ
agwadanilagwo	yigadi	asegwogwo	yinijiweha
I am just ill	if I say	no reason	I would be saying it

iᏞ	ᎩG	ᏽG.	BSᏰW
vhla	kilo	howa	yvgayela
no	no one	would believe it	would not think

ᎾᎯᎵᏥᏚᏚ	DᎬᎤᏉᎬ	ᎾᎯᎵᎣᏚᏚ	iᎬSCᏉᎬ
nagwadvhnadega	agwvsagwo	nagwadvnadega	vgwvdejvgwo
I am here and there	I am just alone	I am getting along	I have just been abandoned

ᏥᏙᏩᏕᎦ	ᎠᏫᏄᏣ	ᎠᏋᏕᏥᎸᏉ	ᎾᏆᏛᎾ
jidowadega	awinuja	agwvdejilvgwo	nagwadvna
I am standing around	young man	he has abandoned me	I am here

ᎾᏉ	ᏑᏕᏘᏴᏓ	ᏑᏓᎵᏃ	ᎢᏯᏅᏙ
nagwo	sudetiyvda	sudalino	iyanvdo
now	one year	and six	months

ᎬᏋᏕᏨᎯ	ᎠᏉᎯᏳᏗ	ᎤᏁᎳᏅᎯ	ᏗᏆᏓᏂᎸᏤᎸᎯ
gvgwvdejvvhi	agwohiyudi	unelanvhi	digwadanilvchelvhi
since he abandoned me	I trust	God	he has accepted him

ᎨᏒᎢ	ᎠᎵᎮᎵᏍᏗ	ᏗᎨᏒ	ᏫᏄᏛᏅ
gesv?i	alihelisdi	digesv	winudvhnv
has	happy	at the place	he is there

ᎠᏉᎯᏳᏗ	ᏧᏅᏟ	ᏧᏩᏛᏛ	ᎨᏒᎢ
agwohiyudi	juhnvhli	juhwahtvdv	gesv?i
I trust	his brothers	he has found them	has

ᎠᏉᎯᏳ	ᎠᎴ	ᎤᎦᏴᎵᎨ	ᎤᏩᏛᏛ
agwohiyu	ale	ugayvlige	uhwahtvdv
I trust	and	his parent	he has found

ᎨᏒᎢ	ᎤᏟᏉ	ᎤᏲᎢᏳ	ᏱᏄᎵᏍᏔᏁ
gesv?i	udligwo	uyo?iyu	yinulstane
has	much more	worse off	he would have been

ᏯᏇᎵᏒ	ᏍᏗᎩᏛ	ᎤᎦᎵᏍᏗ	ᎢᏳᏍᏗ
yagwelisv?i	sdikidv	ugalsdi	iyusdi
I	a little bit	eager	like

ᎢᎦᏓᏅᏓᏗᏍᎪᎢ
igadanvdadisgo?i
habitually

Morpheme by morpheme

ansgvti 31ne 1927 hilv^{4}sgi
may 31Ord 1927 few

ik$\underline{a}^3$nejv d$\underline{a}$-g-owelan-i kohi igo^{4}hi
word Fut 1 write Fut this day

agw-$\underline{a}$d$\underline{a}$ni^{23}l-$\underline{a}$-gwo y$\underline{i}$-g-a^{3}di ase^3-gwo^4 y$\underline{i}$-n$\underline{i}$-j$\underline{i}$-we^{32}h-a
1 ill Pres just nonF 1 say maybe just nonF ni 1 say Pres

v^{4}hla kilo howa^3 yv-g-a^{3}ye^{23}l-a
no someone to-believe nonF 3 think Pres

ni-g-alsdi^{23}s-g-v nagw$\underline{a}$dvn$\underline{a}$de^{32}ga $\underline{a}$gw-v^{23}s$\underline{a}$-gwo n-agw-$\underline{a}$dvn$\underline{a}$de^{32}-g-a
Spec 3 happen distraught 1 alone just Spec 1 get-along Prog
  Prog exP Pres

vgw-v-dej-$\underline{v}^4$-gwo j$\underline{i}$-do^{32}w$\underline{a}$de^{3}g-a a-winu^{4}ja agw-$\underline{v}$-deji^{23}l-v^4-gwo
1Pas abandon exP just 1 stand Pres 3 young-man 1Pas abandon exP just

n-agw-$\underline{a}$dvn-a na^{23}gwo
Spec 1 be-here Pres now

sudet$\underline{i}$yv^{4}aʔv sud$\underline{a}^3$l$\underline{i}$-hno^3 iy$\underline{a}^3$nv^{4}do
one-year six and month

gv-gwv-dej-v^{4}hi agw-ohiyu^{23}di une^{23}l$\underline{a}^3$nvhi d$\underline{i}$-gw$\underline{a}$-d$\underline{a}$nilvche^{23}l-v^{4}hi
since 1Pas abandon 1 trust god Pl 3 accept exP
  exP

ges-v^{4}ʔi $\underline{a}$-lihe^{4}l$\underline{i}$s-di d$\underline{i}$-ge^{3}s-v^4
be exP 3 happy Inf Dst be exP

w$\underline{i}$-n-u-dvhn-v
Tr Spec 3 say exP

agw-ohiyudi j-u-hnvhli j-u-hwahtvd-v ges-vʔi
1 trust Pl 3 brother Pl 3 find exP be exP

agw-ohiyu	ale^{3}	u-gayv^{23}li^{3}ge^{3}	u-hwahtv^{4}d-v
1 trust	and	3 parent	3 find exP

ges-v^{4}?i	udli^{4}-gwo	u-yo?i^{23}-yu	yi-n-u-l^{3}sta^{3}n-e
be exP	away-from just	3 worse-off so-much	nonF Spec 3 happen repP

y-agw-e^{23}lis-v	sdi^{23}kidv	u^{23}-gals-di	iyu^{4}sdi
nonF 1 think exP	a-little	3 abandon Inf	like

i-g-ad^{3}anvdadi^{32}s-g-o^{3}?i
again 1 feel Prog Hab

Syllabary

ᎠᏂᏍᎬᏘ 31Ꮑ 1927 ᎯᏄᏍᎩ ᎢᏍᏁᎲ ᏓᎪᏪᎳᏂ ᎪᎯ ᎢᎪᎯ ᎠᏆᏓᏂᏔᏉ ᏱᏍᎦᏗ ᎠᏎᏉᏉ ᏱᏂᏥᏯᏭ ᎥᏝ ᎩᎶ ᎰᏩ ᏰᎦᏴᎳ ᎾᏆᏛᏏᎦᎦ ᎠᏛᏌᏉ ᎾᏆᏛᎾᎦᎦ ᎥᏛᎦᏨᏉ ᏥᏙᏩᎦᎦ ᎠᏫᏄᏣ ᎠᏛᎦᏥᏄᏉ ᎾᏆᏛᎾ ᎾᏉ ᏈᎦᏘᏰᏓ ᏈᏓᏢᏃ ᎢᏍᏓᏬ ᎬᏛᎦᏨᎯ ᎠᏉᎯᏩᏗ ᏅᏁᏔᏅᎯ ᏗᏆᏓᏂᏄᏤᏄᎯ ᎰᎡᎢ ᎠᎵᎲᎵᏍᏗ ᏗᎰᎡ ᎾᏄᏛᏅ ᎠᏉᎯᏩᏗ ᏧᏅᏨ ᏧᏩᏛᏛ ᎰᎡᎢ ᎠᏉᎯᏩ ᎠᏛ ᏅᎦᏰᎵᎰ ᏅᏩᏛᏛ ᎰᎡᎢ ᏅᏟᏉ ᏅᏲᎢᏳ ᏱᏄᎵᏍᏔᏁ ᏯᏆᎵᏍ ᏍᏗᎩᏛ ᏅᎦᎵᏍᏗ ᎢᏳᏍᏗ ᎢᎦᏓᏅᏓᏗᏍᎪᎢ

English

May 31, 1927: I am going to write a few words on this day. There is no reason for me to say that I am ill because no one would believe me. My life is worthless because I am all alone with no one to stay with me. A young man has left me. It has now been a year and six months since he abandoned me. I have faith that God has accepted him. I have faith that he is in the "happy place," that he has found his brother. I have faith that he has found his parent. When I think about it, he would have suffered if I had left him first. Then I feel a little better.

The Good Samaritan

The story of the Good Samaritan is based on *The New Testament in the Cherokee Language*, published in 1860 by the American Bible Society. This nineteenth-century translation is still read today by Cherokees who are proficient in the Cherokee syllabary. The ease with which the translators completed the New Testament translation is an indication of the power of Cherokee to discuss complex areas of life, including religion and philosophical concepts.

ᏥᏌᏃ	ᏧᏁᏨ	ᎯᎠ	ᏄᏪᏎᎴᎢ	ᎩᎶᎢᏳᏍᏗ	ᏥᎷᏏᎵᎻ
jisahno	juhnejv	hiʔa	nuweseleʔi	kiloiyusdi	jilusilimi
and Jesus	when he answered	this	he said to him	a certain someone	Jerusalem

ᎤᏂᎩᏎ	ᏤᎵᎪ	ᎤᏪᏅᏎᎢ	ᏗᎾᏓᏅᏌᏂᏍᎩᏃ
uhnigise	jeligo	uwenvseʔi	dinadansahvsgihno
he went from	Jericho	he went	and robbers

ᏚᎾᏓᏩᏛᏔᏁᎢ	ᎾᏍᎩ	ᏕᎬᏩᏄᏪᏎ	ᏚᏄᏩᎥᎢ
dunadawatvhtaneʔi	nasgi	degvwahnuwese	duhnuwaʔvʔi
they found each other (accidentally)	they	took his clothes off	the clothes he had on

ᎠᎴ	ᎬᏩᎵᎥᏂᎴᎢ	ᎠᎴ	ᎤᎾᏓᏅᏎ	ᎬᏩᏕᏤ	ᎠᏰᎵ
ale	gvwaliʔvhnileʔi	ale	unadanvse	gvwadeje	ayeli
and	they beat him	and	they departed	they abandoned him	half

ᎢᏴᏛ	ᎤᏲᎱᏒᎯ	ᎨᏎᎢ
iyvdv	uyohusvhi	gese?i
way	dead	he was

ᎠᏰᎵᏃ	ᏄᏩᏔᏅ	ᎩᎶ	ᎢᏳᏍᏗ	ᎠᏥᎸᎨᎶᎯ	ᎾᏂ
ayelihno	nuwvtanv	kilo	iyusdi	ajilvgelohi	nahna
and half	he came	someone	certain	(priest) fire feeder	there

ᏂᎦᏅᏅ	ᏗᎤᎶᏎᎢ	ᎤᎪᎲᏃ	ᎠᏂᏗᏢᏉ	ᏄᎶᏎᎢ
niganvhnv	di?ulose?i	ugohvhno	ahnididlvgwo	nulose?i
down the road	he came	and when he saw him	the other way	he went

ᎠᎴ	ᎾᏉ	ᎠᎵᏫ	ᎾᏂ	ᎡᏙᎲ	ᎤᎷᏤ	ᎤᎦᏔᎮᎢ
ale	nasgwo	aliwi	nahna	edohv	uluhje	uktahe?i
and	also	a Levite	there	he was walking	he came	he looked at him

ᎠᎴ	ᎠᏂᏗᏢᏉ	ᏄᎶᏎᎢ
ale	ahnididlvgw	nulose?i
and	the other way	he went by

ᎩᎶᏍᎩᏂ	ᎢᏳᏍᏗ	ᏌᎺᎵᏱ	ᎡᎯ	ᎠᎢᏒᎢ	ᎤᎷᏤ	ᎦᏅᎢ
kilosgini	iyusdi	sameliyi	ehi	a?isv?i	uluhje	ga?nv?i
but someone	certain	Samaria	dweller	as he walked along	he came to	where he lay

ᎤᎪᎲᏃ	ᎤᏪᏙᎵᏤᎢ
ugohvhno	uwedolije?i
and when he saw him	he had compassion for him

ᎠᎴ	ᏭᎷᏣ	ᎠᎴ	ᏚᎸᎴᎢ	ᏓᏥᏐᏅᎢ	ᎠᎴ	ᎪᎢ
ale	wuluhje	ale	dulv?le?i	dajisonvhnv?i	ale	go?i
and	he came	and	bandaged him	on his wounds	and	oil

ᎩᎦᎨᏃ	ᎠᏗᏔᏍᏗ	ᏓᏍᏚᏞᎮᎢ	ᎠᎴ	ᎤᏩᏒ	ᎤᎩᎸᏙᏗ
gigagehno	aditasdi	dasdudlehe?i	ale	uwasv	ukilvdohdi
and red	drink	he was pouring on them	and	his own	to ride upon

ᎤᎩᎸᏔᏁᎯ	ᏧᏂᏒᏍᏗᏱᏃ
ukilvtane?i	junisvsdiyihno
he sat him upon it	and inn

ᎠᏓᏁᎸ	ᎤᏘᏃᎴᎢ	ᎠᎴ	ᎤᏍᏆᏂᎪᏔᏁ
adanelv	utinole?i	ale	usgwanigotane?i
house	he brought him	and	he took care of him

ᎤᎩᏨᏛᏃ	ᎾᏉ	ᎤᏂᎩᏒ	ᏔᎵ	ᎠᏂᎩᏏ	ᏧᎾᎬᏩᎶᏗ
ugijvdvhno	hnagwo	uhnigisv	ta?li	anigisi	junagvwalhdi
and the next morning	then	when he started out	two	denarii	worth

ᏚᎴᏎᎢ	ᎠᎴ	ᏚᏁᎴ	ᎦᏁᎳ	ᎠᎴ	ᎯᎠ	ᏄᏪᏎᎴᎢ
dulese?i	ale	duhnele	ganel	ale	hi?a	nuwesele?i
he took out	and	he gave to him	the one that lives there	and	this	he said to him

ᎯᏍᏆᏂᎪᏕᏍᏗ	ᎢᎦᎢᏃ	ᏫᎦᎶᏒᏍᏗᏍᎬ
hisgwanigodesdi	iga?ihno	wigalosvsdisgv
keep him	however much	over

ᏣᎫᏳᎯᏙᎸᎢ	ᎢᏥᎷᏨᎲ	ᎢᎬᏯᎫᏴᎡᎸᎲ
jakuyuhidolv?i	ijiluhjvha	igvyaguyv?elvha
your expenses	when I return	I will repay you

ᎯᎠᏃ	ᎾᏍᎩ	ᏦᎢ	ᎢᏯᏂᏛ	ᎨᏒ	ᏂᎯ	ᎭᏓᏅᏖᏍᎬ
hi?ahno	nasgi	jo?i	iyanidv	gesv	nihi	hadanhtesgv
and this	that	three	of them	which	you	your thinking

ᎦᎪ	ᎾᎥ	ᎢᏧᎾᏓᎳ	ᏅᏩᏍᏗ	ᎾᏍᎩ	ᏗᎾᏓᏅᏌᎲᏍᎩ
gago	na?v	ijunadala	nvwasdi	nasgi	dinadanhsahvsgi
who	neighbor	apart	it seems	that	robbers

ᏥᏚᎾᏓᏩᏛᏔᏁᎢ
jidunadawahtvhtane?i
those that found each other by chance

ᎯᎠᏃ	ᏅᏪᏎᎢᎢ	ᏐᎠᏏ	Ꮎ	ᎤᏩᏙᎵᏆᎯ		ᏔᎷᏉᏃ
hi?ahno	nuwese?i	nasgi	na	uwedolijvhi		hnagwohno
and this	he said	that	the	one who had compassion for him		and then

ᏥᏌ	ᎯᎠ	ᏅᏪᏎᎶᎢ	ᏏᎾ	ᎠᏛ	ᏂᎯ	ᏐᎠᏗᏯ	ᏐᏫᏍ
jisa	hi?a	nuwesele?i	hena	ale	nihi	nasgiya	winadvga
Jesus	this	he said to him	go	and	you	the same	go and do

Morpheme by Morpheme

ji^{23}s$\underline{a}^3$-hno	j-u^{23}-hne^{4}j-v	hi?a	n-u-wes-e^{23}l-e^3?i	kilo^3
jesus and	Pst 3 answer exP	this	ni 3 reply Dat repP	someone

iyu^{4}sdi
a-certain

j$\underline{i}$lu^{3}s$\underline{i}$l$\underline{i}$mi	u^{23}-hn$\underline{i}^3$gis-e^3
jerusalem	3 go-from repP

jeligo	u-wenv^{3}s-e^3?i
jericho	3 go repP

di-n-$\underline{a}$da-h^{23}ns$\underline{a}$hvs-g-$\underline{i}^3$-hno	d-u-n-$\underline{a}$da-hwantvh-t$\underline{a}$n-e^3?i
Pl Pl Refl rob Prog Ag and	Pl 3 Pl Refl find accidentally repP

de^{23}-g-v^{3}wahnuwe^{3}s-e^3	d-u-hnuw$\underline{a}^3$?-v^4?i
Pl 3 take-off-clothes repP	Pl 3 wear-clothes exP

nasgi	$\underline{a}$le^3	gvw-$\underline{a}$l$\underline{i}^3$?vhn$\underline{i}^3$l-e?i	$\underline{a}$le^3	u-n-$\underline{a}$d$\underline{a}^3$nvs-e^3
that	and	they/him beat repP	and	3 Pl depart repP

gv-w$\underline{a}$de^{3}j-e^3	$\underline{a}$ye^{4}li
they/me repP	half

iyv^{4}dv	u-yohusv^{4}h-i	ges-e^3-i	$\underline{a}$yel$\underline{i}$-hno
way	3 die exP	be repP and	half and

n-u-wvtan-e^3 kilo^3 iyu^{4}sdi   a-ji^{23}lvge^{23}loh-i   nahna
Spec 3 come repP   someone   type   3 feed-fire Ag   there

ni-ga^{3}nv^{3}hnv   di^3?-u-los-e^3?   u-go^{23}hn-v-hno   a^{3}hni^3-didlv^{3}gwo   n-u^3-los-e^3?i
Lat road   Dst 3 come   3 see exP and   other toward just   Spec 3 go
                repP   repP

ale^3 nasgwo   ali^{23}wi   nahna^3 edo^{3}h-v
and   also   levite   there   walk around exP

u-luh^{3}j-e^3 u-ktahn-e^3?i
3 come repP   3 look-at repP

ale^3 a^{3}hni^3-di^{3}dlv^3-gwo   n-u^{23}-lo^{3}s-e^3?i   kilo^{23}-sgini^3
and   other toward just   Lat 3 go repP   someone but

iyu^{4}sdi   sameli^4-yi   e^{4}h-i   a^3?-is-v^4?i   u-luh^{3}j-e^3
type   samaria from   live Ag   3 walk exP   3 arrive repP

g-a?^{3}n-v^4?i   u-go^{23}h-v-hno   u-wedo^{23}li^{32}j-e^3?i
3 lie exP   3 see exP and   3 pity repP

ale^3 w-u^3-luhj-e^3 ale^3 d-u-lv^3?ei-e^3
and   Tr 3 arrive repP   and   Pl 3 bandage repP

d-a-jisonvhn-v^4?i   ale^3
Pl 3 on-wounds exP   and

go?i
oil

giga^{3}ge^4-hno   a-di^{23}tas-di   d-a-sdu^{3}dleh-e^3?i
red and   3 drink Inf   Pl 3 pour repP

ale^3 u-wa^{23}sv   u-kilv^{3}doh-di   u-kilv^{32}tan-e^3?i
and   3 self   3 ride Inf   3 put-on repP

junisvsdi^{23}yi-hno   adane^{23}lv   u-tino^{23}l-e^3?i   ale^3
inn and   house   3 bring repP   and

u-sgwanigo^{32}tan-e^3?i   ugijv^{23}dv-hno
3 take-care repP   next-morning and

hna^{23}-gwo   u-hni^{3}gi^{4}s-v
then just   3 start-out exP

ta?li   a-ni-gi^{23}si   j-u-n-agv^{23}walh-di
two   3 Pl denarii   Pl 3 Pl be-worth Inf

d-u-le^{3}s-e^3?i   ale^3 d-u-hn-e^{23}l-e^3 ga-ne^{4}l-a
Pl 3 take-out repP   and   Pl 3 give Dat repP   3 live Pres

ale^3 hi?a   n-u-wese^{23}l-e?i
and   this   ni 3 say Dat repP

h-isgwanigo^{32}de^{3}s-di   iga^3?i-hno^3 wi-ga^3-losvsdis-g-v^3
2 keep Inf   however-much and   Tr 3 exceed Prog exP

j-akuyuhi^{23}do^{32}l-v^4?i   i-ji^3-luh^{3}jv^{4}h-a   i-gv^3-yaguyv^3?-elvh-a
2 expenses exP   Rep 1 arrive recP   Rep I/you repay Dat recP

hi?a^3-hno
this and

nasgi   jo?i
that   three

iya^{3}ni^{4}dv   ges-v^3 nihi   h-adanhte^{23}s-g-v
number   be exP   you   2 think Prog exP

ga^{3}go   na?v   iju^{3}nada^{4}la   nvwa^{3}sdi   nasgi   di-n-ada-nhsahvs-g-i
who   close   apart   it-seems   that   Pl Pl Refl find Prog Ag

ji-d-u-n-ada-wahtvh-ta^{3}n-e^4?i   hi?a^3-hno   n-u-wes-e^3?i
Rel Pl 3 Pl Refl find accidental repP   this and   ni 3 say exP

nasgi
that

na³ u̱-wedolij-v⁴hi   hna²³-gwo³-hno   ji²³sa
the   3 pity exP   then just and   jesus

hi̱?a
this

n-u-wes-e²³l-e³?i   h-en-a
ni 3 say Dat repP   2 go Imp

ale   ni̱hi   nasgi-ya   wi-n-nadv³²g-a
and   you   that exactly   Tr Spec do Imp

Syllabary

ᎯᎥᏃ ᏝᏂᏟᎼ ᎠᎠ ᏋᏩᏉᏓᎢᎢ ᏯᏟᎢᏫᎤᎠᏏ ᎯᎷᎻᎮᎲ ᎤᎯᏴ4 ᏤᎮᎠ ᎤᏫᏯᎤᎢ4Ꭲ ᏝᎾᎤᎤᎲᏫᎤᎯᏃ
ᏕᏬᎢᏫᎹᎢ ᎾᏫᏴ ᏕᎬᏋᏉ4 ᏕᏋᏟᎢ Ꮄᛯ ᎬᎬᎱᎯᏂᎤᎢ Ꮄᛯ ᎤᎤᎾᎡᎤ4 ᎬᎬᏕᏤ ᎠᏰᎮ
ᏔᏰᎷ ᎤᎲᎦᎡᎠ Ꮀ4Ꭲ ᎠᏰᎮᏃ ᏋᎦᏪᎤ ᏯᎬ ᎢᏩᎠᏏ ᏪᎯᏋᎷᎬᎠ ᎾᏛ ᎯᏕᎤᎤ ᏟᎤᎬ4Ꭲ
ᎤᎠᏫᏃ ᏕᎯᏑᏆᏤ ᏋᎬ4Ꭲ Ꮄᛯ ᎾᎤ ᎠᎠᎾ ᎾᏛ ᎡᎾᏫ ᎤᎻᏤ ᎤᏕᏫᏟᎢ Ꮄᛯ ᎯᏑᏆᏤ
ᏋᎬ4Ꭲ ᏯᎠᏏᎯ ᏔᎠᏏ ᎤᎤᎢᏬᎶ ᎡᎠ ᎠᎢᎡᎢ ᎤᎻᏤ ᏕᎤᎢ ᎤᎠᏫᏃ ᎤᎠᏤᎡᏤᎢ Ꮄᛯ
ᏟᎷᏓ Ꮄᛯ ᏕᏋᎡᎢ ᎯᎤᏲᎤᎢ Ꮄᛯ ᎠᎢ ᏯᏏᏃᏃ ᏝᏑᏫᎠᏏ ᏓᏗᏕᏞᎢ Ꮄᛯ ᎤᎬᎡ ᎤᏯᏋᏤᏥ
ᎤᏯᏑᏫᏟᎠ ᏜᎯᎡᎤᏟᏒᏃ ᏕᏞᏁᎠ ᎤᏟᏃᎤᎢ Ꮄᛯ ᎤᎤᎢᎯᎠᏫᏟ ᎤᏰᏓᎼᏃ ᎾᎤ ᎤᎯᏯᏒ
ᏫᏞ ᏕᎯᏴᎦ ᏝᎾᎬᎬᎤᏥ ᏚᎼ4Ꭲ Ꮄᛯ ᏕᏟᎾ ᏕᏟᏫ Ꮄᛯ ᎠᎠ ᏋᏩᏉᏓᎢᎢ ᎠᏫᎢᎯᎠᏕᏬᏥ
ᎢᏕᎢᏃ ᎾᏕᏋᎡᏝᏫᎬ ᏤᏝᎯᏫᏋᎢ ᎢᎯᎷᏟᏔ ᎢᎬᏝᏈᎡᏋᏈ ᎠᎢᏃ ᎾᏫ ᎡᎢ ᎢᎾᎯᎼ
ᎰᎡ ᎯᎠ ᏥᏎᎤᎤᎡᏫᎬ ᏕᎠ Ꮎ ᎢᏘᏬ ᎤᎬᎠᏏ ᎾᏫ ᏝᎾᎤᎤᎲᏫᏝᏫ ᎯᏕᏬᎢᏫᎹᎢ
ᎠᎢᏃ ᏋᏩ4Ꭲ ᎾᏫ Ꮎ ᎤᎤᎡᏤᎯᎬᎠ ᏛᏯᏃ ᎯᎤ ᎠᎠ ᏋᏩᏓᎤᎰ ᎠᎾ Ꮄᛯ ᎯᎠ ᎾᏫᏃ
ᎾᎾᎢᏕ.

English

In reply, Jesus said: "A man was going down from Jerusalem to Jericho, when he fell into the hands of robbers. They stripped him of his clothes, beat him, and went away, leaving him half dead. A priest happened to be going down the same road, and when he saw the man, he passed by on the other side. So too a Levite, when he came to the place and saw him, passed by on the other side. But a Samaritan, as he traveled, came where the man was, and when he saw him he took pity on him.

He went to him and bandaged his wounds, pouring on oil and wine. Then he put the man on his own donkey, took him to an inn, and took care of him. The next day he took out two silver coins and gave them to the innkeeper. "Look after him," he said, "and when I return, I will reimburse you for any extra expense you may have." "Which of these three do you think was a neighbor to the man who fell into the hands of robbers?" "The one who had mercy on him." Jesus told him, "Go and do likewise."

How to Make Chestnut Bread

Annie Jessan

"How to Make Chestnut Bread" is an example of a procedural narrative, a set of instructions that teach someone how to do a specific task. Recipes such as this one, provided by Annie Jessan of Cherokee, North Carolina, are an important type of procedural narrative.

ᎠᎬᏱᏃ	ᎠᎬᏱ	ᏕᎦᎵᏍᏗᏍᎪ	ᎠᏎᎨ	ᏅᎩᎭ
agvyhno	agvy	degalisdisgo	asege	nvhgiha
and first	first	I cook them	perhaps	about four

ᎢᏳᏪᏅᏍᏗ	ᏕᎦᎵᏗᏍᎪ	ᏘᎵ	ᎩᎳᏃ	ᏳᏅᏂᏍ
iyuwenvsdi	degalihdisgo	tili	kilno	yunvs
hours	I boil them	chestnuts	then	when they are done

ᏱᎨᎵ	Ꮓ	ᎩᎳ	ᎠᎹ	ᏥᏙᏗᏍᎪ	ᏗᎩᏚᏗᏱ
yigeli	no	kil	am	jitondisgo	digitdiyi
when I think	then	until then	water	I heat water	to bake bread

ᏃᏬᏃ	ᏣᎵᏟᎭᏬᏴ	ᎠᎹ	Ꮓ	ᏕᎦᏑᏴᏍᎪ	ᏘᎵ
nown	jaljihawyv	am	no	degasuyvsgo	til
then	just when it starts to boil	water	then	I mix them in	chestnuts

ᎦᏚ	Ꮎ	ᏯᏋᎫᏍᏔᎾ	ᎢᏣ	ᏃᏬ	ᎩᎳ
gadu	na	yagwvgutan	itsa	now	kil
in bread	that	when I sift	flour	then	until then

ᏘᎸ ᏐᏓ ᏥᎸᏍᎪ ᏃᏭᎴ ᎧᎵᏎᏥ ᏍᎩᏅ
tilv sod jilvsgo nowle kalseji sginv
chestnut soda I put it in also sugar and that

ᏃᏭ ᎠᏉᏰᏂ ᎧᎵ ᎢᎦ ᎦᏐᏳᎩᏍᎪ
now agwoyeni kali iga gasoyugisgo
then my hand full quantity I get a handful

ᏍᎩᎾ ᏐᏊ ᏂᎦᎵᏍᏓ ᎦᏄᎵ ᏌᏊᏃ ᎤᏆᎶ
sgin sogwu nigalsdi ganuli sagwuno ugwalo
that one it happens wrap and one leaf

ᏃᏭ ᎦᏄᎶᏙᏗ ᏍᎩ ᎦᏚ ᎦᏄᎵ ᏃᏭ
now ganulodohd sgi gadu ganul now
then to wrap it with that bread wrapped then

ᏂᎦᎵᏍᏗ ᏃᏭᏅ Ꮟ ᎯᎸ ᏳᏪᏭᏅᏍᏗ
nigalsdi nowhnv si hilv yuwenvsd
it becomes and then still a few hours

ᏗᎵᏥᏍᏙᏗ ᎩᎳ ᎤᏅᏏᏌᏛ ᏂᎦᎵᏍᏗ
dilitsdod kil unvsisad nigalsdi
to boil until well done it becomes

Morpheme by Morpheme

agvy-^{23}hno agvy^{23} de-g-v^{3}nisdi^{3}s-g-o ase^{3}ge^{3}
first and first Pl 1 cook Prog Hab perhaps

nvhgiha
four of them

iyu^{3}wenvsd de-g-a̲^{3}lihdi^{4}s-g-o
hour Pl 1 boil Prog Hab

tili ki̲lo y-u-n-vs^{23}
chestnut then nonF 3 Pl be-done

yi-g-e^{4}li^{32}
nonF 1 think

no   kil   am
then   until   water

ji-to^{3}dis-g-o   di-git-diyi   nown
1 heat-water Prog Hab   Pl bake Inf   then

j-a-lji^{4}hawyv^3
when 3 start-to-boil

am   no
water   then

de-g-a^{32}suyv^{3}s-g-o^3
Pl 1 mix-in Prog Hab

tili
chestnut

gadu^3
bread

na
that

y-agw-v^{3}gutan^3
nonF 1 sift

ihcha   now   kil
flour   then   until

tili   sod^3 ji-lvs-g-o^3 no^{23}wle^3 kalse^{23}ji sgi-no^3
chestnut   soda   I put-in Prog Hab   also   sugar   that and

now^{3}
then

ag-woye^{4}ni kali
1Pos hand full

iga^{3} g-asoyu^{23}gi^{32}s-g-o^{3}
quantity 1 get-handful Prog Hab

sgin sogwu^{3} ni-g-alsdi^{3} g-anu^{4}li sagwu-^{3}no ugwalo^{23}
that one Spec 3 happen 1 wrap one and leaf

now^{3} g-anu^{23}lo-dohd^{3} sgi^{3} ga^{3}du
then 1 wrap Ins that bread

g-anul now^{3}
1 wrap then

ni-ga-lsdi^{3} no^{3}w-hnv^{3} si^{3} hilv^{3} y-u-^{3}wenvsd^{3}
Spec 3 happen then and still a-few nonF 3 hour

di-^{23}lits-dod
Pl boil Ins

kil
until

u-n-si^{4}sad ni-g-alsdi^{3}
3 Pl done Spec 3 happen

Syllabary

ᎠᎨᏴᏃ ᎠᎨᏴ ᎦᏚᎵᏍᏗᏍᎪ ᎠᏎᎰ ᎤᎩᏐ ᎢᏳᏪᏅᏍᏗ ᎦᏚᎵᏗᏍᎪ ᏧᎵ ᎩᎳᏃ ᏳᏅᏂᏍ ᏴᎰᎵ Ᏻ ᎩᎳ ᎠᏩ ᏥᏙᏗᏍᎪ ᏗᎩᏚᏗᏴ ᏃᏊᏃ ᏣᎵᏟᏐᏊᏰ ᎠᏩ Ᏻ ᎦᏚᏭᏰᏍᎪ ᏧᎵ ᎦᏚ Ꮎ ᏫᏋᏧᏍᎳᎾ ᎢᏳ ᏃᏊ ᎩᎳ ᏧᎸ ᏐᏓ ᏥᎸᏍᎪ ᏃᏊᏛ ᎧᎵᏎᏥ ᏍᎩᏅ ᏃᏊ ᎠᏉᏰᏂ ᎧᎵ ᎢᎦ ᎦᏐᏳᎩᏍᎪ ᏍᎩᎾ ᏐᏊ ᏂᎦᎵᏍᏓ ᎦᏄᎵ ᏌᏊᏃ ᎤᏆᎶ ᏃᏊ ᎦᏄᎶᏙᏗ ᏍᎩ ᎦᏚ ᎦᏄᎵ ᏃᏊ ᏂᎦᎵᏍᏗ ᏃᏊᏅ Ꮟ ᎯᎸ ᏳᏪᏅᏍᏗ ᏗᎵᏥᏍᏙᏗ ᎩᎳ ᎤᏅᏏᏌᏛ ᏂᎦᎵᏍᏗ

English

First I cook the chestnuts for about four hours until I think they are done. Then I heat some water to bake the bread. When the water is just beginning to boil, I mix the chestnuts into the batter. I then add soda and sugar. After I have mixed in all the ingredients, I take just a handful and wrap it up in a leaf. They must be boiled a few more hours until they are well done.

Hunting Dialogue

Durbin Feeling

The following is a dialogue between Durbin Feeling and a Cherokee hunter. The story provides insights into an activity that is traditionally important to the Cherokee people.

Durbin:

ᏝᎮ	ᏱᏃᎭᎵᏓ	ᎠᏫ	ᏧᏂᏲᏍᏗ	ᏥᎡᎲ
hlahe	hyinohalida	ahwi	juniysdi	ji?ehv
so	you didn't hunt	deer	season	when it was

Cherokee Hunter:

ᎨᏍᏗ	ᏥᏃᎠᎵᏙᎯ	ᏱᎩ	ᏌᏊᎡᎦ	ᎢᏯᎩᏃᎭᎵᏙᎸ
gesdi	jino?alidohi	yigi	sagwu?ega	iyaginohalidolv
not	I a hunter	am not	once however	I have gone hunting

ᏥᎾᏩᏛᎲᏊᏅ	ᎥᏍᏊ	ᎠᏫ	ᎩᎶ	ᎤᏲᎸ	ᎨᏍᏗ
jinawatvhvgwuhnv	vsgwu	ahwi	kilo	uyohlv	gesdi
I just found it	too	deer	someone	who had shot	not

ᎠᏋᏍ	ᏱᏥᎳ	ᎩᎶ	ᏦᎩᎾᎵᎪᏒ	ᏦᎢᏕ	ᏃᏥᎥ
agwvs	yijila	kilo	joginaligosv	jo?ide	noji?v
myself	I kill	someone	we were together	or three	there were of us

ᎣᏣᎣᏍ
oja?isv
we were walking along

ᎣᎦᏛᎦᏅ	ᎩᎶ	ᏚᏍᏓᏲᎸ	ᎪᎯ	ᎢᏴ	ᏃᏊ	ᏄᏢᏍᏔᏅ
ogatvganv	kilo	dusdayohlv	kohi	iyv	nogwu	nutlvstanv
we heard	some	he shot a gun	after	a while	then	it ran across

ᎢᎬᏱ	ᏝᏍᏊ	ᏲᏥᎪᎡ	ᏭᎶᏒ	ᎢᎬᏱ	ᎣᏣᎢᏒ
igvyi	hlasgwu	yojigo?e	wulosv	igvyi	oja?isv
ahead	and not	we did not see it	(where) it went	ahead	where we walked

ᏥᎦᎾᏏᏂᏐ	ᎢᏳᏍᏗ	ᏂᎦᎵᏍᏗᏍᎬ	ᎯᎠ	ᎢᏗᏜ	ᏭᎿᎷᏒ
jiganasiniso	iyusdi	nigalisdisgv	hi?a	ididla	wuhnalusv
as though dragging it	like	it was	this	toward	it went up a hill

ᎤᎿᏅ	ᏬᎩᎷᏣ	ᏚᎾᏗᏩᏒ	ᎩᎦ
uhnahnv	wogiluhja	dunadiwasv	giga
and there	when we got there	where it had crossed	blood

ᎤᏩᏍᏉᏨᏍᏔᏅ	ᎣᏦᎷᏅᏒ	ᎦᏚᏏᏱ	ᏧᎦᎾᎥ	ᎩᎶ	ᎤᏲᎸ
uwasgwojvstanv	ojoluhnvsv	gadusiyv	jugana?v	kilo	uyohlv
where it dripped along	we trailed it	at the top of hill	it lay	someone	had shot

Durbin:

ᎡᏥᏁᏎ
ejinese?
you took it?

Cherokee Hunter:

i
v
yes

ᎠᏴᏛᏍᏊ	ᏌᏊ	ᏳᏩᎪᏗ	ᏍᏊ	ᏍᎩ
ayvdvsgwu	sagwu	yuwagodi	sgwu	sgi
I also	one	time	also	that

ᏥᏄᎵᏍᏔᏅ	ᎩᎦ	ᏍᏊ	ᏚᏩᏍᏬᏨᏍᏔᏅ	ᏥᎨᏒ	ᎡᎵᎠᏯ
jinulistanv	giga	sgwu	duwaswojvstanv	jigesv	eliʔaya
it happened	blood	also	it had dripped along	it was	quite

ᎢᏅᎯ	ᎣᏍᏙᎷᏅᏒ	Ꭸ	ᏥᎦᏅ	ᏦᏍᏗᏁᏒ	ᎤᏂᏅ	ᎣᏍᏕᏙᎲ
invhi	osdolunvsv	ge	jigaʔnv	josdinesv	uhnahnv	osdedohv
far	we trailed it	there	it lay	we took it	and there	where we were

ᎾᎥ	ᎯᏗᏜ	ᎨᏓᎵ	ᎤᏂ	ᏓᏥᏍᏓᏲᎸ	ᎠᏴ	Ꮭ
naʔv	hididla	kedali	uhna	dajisdayohlv	ayv	hla
near	this toward	bottom of hill	there	it was shot at	I	not

ᏱᏗᏥᏍᏓᏲᎴ	ᎩᎦ	ᎣᏍᏙᎷᏅᏒ	ᎨᏴ	ᏬᏍᏗᎾᏩᏛᎲ
yidijisdayohle	gig	osdolunvsv	geyv	wosdinawatvhv
didn't shoot at it	blood	we trailed it	way over more	we found it

ᎯᎠᏅᏍᏊ	Ꮠ	ᏥᏛᏟᎢᎵᏒ	Ꮎ	ᎡᏥ	ᏦᎢᏁ	ᏗᎾᏓᎸ	ᎤᏪᏥ
hiʔanvsgwu	soʔ	jidvhliʔilisv	na	eji	joʔine	dinadalv	uwej
this also	last	week	that	my mother	third	her sister	her offspring

ᎠᏧᏣ	ᎯᎠᏴ	Ꮲ	ᏂᎠᏔ	ᎣᎢᏂᏃᎭᎸᏒ	ᏙᏓᏫᏕᎾ
achuja	hiʔyv	dlv	niʔata	oʔininohalvsv	dodawidena
boy	this much	about	his height	we went hunting	Saturday

ᏥᎡᎲ	ᎾᏅ	ᏓᏁᎸ	ᎨᏓᎵ	ᏅᏲ	ᎧᏃᎾ	ᏗᎠᎧᎲ
jiʔehv	nanv	danelv	kedali	nvyo	kanon	diʔakahv
when it was	and that	at home	bottom of hill	rocky	canyon	where it sits

ᎣᏣᏗᏍᎪ	ᎤᏂᎾ	ᎤᏂ	ᎣᎢᏂᎦᏐᏏᏗᎲ	ᏚᎴᏅ	ᎠᏫ
ojadisgo	uhnana	uhna	oʔinigasosidihv	dulehnv	ahwi
we say	there	there	we were going down the hill	it got up	deer

ᏥᏲᎮᎸ	ᏙᏍᏗᏍᏓᏲᏏᎶᎥ	ᏫᏙᎢᏂᎩᏴ	ᎣᎢᎾᏂᎢᏒ
jiyohelv	dosdisdayosiloʔv	widoʔinikiyv	oʔinahniʔisv
I told him	we shot at it repeatedly	it got away from us	we started out

ᏐᎳᎩᏬ	Ꮝ	ᏂᎠᏫᎿ	ᎤᎾ	ᏍᏍᏬ	ᏗᏜ	ᎤᎾ
nelaginv	so	ni?anvhna	uhna	gadus	didla	uhna
other	another	a road is there	there	top of hill	toward	there

ᎤᏙᎯᏔᏒ	ᎤᏴ	ᎠᏗᏡ	ᎥᏙᎯᏂᎯᏬᏒ	ᎠᎲ
wo?inahni?isv	nvno	adidlv	do?ininadiwisv	ahwi
we started out	road	there toward	we crossed	deer

ᏙᏍᏙᎷᎲᏒ		ᏥᎬᎢᏙᎲ	ᏃᏭᎴ	ᏥᏙᏍᏖᏍᏔᏅ	ᎤᎾ
dosdoluhnisv		tsigwisdohv	nowule	jidostestanv	uhnana
we were on the trail of		a lot of them	also	we spooked them	there

ᏃᏭ	ᎬᎤᎦᏘ	ᏕᎠᏲᏂᎩᏴ	ᏧᎨᏓᎵᏴ	ᏗᏜ
nowu	gvwagati	de?o?inikiyv	jukedaliyv	didla
then	forever	we lost them	bottom of hill	toward

ᎠᏫᏂᎶᎲ	Ꮅ	ᎤᎦᎵ	ᏲᏍᏗᎪᏁ
dv?o?inilohv	dlv	saloli	yosdigo?e
we came back through	somewhere	squirrel	we didn't see it

Morpheme by morpheme

Durbin:

hla-he^{32}	h-y-noh$\underline{a}$lid-a^{23}	$\underline{a}$hwi	juniyosdi^3	ji?-eh-v^3
not or	2 nonF hunt Pres	deer	season	Pst be exP

Cherokee Hunter:

gesd^{23}	ji-n$\underline{o}$?$\underline{a}$lido^{4}h-i	y-ig^3	sagwu^{23}?e^{32}ga	i^{2}y-$\underline{a}^3$ginoh$\underline{a}$lidol-v^3
not	1 hunt Ag	nonF be	one however	1 hunt exP

ji-nawa^{32}tvhv^{23}-gwu^3-hnv^3	vsgwu	ahwi	kilo^3	u-yohl-v^{23}	gesd^{23}
1 find exP just and	too	deer	someone	3 shot exP	not

$\underline{a}$gw-vs^{23}	y$\underline{i}$-ji-l^3	kilo	j-ogi-n-ali^{3}gos-v^3
1 self	nonF 1 kill	someone	Pst he-and-I be-together exP

jo?i³-de³ n-oj-i³?-v³   oj-a³?is-v³   ok-tvga³²n-v³
three or   Spec they-and-I number exP   they-and-I walk exP   they-and-I hear
                                                                     exP

kilo³   d-u-sdayohl-v³   kohi³ iyv³   no²³gwu³   n-u-tlv³stan-v   igvy²³
some   Pl 3 shoot exP   after a while then   Lat 3 run exP   ahead

hla³-sgwu³   y-oji³-go?-e   n-u-los-v³   igvy²³   oj-a³?is-v³
not also   nonF they-and-I see   Lat 3 pass-by exP   ahead   they-and-I
             repP   walk exP

ji-gansi²³ni³²s-o³   iyusd²³   ni-g-alsdi²³s-g-v³   hi?a³
1 drag Hab   like   Spec 3 happen Prog exP   this

idi³dla³   w-u-hnalus-v³   uhna³-hnv³
toward   Tr 3 ascend exP   there and

w-o²³gi³-luhj-a   d-u-n-adi²³ws-v   gig²³
Tr they-and-I arrive Pres   Pl 3 Pl cross exP   blood

uw-a³sgwojvs-tan-v³   oj-olu²³hnv²³s-v³   gadu³si³²-yv³   j-u-gana³?-v³
3 drip-along accidentally   they-and-I see exP   hill on-top   Pst 3 lie exP
  exP

kilo³   u-yohl-v³
someone   3 shoot exP

Durbin:

eji-ne³s-e³?
you Pl Ex take repP

Cherokee Hunter:

v
yes

ay-dv³-sgwu³   sagwu³   yuwagd²³   sgwu³   sgi³
I Emp also   one   time   also   that

ji-n-u-list$\underline{a}$n-v^3 gig^{23} sgwu^3 d-u-wa^{3}swojvstan-v^3 ji-ges-v^3
Pst Spec 3 happen exP blood also Pl 3 drip-along exP Pst be exP

eli$\underline{?}$aya^3 invhi^3 osd-olu^{3}nvs-v^3 ge ji-g-a?n-v^3
quite far he-and-I trail exP there Pst 3 lie exP

j-osd-ine^{3}s-v^3 uhna^3-hnv^3 osd-e^{23}do^{32}h-v^3 n$\underline{a}$?v^3
Pst he-and-I take exP there and he-and-I be exP near

hi-didl^3 ked$\underline{a}$li^3 uhna^3 d-aji-sd$\underline{a}$yohl-v^3 $\underline{a}$yv^3 hla^3
this toward bottom-of-hill there Pl 3Pas shoot exP I no

y$\underline{i}$-d-iji^3-sd$\underline{a}$yohl-e^3 gig^{23} osd-olu^{3}nvs-v^3 ge^{32}yv^3
nonF 2Pl you shoot repP blood he-and-I trail exP way-over-more

w-osd-ina^{32}watvh-v^3 h$\underline{i}$?a-n^3-sgwu^3 so?^{3} j$\underline{i}$dvhl$\underline{i}$?$\underline{i}$li^{3}sv
Tr he-and-I find this and also the other week

na^3 e-ji^3 j$\underline{o}$?i-ne^3 d-in$\underline{a}$dalv^3 $\underline{u}$-wej^{23} a-chuj^{23}
that 1Pos mother 3 Ord Pl 3 sister 3 offspring 3 boy

h$\underline{i}$?yv^3 dlv^3 n$\underline{i}$?at^{23} o?$\underline{i}$ni-noh$\underline{a}$lv^{3}s-v^3 dod$\underline{a}$widen^{23}
this-quantity about this-height they-and-I hunt exP saturday

ji-?eh-v^3 na-nh^3 da^{3}nelv^3 ked$\underline{a}$li^3 nvy-o^3 k$\underline{a}$non^{23}
Rel be exP that and at-home bottom-of-hill rock Loc canyon

di-?a^{23}-k$\underline{a}^3$h-v^3 o?^{23}-atd uhna^3-na^3 o?$\underline{i}$ni-kso^{3}si^{23}di^{32}h-v^3
Dst 3 sit exP he-and-I say there and he-and-I descend exP

d-u-lehn-v^3 $\underline{a}$wh jiy-oh-e^{23}l-v^3 d-osd-isd$\underline{a}$yos-i^{23}-lo^3-?v^3
Pl 3 arise exP deer 1 tell Dat exP Pl he-and-I shoot repeatedly exP

w$\underline{i}$-d-$\underline{o}$-?-$\underline{i}$n-iki^{3}y-v^3 $\underline{o}^3$?$\underline{i}$n-a^{23}hn$\underline{i}^3$?is-v^3 so^3 ne^{23}l$\underline{a}$gin^3
Tr Pl Ex 1 Pl he-and-I start-out exP other leave-alone

ni^{23}?$\underline{a}^3$nvhn uhna^3 g$\underline{a}$dus^3 didl uhna^3
Lat road-is-there there hill-top-of toward there

w-o̲^{3}ʔi̲-na^{23}hni̲^{3}ʔis-v^{3}	nvno^{3}	a^{3}di^{3}	dlv	d-oʔi̲n-indi^{32}hs-v^{3}
Tr he-and-I start-out exP	road	there	toward	Pl he-and-I cross exP

a̲hw	d-osd-olu^{23}hni^{32}s-v^{3}	tsigwisd-o^{23}hv
deer	Pl he-and-I trail exP	many really

nowu^{3}le^{3}	ji̲-d-o^{3}st-e^{3}sta̲n-v^{3}	uhna-n^{3}	now^{23}
also	Pst Pl he-and-I startle exP	there and	then

gv^{23}wakt	de-ʔo^{3}ʔi̲n-i^{3}-ki^{3}y-v^{3}	ju^{23}ke^{3}da̲liyv^{3}	didl^{3}
forever	Pl he-and-I lose-trail exP	bottom-of- hill	toward

d-v̲^{3}ʔ-oʔi̲n-iloh-v^{3}	dlv	sa̲lol^{23}	y-o^{23}sd-i^{3}go̲ʔ-e^{3}
Pl Rep he-and-I return exP	somewhere	squirrel	nonF he-and-I see repP

Syllabary

Durbin: ᏝᏢ ᏱᏃᎮᎵᏓ ᎠᏫ ᏧᏂᏲᏍᏗ ᏥᎡᎲ

Cherokee Hunter: ᎨᏍᏗ ᏥᏃᎠᎵᏙᎯ ᏱᎩ ᏌᏊᏑᎡᏕ ᎢᏑᎩᏃᎮᎵᏙᏆ ᏥᎾᏩᏛᎲᏊᏅ ᎥᏍᏊ ᎠᏫ ᎩᎶ ᎤᏲᏢ ᎨᏍᏗ ᎠᏋᏍ ᏱᏥᎳ ᎩᎶ ᏦᎩᎾᎵᎠᎡ ᏦᎢᏕ ᏃᏥᎥ ᎣᏣᎣᏍ ᎣᏕᏛᏕᏅ ᎩᎶ ᎦᏍᏓᏲᏢ ᎪᎯ ᎢᏴ ᏃᏊ ᏆᏢᏍᏔᏅ ᎢᎬᏱ ᏝᏍᏊ ᏲᏥᎪᎡ ᏭᎶᏒ ᎢᎬᏱ ᎣᏣᎢᏒ ᏥᏕᎾᏏᏂᎰ ᎢᏳᏍᏗ ᏂᎦᎵᏍᏗᏍᎬ ᎯᎠ ᎢᏗᏜ ᏭᎿᎷᏒ ᎤᎿᏅ ᏬᎩᎷᏣ ᎦᎾᏗᏩᏒ ᎩᏕ ᎤᏩᏍᏉᏨᏍᏔᏅ ᎣᏦᎷᏅᏒ ᏕᎦᏏᏱ ᏧᏕᎾᎥ ᎩᎶ ᎤᏲᏢ

Durbin: ᎡᏥᏁᏎ

Cherokee Hunter: Ꭵ ᎠᏴᏛᏍᏊ ᏌᏊ ᏳᏩᎪᏗ ᏍᏊ ᏍᎩ ᏥᏆᎵᏍᏔᏅ ᎩᏕ ᏍᏊ ᎦᏩᏍᏬᏨᏍᏔᏅ ᏥᎨᏒ ᎡᎵᎠᏑ ᎢᏅᎯ ᎣᏍᏙᎷᏅᏒ Ꭸ ᏥᏕᏅ ᏦᏍᏗᏁᏒ ᎤᎿᏅ ᎣᏍᏕᏙᎲ ᎾᎥ ᎯᏗᏜ ᎨᏓᎵ ᎤᎿ ᏓᏥᏍᏓᏲᏢ ᎠᏴ Ꮭ ᏱᏗᏥᏍᏓᏲᏓ ᎩᏕ ᎣᏍᏙᎷᏅᏒ ᎨᏴ ᏬᏍᏗᎾᏩᏛᎲ ᎯᎠᏅᏍᏊ Ꮀ ᏥᏛᏣᎢᎵᏒ Ꮎ ᎡᏥ ᏦᎢᏁ ᏗᎾᏓᏆ ᎤᏰᏥ ᎠᏧᏣ ᎯᎠᏴ Ꮲ ᏂᎠᏔ ᎣᎢᏂᏃᎮᏆᏒ ᏙᏓᏫᏕᎾ ᏥᎡᎲ ᎾᏅ ᏓᏁᏆ ᎨᏓᎵ ᎤᎯ ᎧᏃᎾ ᏗᎠᎧᎲ ᎣᏣᏗᏍᎪ ᎤᎿᎾ ᎤᎿ ᎣᎢᏂᏕᎰᏏᏗᎲ ᎦᎴᏅ ᎠᏫ ᏥᏲᏢᏆ ᏙᏍᏗᏍᏓᏲᏏᎶᎥ ᏫᏙᎢᏂᎩᏴ ᎣᎢᎾᏂᎢᏒ ᏁᎳᎩᏅ Ꮀ ᏂᎠᏅᎿ ᎤᎿ ᏕᎦᏍ ᏗᏜ ᎤᎿ ᏬᎢᎾᏂᎢᏒ ᏅᏃ ᎠᏗᏢ ᏙᎢᏂᎾᏗᏫᏒ ᎠᏫ ᏙᏍᏙᎷᏂᏒ ᏥᏈᏍᏙᎲ ᏃᏭᎴ ᏥᏙᏍᏖᏍᏔᏅ ᎤᎿ ᏃᏭ ᎬᏩᏕᏘ ᏕᎣᎢᏂᎩᏴ ᏧᎨᏓᎵᏴ ᏗᏜ ᏛᎣᎢᏂᎶᎲ Ꮲ ᏌᎶᎵ ᏲᏍᏗᎪᎡ

English

Durbin: Did you not go hunting during deer season?

Cherokee Hunter: I don't hunt. One time, though, I did go hunting. I just found a deer, too, that someone had shot. I didn't kill it. I was with someone, I mean there were three of us. We were walking along, and we heard someone shooting. Pretty soon we heard one cross the path in front of us, but we didn't see it. It sounded like it was dragging something, and it went up a hill. When we got to the place where it had crossed our path, we saw some blood where it had bled as it walked. We trailed it, and we found it at the top of the hill. Someone had shot it.

Durbin: Did you take it?

Cherokee Hunter: Yes, that happened to me once. I saw a trail of blood. We trailed it a long way, and we found it lying way out there. We took it. When we heard someone shoot it and found the trail of blood, we trailed it until we found it. And just last week, my mother's sister's boy—he's about this tall—he and I went hunting on a Saturday. Close to where I live there's a place we call "Where Kanun Sits." We were walking down the hill there, and a deer jumped up in front of us. "Deer!" I yelled. We shot at it, but it got away from us. We started out again, and there's another trail on top of the hill. We took that trail and crossed to the other hill trailing deer. And we scared off a bunch more there. We lost them, too. We came back through a ravine, and we did not even see a squirrel.

Rabbit and Buzzard

Charley Campbell

"Rabbit and Buzzard" is a classic example of a trickster tale, a story in which a roguish mythical figure plays clever tricks on others. This story was related by Charley Campbell, who lived near Proctor, Oklahoma, east of Tahlequah.

ᎢᏈᎯᏳᏃ	ᏥᎨᏒ	ᏑᎵᏃ	ᏗᏓᏅᏫᏍᎩ
ilvhiyuhno	jigesv	sulihno	didahnvwisgi
and way back	when it was	buzzard and	one that cures

ᎡᎮ	ᏑᎵ	ᎦᏃᎯᎵᏙᎯ	ᏥᎩ	ᏥᏍᏚᏃ
ehe	sul	ganohilidohi	jigi	jisduhno
he lived	buzzard	one that flies around	which is	rabbit and

ᏣᏁ	ᎤᏂᏠᏲ	ᎤᏢᏤ	ᏃᏭᏃ	ᎤᏂᏯᎴ
jane	unihloy	udlvje	nowuhno	unihyale
who live	their kind	became sick	and so	they searched for

ᎤᏅᏫᏍᎩ	ᎤᏂᏩᏛᎭᏃ	ᏑᎵ	ᎤᏂᏩᏛᎮ
uhnvwisgi	unihwatvhahno	suli	unihwatvhe
one to cure him	and when they found him	buzzard	they found him

ᏥᏏᎾᏍᏓᏛ	ᏗᏩᏓᏅᏬᏗ	ᎥᏍᎩ	ᎢᏳᏍᏗ
jisinasdadv	diwadahnvwodi	vsgi	iyusdi
I am very knowledgeable	at curing	that	kind

ᎤᏛᏁᏃ	ᏑᎵ	ᏙᏅ	ᎯᏅᏮᎦᏗᎲ
udvhnehno	sul	dohnv	hinvwvgadihv
so he said	buzzard	and sure enough	so cure him

ᏥᏍᏚ	ᎠᎪᏎᎴ	ᎤᏪᎾ	ᏭᎷᏤ
jisdu	agosel	uwena	wuluhje
rabbit	he was told	when he went	he arrived there

ᏃᏭᏅ	ᎠᎭᏂᏛ	ᏱᏬᎩᏂᏴᏝ	ᎦᎶᎯᏍᏗ
nowuhnv	ahandv	yiwoginiyvhla	galohisdi
and so now	here	if we go in	door

ᎧᏅᏑᎸ	ᏱᏬᎩᏂᏴᏝ	ᎢᏥᏍᏚᏅᏃ	ᏃᏭᏃ
kanvsulv	yiwoginiyuhla	ijisduhnvhno	nowuhno
room	if we go in	and close it	and then

ᎡᎵᏭ	ᎦᏛᏅ	ᎢᏥᏍᏚᎢᏒ	ᎨᏅ	Ᏼ
eliw	gadvnv	ijisdu?isv	genh	yv
okay	when I say	you open it	and over there	distance

ᏫᏥᏃᎢᎵᏎᏍᏗ	ᎩᎳ	ᏫᏥᏴᎵ	ᎤᏛᏁᏃ
wijino?ilisesd	kil	wijiyvhlv	udvhnehno
when I have flown	then	you go in	he said

ᏑᎵ	ᏙᏅ	ᎪᎯᏴ	ᏃᏭ
suli	dohnv	kohiyv	now
buzzard	sure enough	after a while	then

Ꭷ	ᏧᏩᏂᎴ	ᏃᏭᏃ	ᏭᏂᏍᏚᎢᏌ	ᏧᏄᎪᏣ
ka	juwahnile	nowuhno	wunisdu?isa	junugoja
now	he knocked	and when	when they opened	he came out

ᎤᏝᏫᏛᎮ	ᎨᏅ	Ᏼ	ᏫᎦᏃᎯᎵᏒ
uhlawidvhe	genh	yv	wiganohilisv
he flew	there	distance	as he was flying away

ᎤᏂᏴᏞ	ᎠᏩᏁᎪᏃ	ᏔᏏ	ᏕᏥᏰᏈ
wuniyvhle	kolawuhno	iga	dejiye
they went in	and just bones	that is all	they were lying there

ᎠᏥᎴᏍ	ᏥᏍᏓ	ᏣᏫᏯᎣᎲᎤ	ᏍᎩᏯᏔ		ᎤᏌᎻᏗ	ᏑᎵ
ajile	jisd	wajiya?ehnv	sgiya		asamadi	suli
he was killed	rabbit	and he was eaten up	that is how much		he is smart	buzzard

Morpheme by Morpheme

ilvhiyu^{23}-hno   ji-ges-v   suli-hno   di-d-a-hnvwi^{3}-s-g-i   eh-e^{3}
long-ago and   Rel be exP   buzzard and   Pl Pl 3 cure Prog Ag   live repP

sul   ga-nohili-do^{3}h-i   j-i^{3}gi   jisdu^{3}-hno
buzzard   3 fly place-to-place Ag   Rel be   rabbit and

j-a-ne^{23} u-ni-hloy^{3} u-dlvj-e   nowu^{3}-hno   u-ni-hyal-e^{3}
Rel 3 live   3 Pl same-kind   3 sick repP   so and   3 Pl search repP

u-hnvwi^{3}s-g-i   u-ni-hwatv^{23}h-a-hno   suli   u-ni-hwatvh-e^{3}
3 treat Prog Ag   3 pl find Pres and   buzzard   3 pl find repP

ji-sina^{3}sd-a-dv   diw-a-d-anvwo^{32}-di   vsgi   iyu^{23}sdi
1 skilled Pres Emp   Pl 3 Pl treat Inf   that   kind

u-dvhn-e^{3}-hno   sul   do^{23}hnv   hi-nvwvgadi^{3}h-v^{3}
3 say repP and   buzzard   indeed   2 treat Fut-Imp

jisdu ag-ose^{23}l-e   u-we^{23}n-a   w-u^{3}-luhj-e^{3}
rabbit he/me say repP   3 go imP   Tr 3 arrive repP

nowu^{3}-hnv   a^{3}han-dv^{3} yi-w-ogi^{3}-niyv^{23}hl-a   galosdi
so and   here Emp   nonF Tr they-and-I enter Pres   door

kanv^{3}sulv^{3} yi-w-o-gi^{3}-niyv^{23}hl-a   iji-sdu^{3}hn-v-hno   nowu^{3}-hno
room   nonF Tr they-and-I enter Pres   you/all exP and   then and

eli^{23}wu   g-advn-v   i-ji-sdu̲^{3}ʔis-v^3 ge^{23}-nh   yv
okay   1 say exP   you-all open Fut-Imp   there and   distance

wi-ji̲-no̲^{3}ʔi^{23}li^{32}s-e^{3}sd   kil   w-iji-yv^{3}hl-v   u-dvhn-e^3-hno
TR 1 fly-in Fut-Prog   then   Tr you-all go-in Fut-Imp   3 say repP and

suli   do^{23}hnv   kohi^{32}yv   now^{23}
buzzard   in-fact   after-a-while   then

ka^3 j-u̲-wa^{3}hni̲l-e^3 nowu^3-hno   w-u-ni^3-sdu̲ʔi^{3}s-a   j-u-n-u^{3}go^{4}j-a
okay   Rel 3 knock repP   when and   Tr 3 pl open Pres   Rel 3 Pl exit Pres

u-hli̲widvh-e^3 genh   yu   wi̲-ga̲-no^{3}hilis-v^3
3 fly repP   there   distance   Tr 3 fly exP

w-u-ni^3-yvhl-e^3 kola̲^{3}-wu^3-hno   i^{23}ga   de-ji^{3}y-e^3
Tr 3 pl go-in repP   bone just and   all-be   Pl lie-there repP

a-ji-l-e^3 jisd   w-a̲^{3}ji-ya^{3}ʔ-e^3-hnv   sgi-ya^3
3Pas kill repP   rabbit   Tr 3Pas eat-up repP and   that degree

a-samadi^3 suli
3 smart   buzzard

Syllabary

ᎢᏉᎠᏃ ᏂᎵᎡ ᎨᏢ ᎠᏞᏫᏎᏯ ᏣᏢ ᎨᏢ ᏎᏣᏅᎥᎠ ᏂᏴ ᏂᏎᏃ ᏣᎾ ᎤᏂᏛᏬ ᎤᏢᎥ
ᏃᎥ ᎤᎭᏍᏛ ᎤᎤᏫᏎᏯ ᎤᎭᎬᏓᏃ ᎨᏢ ᎤᎭᎬᎽ ᏂᏦᏫᏞᎽ ᏣᎬᏆᎤᎥᏣ ᎢᏫᏯ
ᏔᎬᏫᏣ ᎤᎽᏁᏃ ᎨᏢ ᏴᎤ ᎠᎤᎲᏍᏣᏬ ᏂᏫᏍ ᎠᎯᏙᎤ ᎤᏴᎦ ᏆᎽᏫ ᏃᎤ ᎠᏫᎭᎽ
ᏌᎤᏴᏂᏌᏟ ᏍᎬᏅᏫᏣ ᎠᎤᎩᎣ ᏌᎤᏴᏂᏌᏟ ᏔᏂᏎᏍᎤᏃ ᏃᎥ ᏞᏫᎦ ᏎᎽᎤ ᏔᏂᏎᏔᎡ
ᏂᎤ Ꭾ ᎤᏂᏃᏔᏢᏅᏬᏣ ᏴᏫ ᎤᏂᎡᏆ ᎤᎽᏁᏃ ᎨᏢ ᏴᎤ ᎠᏁᏆ ᏃᎢ Ꭰ ᏣᎦᎭᏛ ᏃᎥ
ᏌᏂᏫᏍᏔᎤ ᏠᎠᎦᎦ ᎤᏟᎤᎽᏢ ᏂᎤ Ꭾ ᎤᏎᏃᏅᏟᎡ ᏌᏂᏆᏟ ᎠᏫᏃᏃ ᏔᏎ ᏏᏂᏆ ᎠᏂᏍᏛ ᏂᏫᏍ
ᏣᏂᎡᎡᎤ ᏅᏯᎠ ᎠᏳᏉᏣ ᎨᏢ

English

Way back a long time ago, there was a Doctor Buzzard. One day a rabbit became ill, and the other rabbits searched for a doctor to cure his illness. The rabbits found this Doctor Buzzard. "I'm good at doctoring that type of illness," the buzzard said. "Then doctor the rabbit," he was told. Doctor Buzzard started out, and when he arrived, he told the others to allow him some privacy in the room where the rabbit was. "When I have finished, then you can let me out, and I'll be on my way," said Doctor Buzzard. "But you must not go into the room until I have flown out of sight," he told the others. Sure enough, when Doctor Buzzard came out and flew away, the others just stood there until he was out of sight. When they entered the room where the rabbit was, all they found were bones, because Doctor Buzzard had eaten the rabbit.

Legal Document

John Littlebones

Written in 1900, "Legal Document" is an example of Cherokee legal language that would have been used in the nineteenth-century Cherokee Nation court system. This letter was written by John Littlebones. It was donated to Durbin Feeling for his personal collection.

JGꞰT
kuwayoꞋiꞋ
Pryor Creek

DOꞋꞆ	18	1900
anvhyi	18,	1900
March	18,	1900

SꞆꞆY	ꞀGꞀ
gasuyogi	gritts
Gasuyogi	Gritts

ꞄꞨPT
ginaliꞋi
you my friend

ꞋSP	27	KꞨWOꞋꞨ	AꞨP
kagali	27	johwelanvhi	gowehli
February	27	what you have written	letter

DYℂi	TᎩ	ᎭDⱷZ	OᏞᏂℛb	EⱷᎤTℙBℛⱷ
akhla?v	igi	hi?agwuhno	nvdajiwesi	gvyawo?iliyvehv
I have on a table	it is	and just this	I will say	my response to you

ⴱⱷᎩ	ꮖⱷⴹ	GⱼᎩSᏫOᏔ		james	shavehead
nasgi	nusdv	wagikdvhnv?i		james	shavehead
that	way it is	I went and checked it out		James	Shavehead

ꮝ	SVℛ	DⱷⱷᎩ	ꮖ4	JᎻꮒ
ke	dudo?e	ayawsgi	gese	kusani
was it	his name was	soldier	he was	Kusani

ⴱ꘡ⱷꙄ	ꮖꮖℛ	OᏂᎡ4ꮖ	Dơ	JⱷꮖᏫꙄ
dahnawohi	jigesv	uyoseke	ale	juwejidvhi
war	when it was	or did he die	and	his (surviving) children

OⱷⱷꮒᏰT	ⱷⱷᎩZ	Gꮒ	mills	JVTᏫ
unadaniye?i	nasgihno	jani	mills	judo?idv
they were orphaned	and that	John	Mills	named

SSⱼꙄT	ⱷⱷᎩZ	ⴱSⱼB
duktide?i	nasghino	daktiyv
took care of them	and so	taking care of them

OⱵⱷℙVơ	ⱷⱷᎩ
udahilidole	nasgi
he filed a custody suit	that

james	shavehead	JVTᏫ		OⱷGℛ	Dơ
james	shavehead	judo?idv		uwasv	ale
James	Shavehead	by the name of		himself	and

SS	JⱷJ	Dơ	Dⴱ4AᎩᏫ	ꮒOⱷℙⱷWꙄT
gadu	dihlohdi	ale	adasehgogidv	ni?ulstane?i
on top of	to lie down	and	won case	it happened

DSꝗ	Jⱷ4ꞆⱷVꟷ	OⱷV	OⱷꙆ	DSJBⴱꙆⱼ
adelv	disehisdohdi	udo	uhne	agaguyvdanedi
money	to draw with	his sister	he gave	his fee

john	mills	ᏗᏂᏲᏟ	ᏗᎦᏘᏯ	ᏄᏛᏅᎢ	ᎠᏎᏃ
john	mills	diniyohli	diktiya	nudvhnvʔi	asehno
John	Mills	children	custodian	his situation	however

ᎾᏊ	ᏄᏍᏆᎸᏛ	ᎠᎫᏴᏗ	ᏥᏚᏪᎾᏒ	ᏂᎦᏛ
nagwu	nusgwalvdv	akuyvdi	jiduwenasv	nigadv
now	before time	to pay	froze	all

ᎾᏍᎩ	ᎢᎬᏩᏍᏗᏓᏂ	ᎨᏒ	ᏫᏚᏨᏎᏊ	ᎾᏍᎩ
nasgi	igvwasdidani	gesv	widujvsegwu	nasgi
that	remaining situation	which was	they were returned	that

ᏧᏚᎦᏔᏅᎯ	ᎪᎯᏃ	ᏥᎩ	ᎾᏊ	ᎾᏍᎩ
juduktanvhi	kohihno	jigi	nagwu	nasgi
judgment	and now	which is	now	that

john	mills	ᏛᎾᏣᏂ	ᏥᏲᏎ	ᎤᏣᏘ	ᎣᏍᏛ
john	mills	dvnajani	chiyose	ujati	osdv
John	Mills	name	what you call him	much	good

ᎤᏓᏚᎬ	ᏂᎦᎵᏍᏗᎭ	ᎤᏲᎱᏒᎯᏃ	ᏥᏂᎦᎵᏍᏗᎭ
udatugv	nigalsdiha	uyohusvhihno	jinigalsdiha
he was owed	as it happens	and dead	since he happens to be

ᎾᏊ	ᏭᏓᎪᎾᏛᏛ	ᎾᎥ	ᎪᎱᏍᏗ	ᎤᏩᏅ
nagwu	wudagonatdv	naʔv	gohusdi	uwahnv
then	very	near	something	to him

ᎡᎲ	ᎤᏘᏯᏍᏓᏁᎲ	ᏂᎦᎵᏍᏗᎭ	ᎤᏁᏍᏓᎳ	ᎤᏩᏒ
ehv	utiyasdanehv	nigalsdiha	unesdala	uwasv
he lives	his inheritance	it happens	Ice	himself

ᎠᏎ	ᏧᎸᏫᏍᏓᏁᏗ	ᎡᎲᏃ	ᏥᏂᎦᎵᏍᏗᎭ	ᎾᏊ
ase	julvhwisdanedi	ehvhno	jinigalsdiha	nagwu
must	for him to work	his life	as it happens to be	then

ᎯᎠ	ᏫᏂᏥᏪᏎᎭ	ᏓᎩᎾᎥ	ᎪᏪᎵ
hiʔa	winijiweseha	daginaʔv	gohweli
this	I am saying to him	in my possession	papers

ᎠᏆᎮᏍᎩ   ᎤᏴᏣᏂ
kanohesgi   dvnajani
it tells   Dvnajani

Morpheme by Morpheme

john   littlebones
john   littlebones

kuway-o^4?
pryor-creek Loc

anvhyi   18,   1900
march   18,   1900

gasuyogi   newadv
gasuyogi   newadv

gin-ali^4?i
he-and-I friend

kagali	27	j-ohwe^{23}la^{32}n-v^{4}vhi	gohweli
february	27	2 write exP	letter

ak-hla^3?-v	i^{23}gi	hi?a-gwu^3-hno	nv-da-ji^3-wes-i	gvy-awo^3?ili^{23}yv^{3}eh-v
I have-on table exP	be	this just and	Spec Fut 1 say Fut	I/you reply exP

nasgi	nusdv	w-agi^3-kdv^{4}hnv-v?i	james	shavehead
that	way that it is	Tr 1 check-out exP	james	shavehead

ke^3	d-u-do^3?-e^3	a^3-yaws-g-i	ges-e	kusani
maybe	Pl 3 be-named repP	3 soldier Prog Ag	be repP	kusani

dahnawo^{4}hi	ji-ges-v
at war	Pst be exP

u-yos-e-³ke   ale³   j-u-wejidv⁴h-i
3 die repP or   and   Pl 3 child Ag

u-n-a³daniy-e³ʔi   nasgi-hno³ jani mils   j-u-do³ʔid-v
3 Pl be-orphaned repP   that and   john mills Pl 3 be-named exP

d-u-kti³d-e³ʔi   nasgi-hno d-akti²³y-v
Pl 3 take-care repP   that and   Pl take-care exP

u-dahil²³ido³²l-e³   nasgi james shavehead
3 file-custody-suit repP that   james shavehead

j-u-do³ʔid-v   u-wasv ale³ john littlebones
Pl 3 be-named exP   3 self   and john littlebones

di-²³hloh-di   ale³ a-dasehgogi⁴d-v ni³ʔ-u-lstan-e³ʔi
Pl lie-down Inf and 3 when-case exP Spec 3 happen recP

ade²³lv d-ise³hisd-oh-di u-do   u-hn-e³   a-gaguyv³danedi
money Pl draw Inst Inf 3 sister 3 give repP 3 fee

john mills diniyo⁴hli dikti⁴ya n-u-d-vhn-v⁴ʔi   ase-³hno
john mills children   custodian Spec 3 situation exP however

na²³gwu n-u-sgwa³lv⁴d-v   a-kuy-di⁴hi ji-d-u-we³nas-v   niga⁴dv
now   Spec 3 before-time exP 3 pay Inf Pst Pl 3 return exP all

nasgi igv³wasdi²³dani   ges-v   wi-d-u-³jv³s-e-³gwu   nasgi
that   remaining-situation be-exP Tr Pl 3 be-return repP just that

j-u-duktan-v⁴hi kohi-hno
Pst 3 judge exP now and

j-i-⁴gi nagwu nasgi john mills dvnajani chi-yos-e u³jati o⁴sdv
Rel be now   that   john mills dvnajani you/him much good
                                              call repP

u-datu^{3}g-v ni-g-alsdi^{3}h-a u-yohus-v^{23}hi-hno ji-ni-g-alsdi^{4}h-a
3 owe exP Spec 3 happen Pres 3 die exP and since Spec 3 happen Pres

na^{23}gwu w-u-da^{3}gonatd-v na?v gohu^{4}sdi u-wa^{23}hn-v
then Tr 3 extremely exP near something 3 related exP

eh-v u-tiya^{32}sdaneh-v ni-g-alsdi^{3}h-a une^{23}sda^{3}la u-wa^{23}sv
live exP 3 inherit exP Spec 3 happen Pres ice 3 self

ase^{3} j-u-lv^{23}hwisdaneh-di eh-v-^{4}hno ji-ni-g-alsdi^{4}h-a nagwu
must Pl 3 work Inf live exP and Rel Spec 3 happen Pres then

hi?a wi-ni-ji-^{23}w-e^{32}se^{3}h-a d-agi-na?-v gohweli
this Tr Spec 1 say Dat Pres Pl 1Pos exP paper

ka-nohes-g-i dvnajani
3 tell Prog Ag dvnajani

Syllabary

ᎫᏩᏲᎢ
ᎠᏅᏱ 18, 1900
ᎦᏬᏲᎩ ᏁᏩᏓ
ᎩᎾᎵᎢ

ᎧᎦᎵ 27 ᏦᏪᎳᏅᎯ ᎪᏪᎵ ᎠᎩᏞᎥ ᎢᎩ ᎯᎠᏊᏃ ᎤᏓᏥᏪᏏ ᎬᏯᏌᎢᎵᏰᎡᎲ ᎾᏍᎩ ᏄᏍᏛ ᏩᎩᎦᏛᏅᎢ James Shavehead Ꮀ ᏚᏙᎡ ᎠᏯᏏᏍᎩ ᎰᏎ ᎫᏌᏂ ᏓᏖᏑᎯ ᏥᎰᎡ ᎤᏲᎱᏎᎰ ᎠᎴ ᏧᏪᏥᏛᎯ ᎤᎾᏓᏂᏴᎢ ᎾᏍᎩᏃ ᏣᏂ Mills ᏧᏙᎢᏛ ᏚᎦᏘᎦᎢ ᎾᏍᎩᏃ ᏓᎦᏘᏰ ᎤᏓᎯᎵᏙᎴ ᎾᏍᎩ James Shavehead ᏧᏙᎢᏛ ᎤᏩᏒ ᎠᎴ ᎦᏚ ᏗᏌᏗ ᎠᎴ ᎠᏓᏎᎪᎩᏛ ᏂᎤᎵᏍᏔᏁᎢ ᎠᎦᏄ ᏗᏎᎯᏍᏙᏗ ᎤᏙ ᎤᏁ ᎠᎦᎫᏰᏓᏁᏗ John Mills ᏗᏂᏲᏟ ᏗᎦᏘᏯ ᏄᏛᏅᎢ ᎠᏎᏃ ᎾᏊ ᏄᏍᏆᏄᏛ ᎠᎫᏰᏗ ᏥᏚᏪᎾᎡ ᏂᎦᏛ ᎾᏍᎩ ᎢᎬᏩᏍᏗᏓᏂ ᎰᎡ ᏫᏚᏨᏎᏊ ᎾᏍᎩ ᏧᏚᎦᏔᏅᎯ ᎪᎯᏃ ᏥᎩ ᎾᏊ ᎾᏍᎩ John Mills ᏛᎾᏣᏂ ᏥᏲᏎ ᎤᏟᏘ ᎣᏍᏛ ᎤᏓᏚᎬ ᏂᎦᎵᏍᏗᎭ ᎤᏲᎱᏒᎯᏃ ᏥᏂᎦᎵᏍᏗᎭ ᎾᏊ ᏭᏓᎪᎾᏛᏛ ᎾᎥ ᎪᎱᏍᏗ ᎤᏩᏅ ᎡᎲ ᎤᏘᏯᏍᏓᏁᎲ ᏂᎦᎵᏍᏗᎭ ᎤᏁᏍᏓᎳ ᎤᏩᏒ ᎠᏎ ᏧᎸᏫᏍᏓᏁᏗ ᎡᎲᏃ ᏥᏂᎦᎵᏍᏗᎭ ᎾᏊ ᎯᎠ ᏫᏂᏥᏪᏎᎭ ᏓᎩᎾᎥ ᎪᏪᎵ ᎧᏃᎮᏍᎩ ᏛᎾᏣᏂ

English

Pryor Creek
March 18, 1900

I have in my possession your letter of February 27. I am going to tell you what I think in regard to what you have asked. Do you suppose that his name was James Shavehead?

Kvsani was reportedly a soldier during the war. Or did he die and leave his children as orphans, a man named John Mills took custody of them, and while in his custody this man named James Shavehead, an ex-soldier, took court action and won a judgment and an initial payment, and a check was made out to John Mills, a juvenile officer. However, before payment was made, the money was frozen, and the judgment was overturned. And now it turns out that this man, John Mills, whom you call Dvnajani, has a substantial sum of money owed to him, and since the records show that he is deceased, it is left up to a close relative to take action.

Since Ice is still living, he should be the one to take action. So I would advise him that I do have the necessary papers and that an initial payment of three dollars will be sufficient to begin the paperwork. Ask him to send that amount and include with it the documents showing the number and names of Dvnajani's children and the dates of their deaths. Also the number and names of Dvnajani's brothers and the dates of deaths for the ones who are dead. (Is Ice the only surviving brother?) Daloge lives here close by and would be a good informant concerning the history/obituary of Dvnajani. Ask Ice to complete all that he needs to do concerning what I mentioned about the initial payment and anything else that might remain to be done. I surely plan to use Daloge (ask for his assistance). Since there is evidence that this money exists, then a portion of it, thirty-five cents from each dollar, will be given to the collector as consignment for his work when we secure it. He was the one who made possible the disclosure of the money that is due James Shavehead for expenses incurred upon him.

Your friend,
John Littlebones

Reminiscence

Mose Killer

"Reminiscence" is a commentary on changes in the Cherokee way of life brought about by contact with Euro-Americans. In particular, the speaker laments what he considers to be an excessive preoccupation with deadlines. In "Reminiscence," Mose Killer recalls the Cherokee way of life when he was a child, and how the widespread use of the automobile has brought about major changes in the lives of Cherokees today. Linguistically, "Reminiscence" is interesting because of Killer's use of code switching at a number of places in the narrative. Code switching is widespread in bilingual communities throughout the world and is rule governed. "Reminiscence" reveals points at which Cherokee speakers can appropriately switch between Cherokee and English.

back	when	I	was	at	home
back	when	I	was	at	home
back	when	I	was	at	home

KⱠWƟⱠV	ⱠᏉ&	we	traveled	at	least
jojilawijido	jigehv	we	traveled	at	least
we churchgoers	when it was	we	traveled	at	least

a	good	3–5	miles	ᏤMᏏᏫ	ᏦhWƟᏖᏍ
a	good	3–5	miles	saluyigw	junilawsdi
a	good	3–5	miles	through the woods	to church

Sunday	mornings	AᏏZ	ⱠᎩ	cars	ⱠᏚᎩᏈ
Sunday	mornings	kohin	jig	cars	jidegih
Sunday	mornings	now	which it is	cars	we have cars

you	know	people	Ⴆ	DhꙨ⎰ꞖᏚ	ᏂhWꙨᏍᏗ
you	know	people	si	anina?liyoga	junilawsdi
you	know	people	still yet	they are lazy	to church

Ꝍ⎰Ꮍ⎰Ꮧ	and	back	we'd	go	visit
unedasdi	and	back	we'd	go	visit
to attend	and	back	we'd	go	visit

our	aunts	we'd	go	visit	our
our	aunts	we'd	go	visit	our
our	aunts	we'd	go	visit	our

uncles	and	they	lived	2–3 miles
uncles	and	they	lived	2–3 miles
uncles	and	they	lived	2–3 miles

away	RWᏠꙨ	AᏠZ	hꓬ	cars	Ꮪꓬꝛ
away	eldigw	kohin	jig	cars	degih
away	on foot	now	which it is	cars	we have

we	don't	even	think	about	going
we	don't	even	think	about	going
we	don't	even	think	about	going

over	there	and	it	takes	3–5
over	there	and	it	takes	3–5
over	there	and	it	takes	3–5

minutes	to	get	there	and	back
minutes	to	get	there	and	back
minutes	to	get	there	and	back

then	it	took	you	one	to
then	it	took	you	one	to
then	it	took	you	one	to

two	hours	to	walk	that	so
two	hours	to	walk	that	so
two	hours	to	walk	that	so

what	ᏂᎯᎾ	ᏱᎬᏯᏛᏛᏅ	what	has	happened
what	nihina	yigvyatvdvnh	what	has	happened
what	what about	if I asked you	what	has	happened

with	our	Cherokee	people
with	our	Cherokee	people
with	our	Cherokee	people

ᏍᎩᏃ	ᎠᏂᏲᏁᎦ	ᏄᎾᏍᏛ	the	influence	a
sgihno	aniyoneg	nunsdv	the	influence	a
because of	white people	how they are	the	influence	a

lot	of	it	ᎦᏣᏄᎵ	ᎠᏂᎩᏍᏗ	ᎨᏒ
lot	of	it	ganjanul	anigisdi	gesv
lot	of	it	fast	to walk	which is

ᏃᏊᎴ	ᏩᏥ	ᏂᎪᎯᎸ	ᎾᏅ	ᏂᏕᎩᏅᏅ	ᏩᏥ
nogwule	waji	nigohilv	nanv	nideginvnh	waj
also	watch	all of the time	look at	how we have them on	watch

you	know	this	is	what	runs
you	know	this	is	what	runs
you	know	this	is	what	runs

our	lives	anymore	ᎩᎳᏊᏅ	ᎢᏳᏍᏗ	I've
our	lives	anymore	kilagwun	iyusd	I've
our	lives	anymore	in just a while	a little	I've

got	to	go	ᏓᎬᏲᏎᎵ	ᏂᎴᏱᎩ	ᏍᎩ
got	to	go	dagvyosel	nileyig	sgi
got	to	go	I will tell you	or you	that

ᏂᏓᏍᎩᏪᏎᎵ	I have	got	to	go	and
nidasgiwesel	I have	got	to	go	and
you will tell me	I have	got	to	go	and

start something else five o'clock DCTGP ZⱭ it is time
start something else five o'clock ahliʔilohlv nogw it is time
start something else five o'clock when time comes when it is time

to go iⱭꙆZ DhⰂꙆS TEⱭ ꚒhM𑅇
to go vsgihno aniyoneg igvyi juniluhje
to go and that's white people at first when they arrived

DⱫBC DhBⵀⱭ DꙆ౸ ⱭꙆOⱴ TGⱭꚒ ShⰂL
ameyehl aniyvwiya anehv sginv iyusd dunihyohle
in the United Indians where they and like they brought
  States   live   that   with them

we did not sunup to sundown ⱭꚒSꙄWⴱ
we did not sunup to sundown yijuksatan
we did not sunup to sundown when it came up

OⱴV ⱭVꚒⵀⴳ ꚒSꝮⱭⱭLꙆꚒ ⰂR Oⴳ DLⴴhⱭⰂ
nvd yidojulehna digalvwsdanhdi gesv uhna adalenisge
sun when it rose to work it was there it would begin

ⱭꝮSⱣCOⱴ TAꙆL
yiwudelijahnv igohid
when it went down until

DBⱣOⱴ ⱭⱭ SOⱴLꚒⱭA ⱭꙆ TⰂGꙅꚒ ⰂⰂR
ayvhen sgwu gandadisgo sgi iyojadvne jigesv
now me also I remember that we would do it was

RꙆBⱭ ⰂChꙆ ⱭVⰂGꙅTS ⰂR Ɵi TKSLⱣ
svhiyey yojahnig yidojihwahtvhug gesv naʔv ijogadal
evening we would leave we would go to it was near we apart
    visit them

P RZⱭ TAꙆL ⱭⱱVL ⰂR they would
dlv svnoy igohid yiwojed gesv they would
somewhere midnight until we would go it was they would

just	sit	around	and	talk	ᏱᏚᏂᎦᏒᏍᏗ	ᏱᎩ
just	sit	around	and	talk	yiduniksvsdi	yig
just	sit	around	and	talk	or they would build fire	for example

ᏙᏑ	ᏚᏂᏖᏍᏛ	ᏗᏂᏲᏟᏅ	ᎾᎥ	ᏯᎾᏝᎢᏙ
dos	dunitesdv	diniyohlinv	na?v	yanatla?ido
mosquito	repelling	and the children	near	they would run around

ᏱᏓᎾᏁᎶᎲᏍᎦ	ᏒᏃᏱ	ᎢᏴ	ᏱᏛᎣᏣᏂᎩ	ᎨᏒ	ᎨᏍᏗ
yidananelohvsg	svnoy	iyv	yidv?ojahnnig	gesv	gesd
they would play around	midnight	then	we would start back	was	not

ᏩᏥ	ᏱᏙᎦᎦᏎᏍᏕ
waj	yidogaksesde
watch	we would not keep an eye on

Morpheme by Morpheme

back	when	I	was	at	home
back	when	I	was	at	home

j-oji-lawijido	ji-geh-v	we	traveled	at	least
Pl they-and-I attend-church	Rel be exP	we	traveled	at	least

a	good	3–5	miles	salu^{3}yi-gw	j-u-ni-laws-di
a	good	3–5	miles	woods just	Pl 3 Pl attend-church Inf

sunday	mornings	koh-in^{3}	j-ig	cars	j-id-e^{3}gih^{34}
sunday	mornings	now	Rel be	cars	Pl you Pl-and-I have

you	know	people	si^{3}	a-ni^{3}-na^{3}?liyo^{3}	j-u-n-laws-di^{3}
you	know	people	still-yet	3 Pl lazy	Pl 3 Pl attend-church Inf

u-n-edas-di^{3}	and	back	we would	go	visit
3 Pl attend	and	back	we would	go	visit

our   aunts   we'd   go   visit   our
our   aunts   we'd   go   visit   our

uncles   and   they   lived   2–3 miles
uncles   and   they   lived   2–3 miles

away   eldi-gw^3 kohi-n^3 j-ig   cars   d-e^{3}gih^{23}
away   on-foot just   now and   Rel be   cars   you Pl-and-I have

we   do not   even   think   about   going
we   do not   even   think   about   going

over   there   and   it   takes   3–5
over   there   and   it   takes   3–5

minutes   to   get   there   and   back
minutes   to   get   there   and   back

then   it   took   you   one   to
then   it   took   you   one   to

two   hours   to   walk   that   so
two   hours   to   walk   that   so

what   nihi^4-na   yi-gv^{23}y-a^{32}tv^{23}dvnh^{34} what   has   happened
what   you what-about   nonF I/you-all ask   what   has   happened

with   our   cherokee   people
with   our   cherokee   people

sgihno   a-ni-yo^{3}neg   nunsdv   the   influence   a
because-of and   3 Pl white   as-they-be   the   influence   a

lot   of   it   ga-n-janul^{23} a^{23}-ni^3-gi^{4}s-di   ges-v^3
lot   of   it   3 Pl fast   3 Pl pace Inf   be exP

no^{23}gwu^{3}le^3 wa^{23}ji   nigo^{23}hi^{3}lv   na^{3}nhv^3 nide^{23}gi^{3}nvnh   waj^{23}
also   watch   always   look   Spec Pl how we-and-   watch
   they have-on and

you know this is what runs
you know this is what runs

our lives anymore kilagwu-n^3 i^{3}yusd^{34} I've
our lives anymore right-away and a-little I've

got to go da-gv^{23}y-o^{32}sel^{23} ni-le^3-yig sgi^3
got to go Fut I/you tell you-or that

ni-da-sgi^3-wes-el^{23} I have got to go and
Spec Fut you-me tell Dat I have got to go and

start something else five o'clock a-hli^{3}ʔilo^{23}hl-v
start something else five o'clock 3 time-come exP

nogwu^{23} it is time
when it is time

to go vsgi-hno^3 a-ni-yo^{3}neg igvyi j-u-ni^3-luhj-e
to go that and 3 Pl white-people at-first Rel 3 Pl arrive repP

ame^{3}yehl^3 a-ni-yvwi-ya a-neh-v sgin-v^3 iyusd^{23} d-u-ni-hyo^{23}hl-e^3
in-the-u.s. 3 Pl person pure 3 live that-and like Pl 3 Pl bring-along
                                    exP   repP

we did not sunup to sundown yi-j-u^{23}-ksatan
we did not sunup to sundown nonF when 3 come-up

nvd yi-do-j-u^{23}-le^{4}hn-a di-ga-lv^{23}wsdanh-di ges-v^3
sun nonF Dst when 3 face recP Pl 3 work Inf be exP

uhna^3 a-da-leni^{23}s-g-e yi-w-u^{23}-delijahn-v^3 i^{23}go^{3}hid^{34}
there 3 Refl begin Prog repP nonF Tr 3 go-down exP until

ayv^3-hen^{23} sgwu^3 ga-ndadi^{32}s-g-o^3 sgi^3
I now also 1 remember Prog Hab that

iy-o^{3}j-advn-e^{34}	ji-ges-v^{3}	svhiyey^{23}
nonF 1Pl do repP	Pst be exP	evening

y-oj-a^{23}hnig^{3}	yi-d-oji-hwahtvhug^{32}	ges-v^{3}	na?v^{3}	ij-o^{3}gadal^{3}
nonF we/they leave	nonF Pl they-and-I go-visit	be exP	near	youPl-and-I apart

dlv^{3}	svnoy^{23}	i^{23}go^{3}hid^{34}	yi-w-oj-ed^{23}	ges-v^{3}	they would
somewhere	midnight	until	nonF Tr 1Pl go	be exP	they would

just	sit	around	and	talk	yi-d-u^{3}-n-iksv^{23}sdi^{3}	y-igi
just	sit	around	and	talk	nonF Pl 3 Pl build-fire	nonF or

dos	d-u-ni-te^{3}sd-v	di-ni-yo^{23}hli-nv^{3}	na?v^{3}	y-a^{3}-n-atla^{3}?-id-o^{3}
mosquito	Pl 3 Pl repel exP	Pl Pl child and	near	nonF 3 Pl run around Hab

yi-d-a^{3}-n-a^{3}-nelo^{23}hvsg^{3}	svnoy^{23}	iyv^{3}	yi-dv^{3}?-oj-a^{23}hnig^{3}
nonF Pl 3 Pl play-around	midnight	then	nonF Dst 1Pl return

ges-v	gesd	waj^{23}	yi-d-o^{23}g-a^{3}ksesde
be exP	not	watch	nonF Pl they-and-I watch

Syllabary

Back when I was at home ᏦᏥᎳᏫᏥᏙ ᏥᎨᏐ we traveled at least a good 3–5 miles ᏌᎷᏱᏉ ᏧᏂᎳᏫᏍᏗ Sunday mornings ᎪᎯᏃ ᏥᎩ cars ᏥᎦᎩᏘ you know people Ꮟ ᎠᏂᎾᎵᏲᎦ ᏧᏂᎳᏫᏍᏗ ᎤᏁᏓᏍᏗ and back we'd go visit our aunts we'd go visit our uncles and they lived 2–3 miles away ᎡᎳᏗᏉ ᎪᎯᏃ ᏥᎩ cars ᎦᎩᏘ we don't even think about going over there and it takes 3–5 minutes to get there and back then it took you one to two hours to walk that so what ᏂᎯᎾ ᏱᎬᏯᏛᏛᏖ what has happened with our Cherokee people ᏍᎩᏃ ᎠᏂᏲᏁᎦ ᏄᎾᏍᏛ the influence a lot of it ᎦᏟᏄᎵ ᎠᏂᎩᏍᏗ ᎨᏒ ᏃᏉᏍᏅ ᏣᏥ ᏂᎪᎯᏄ ᎾᎤ ᏂᎦᎩᎤᏖ ᏣᏥ you know this is what runs our lives anymore ᎩᎳᏉᎤ ᎢᏳᏍᏗ I've got to go ᏓᎬᏲᏎᎵ ᏂᏅᏱᎩ ᏍᎩ ᏂᏓᏍᎩᏬᏎᎵ I have got to go and start something else five o'clock ᎠᏟᎢᎶᏢ ᏃᏉ it is time to go ᎢᏍᎩᏃ ᎠᏂᏲᏁᎦ ᎢᎬᏱ ᏧᏂᎷᏤ ᎠᏜᏰᏟ ᎠᏂᏴᏫᏯ ᎠᏁᏐ ᏍᎩᎤ ᎢᏳᏍᏗ ᏚᏂᏲᏓ we did not sunup to sundown ᏱᏧᎦᏌᏔᎾ ᎤᏙ ᏱᏙᏧᏅᏖ ᏗᎦᏄᏫᏍᏓᏁᏗ ᎨᏒ ᎤᏖ ᎠᏓᏅᏂᏍᎨ ᏱᏭᎦᎵᏟᎤ ᎢᎪᎯᏓ ᎠᏰᎵᎤ ᏍᏉ ᎦᎤᏓᏗᏍᎪ ᏍᎩ ᎢᏲᏟᏛᏁ ᏥᎨᏒ

RᎯᏰᏉ ᏂᏣᏂᎩ ᏉᎶᏂᏀᎪᎵᏒ ᏨᎡ ᎤᎥ ᎢᏍᏂ᏶ Ꮅ ᏒᏃᏉ ᎢᎪᏭᏞ ᏉᏫᏴᏞ ᏨᎡ they
would just sit around and talk ᏉᏍᏂᏍᏒᎣᎫ ᏉᎩ ᏪᏫ ᏍᏂᏞᎣᏁ ᏛᏂᏂᏥᎥ ᏕᎥ ᏁᏫᏞᏘᏫ
ᏉᏞᏫᎠᎬᎫᏫᏍ ᏒᏃᏉ ᎢᏰ ᏉᏁᎲᏣᏂᎩ ᏨᎡ ᎢᎣᎫ ᏣᏨ ᏉᏪᏍᏍ4ᏫᏍ

English

Back when I was at home, when we used to attend church, we traveled at least a good three to five miles through the woods to church on Sunday mornings. Now that we have cars, you know, people are still too lazy to attend church. And back then we'd go visit our aunts, we'd go visit our uncles, and they lived probably two to three miles away. Now we have cars, and we don't even think about going over there, and it takes about three to five minutes to get there and back. Then, it took you one to two hours to walk that. So, what about you, I'm asking you, what has happened with our Cherokee people?

A lot of it has to do with the white man's influence. The everyday fast pace—and these watches—you know this is what runs our lives anymore. In a little while I am going to tell you I've got to go, or you are going to tell me that. I've got to go and start on something else. When five o'clock comes, it's time to go. That's what the white man has brought to the Indians of America. We didn't have anything like that. Our ancestors didn't. Sunup to sundown; when the sun came up, the work began until it went down.

I also remember we used to go and visit our neighbors. We'd go in the evening and stay until late at night. They would just sit around and visit and maybe build a fire to make some smoke to repel the mosquitoes, and the children would play around, and then when we thought it was getting late, we would come home. We didn't have our eyes on our watches.

Interview with Wilbur Sequoyah

Durbin Feeling

"Interview with Wilbur Sequoyah" is a dialogue between Durbin Feeling, who uses a Western Cherokee dialect, and Charles Wilbur Sequoyah, who uses the Eastern Cherokee dialect. This dialogue took place at the Cherokee Nation offices near Tahlequah, Oklahoma.

Durbin:

ᎠᏍᏏᎥᏃ	ᏍᏏᎵ	ᏩᏍᎪᎯᏍᎾᎠ
kohigahno	duninhdi	talsgohineka?
today is	October	tenth isn't it?

Wilbur:

i

v

yes

Durbin:

ᏩᎵᏍᎣᎯᏍᎵ	ᏠᏍᏪᏍ	ᏔᏍᎣᎯᏍᏍᏫ	ᏍᏬᏍᎣᎯ	ᏩᎵ
talsgohine	sohneladu	isgohitsgwi	nelsgo	ta?li
tenth	nineteen	hundred	eighty	two

ᎤᏍᏣᏪᎤᏓᎡ	ᏣᏩᏯ	ᎤᏍᏪᏔ	ᎠᏍᎵ	ᎠᏍᎵᎥ
udetiyvsadisv	jalag	uweti	aneh	anedoh
the year of	Cherokee	old	dweller	they are here

DhWⱤᏇ	SⱢGᏙ	ᏚVT	ᎻᏫ
anitaʔliha	galhjaʔdi	judoʔid	sagwu
two of them	"Bo"	he is named	one

Wilbur:

DⱢGVⱭᏧᏍᏱ
alhjadohvsgi
a preacher

Durbin:

DⱢGVⱭᏧᏍᎩ	ᎿᎫZ	SV	ᎠGV
alhjadohvsg	nihinh	gado	dejadoʔ
a preacher	and you	what	you are named

Wilbur:

ᎾⱢH	ᏏᏉᏯᏙ
wilimi	sigwoyi
Wilbur	Sequoyah

Durbin:

ᎾⱢ	ᏏᏉᎿ
wil	sigwoyi
Wil	Sequoyah

Wilbur:

ᎾⱢH
wilimi
Wilbur

Durbin:

ᎾⱢH
wilimi
Wilbur

Wilbur:

DEᏉZ	ꮀᏑᏚ	OʻhᏛᎢꭲᏱ	charles	wilbur
agvyino	yoneg	uhne?isd	charles	wilbur
first	white person	language	Charles	Wilbur

ᏏᏫᎥᏉ	ᏝᎡᏙ	ꭲᏯᏰ	DᏰᏈ	ᏝᎡᏙꭲᏛ
sequoyah	dagwado	sgina	ayelh	dagwadosdv
Sequoyah	I am named	that	middle	what I am named

ꭵ	TS	ꭲᏯᏰhꭲA	ᏰᏈH	EᏫᎥ4ꭵ
ji	iga	vkiyanisgo	wilimi	gvgwoseho
more	of	I am called by	Wilbur	they call me

Durbin:

ᏍᏯᏗ	B	ꭲᏛᎷᏙ	ᏍᏚᏔꭵᎲ
hilahv	yv	sdiluhje	ogalahoma
when	time	you arrived	Oklahoma

Wilbur:

ᎳᏈᎲ	ꮼR	ᎢᏀ	ꭵꭵᏗ
taliha	nuhsv	iyu	jigehv
two of them	days	then	when it was

OʻᏗR	4ᏑW	ᎢᏀ	ᎢᏀᏀhꮼ
uhsv	sohnel	iyu	iyuwahnilv
at night	nine	about	o'clock

Durbin:

ᏍAᏗ	RꭲᎷᏀᏒᎲᏙ
gagohv	esdiwahtvhido?
who	you two are visiting?

Wilbur:

DᏰZ	ꭵR	DhᏰᏰꭲ	hᏍᏙᏫᎥ	ᏍꭵᏀᏒᎲᏙ
ayhno	gesv	aniyvwiya	nigadogw	dejiwahtvhido
as for me	which	Indians	just everyone	I am visiting them

ᏂᎫᏍᏬᎥᏗ   Ꭿ   ᎠᎬᏵ   ᎩᏗ   ᏀᎥ
ndigalsdohdi   hi?   agvyi   kil   gedo?
because   this   for the first   time   I am here

ᎠᏲᏂ   ᎤᏍᏪᎯᏛ   ᎤᎲᏬᏫᎠ   ᎠᎢᎶᏍᎤ   Ꭿ
ahan   ogalahoma   utsgwiya   aktvganv   hi
here   Oklahoma   much   I have heard   this

ᏍᏯᏁ   Ꮿ   ᏣᎳᎩ   ᏁᏁ   ᏝᏂ
sgina   ha   jalag   nana   han
that   [hesitation]   Cherokee   there   here

ᎤᏬᏗ   ᏂᏓᏳᏂᎶᏒ   ᎠᏁᎲ   ᏍᎩᎬ   ᎠᎩᎧᏛᏂᏙᎭ
uweti   ndayunilohsv   anehv   sgigw   agikdvnidoha
old place   they came from   those living here   just that   I am checking

ᏄᏅᎭᏕᎬ   ᏃᎵ   ᏔᏳᎥᏗ   i   ᏔᏳᎥᏗ
nundvhnadegv   nole   iyuhsd   v   iyuhsd
how they are   and   what   uh   what

ᏄᏅᎭᏕᎬ   ᏍᏯᏁ   ᏁᏔ   ᏗᏂᏁᎩᎸ   ᏗᏂᏁᎸ
nundvhnadegv   sgina   nahna   aninegilv   aninelv
how they are   that   and those   who live   those who live

ᏒᏙᏓᎬᏓ   ᏔᏳᎥᏗ   ᏁᏅᎮᎵᏙᎲ   ᏍᏯᏍ   ᏚᎵᏍᎯᎥᏓᎬ
dudodagwvd   iyuhsd   nandvnelidohv   sgino   judalehnvdagw
daily   what   their activities   and that   just different things

ᏍᏱ   ᏔᎬᏩᎵᏍᏬᎤᎵ   ᏍᏟᏩ   ᏈᏂᎬᏁᎵ   Ꭿ   ᏈᏂᏥᏫ
sgi   igvwalstanvda   sgwala   yinigvnel   hi?   yinjiwi
that   etcetera   short   if you made it   this   I would say

ᏔᏳᎥᏗ   ᏄᏅᎭᏕᎬ   i   ᏚᏙᏓᎬᏙ   i
iyuhsd   nundvhnadegv   v   judodagwvd   v
what   how they are   uh   daily   uh

DhᏮᏁᎤ   DᎾTR   TS   ᏚᏞᏍᎤᎶ   ZᏍ   i
aninelv   ana?ihsv   iga   judlehnvd   nowle   v
they live they walk   daily   different things   and   uh

ᏚhWᎾᏍᎫ   ᏑᎴ   ᏍᎤ   BᎾ   TGᏍᎫ
junilawisdi   geho   sgwu   yvw   iyuhsd
church   included   also   people   what

hᎴSᎶᏁᏍ   ᏍᎩ   hᏚ   TEGᏞᏍWᎤᎶ   ZᏍ
nigegadvhnehv   sgi   nigad   igvwalstanvd   nowle
being done for them   that   all   etcetera   and

i   ᎧZᏁ   ᏑᎴ   ᏍᎾᎶᎩ   ᎤᏍᎤ
v   kanohed   geso   yanhtvgi   osd
uh   news   included   if they here   good

ᎧZᏁ   ᏯᎩ   ᏍᎩᎾ   Ꭽ   ᏍᎩᎾ
kanohed   yig   sgina   ha   sgina
news   if it is   that   [hesitation]   that

Ꭽ   ᏯEGᏞᏍWᎤᎶ   ᏍᎩᏫ   GᏍᎫ   ᎭᏯᎧᎶhV   DB
ha   yigvwalstanvd   sgiw   yuhsd   hagikdvhnido   ay
interjection   and so forth   just that   what   I am checking on   me

Durbin:

SᏚᎶᏛDᎴ   i   DᎭh   ZᏍ   ᏚᏉᎤR
dudalehna?ake   v   ahan   nole   dijenvsv?
is there a difference   uh   here   and   where you come from

Wilbur:

iᏔZ   Ꮧ   TS   ᏍᎩᎾ   BᎾ   ᏓᏍᎫ
vhnahno   ji   iga   sgina   yvw   nuhsd
there yes   more   quantity   that   people   is

ᎤᎾhᏯᏍᎫ   ᏑR   G   ᏔᏍ   ᎾᏍᏯh
unanigisdi   gesv   ja   dale   nasgin
that path   gesv   no   different   but that

i	TG∞Ꮢ	i	VᏒ	G∞ᏒZ	Bↄ		∞ᎩꝊ
v	iyuhsd	v	dodi	yuhsdhno	yvda		sgina
uh	that	uh	what	it is	one would say		that

ᏒᏛ	RᏒ∞Ꮢ	i	hSↄ	Ꝋ&ↄ	Ꮎ
dige	elisd	v	nigad	gehv	na
not	supposedly	uh	all	which	that

O·∞Ꮢ	iG	Ꮖ	ᏙSↄ↺Ꝝ
uhsd	vja	hi?	yidudaleha
that	no	this	no difference

∞ᎩᏍ	TS	hᏛSꝟᏁ&
sgiw	iga	nigegadvhnehv
just that	quantity	being done for them

hSSᏒZᏒᏒV&	O·R	TS	EᏒ↺O·ↄ
jidegalnoheldohv	uhsv	ig	gvgwalenvda
my conversation	yesterday	noon	since

i	∞ᏒᎩↄZ	TSↄ	Ꝋ∞Ꮢ	i	TG∞Ꮢ
v	sdikidno	igad	gesd	v	iyusdi
uh	and a little	all	not	uh	that

TꝊSꝟᏁᏒ	hꝊSꝟᏁ		TG∞Ꮢ	∞hᎩD
igegadvhnehd	nigegadvhne		iyuhsd	yanigi?a
to be done for them	not being done for them		that	they are not getting

TSↄ	Ꮩb	ꝗꝊꝟO·Ꮖ	Z↺
igad	ohsi	nundvhvnh	nole
some	fair	they are	and also

TSↄ	O·ᏒT	ꝗꝊꝟO·	SꝟᎩD
igad	uyo?i	nundvhnv	gatvgi?a
some	poorly	they are	I am hearing

∞ᎩZ	hSᏒ	Ꝋ∞Ꮢ	DB	ᏙAᏒS
sgihno	jigadi	gesd	ay	yigolihga
and so	as I say	not	I	I not understand

Ꮟ	ᎠᏋᏌᏃ	ᏗᏥᎦᏙᎵ	ᏯᏋᏔᏁ	ᏱᏥᎦᏔᎮ
si	agwvhsano	dijigatol	yahktan	yijigahtahe
yet	and I myself	my eyes	if I use	I would know

ᎢᎤᏍᏗ	Ꭵ	ᏗᏓᎴᏂᏍᎬ	ᎨᎵ
iyuhsd	v	didalenisgv	geli
that	uh	the origin of	I think

Ꮟ	ᎢᎦᏓ	ᎨᏍᏗ	ᏰᎵ	Ꭵ	ᎠᏂᏐ
si	igad	gesd	yeli	v	aniso
set	some	not	able	uh	others

ᏄᎾᏍᏛ	ᎢᎦ	ᏯᏂᎩ	ᎢᏳᏍᏗ
nunhsdv	iga	yanigi	iyuhsd
condition	that much	not receiving	that

ᎤᏂᎩᏍᏗ	ᎨᏒ	ᎤᎾᎵᏍᏕᎸᏙᏗ	ᎨᏒᎢ
unigisd	gesv	unalhsdelhdodi	gesv?i
for them to receive	which	their livelihood	which

ᏓᏂᏁᎩᎸ	ᎤᏲ	ᏄᎾᏛᏅ	ᎠᎾᏗᏍᎪ	Ꭿ
daninegilv	uyo	nundvnv	andihsgo	hi?
where they live	had	their condition	they say	this

Ꮲ	ᎢᏅᎯ	ᎨᏒ	ᎠᏙ	ᏗᎨᏒ
dlv	invhi	gesv	adoh	digesv
somewhere	far away	which is	in the words	there

ᎢᏴ	ᏗᏂᏁᎵ	ᎨᏒ	ᎡᏍᎦᏊ	Ꭿ
iyv	dinineli	gesv	esgagwu	hi
distance	dweller	which	not as	much

ᎡᏍᎦᏂ	ᏗᏂᏁᎵ	ᎦᏚᎲ	ᎾᎥᏂᎨ	ᏱᎩ
esgahni	dininel	gaduhv	na?vhnige	yigi
nearby	dweller	from	closer	if it is

ᎢᏳᏍᏗ	ᎦᏛᎩ	ᎥᏣᏃ	ᏱᏥᎦᏔ	ᏍᎩᎾ	Ꭽ
iyuhsd	gatvgi	vjano	yijigahta	sgina	ha
that	I am hearing	and not	I don’t know	that	[hesitation]

ᎤᏥᏘᏯ	ᎠᏆᏓᎴᏤᎭ	Ꭵ	ᏙᏂᏳᏍᏗ	ᎠᏓᎴᏂᎭ
utsgwiya	agwadalecheha	v	doniyuhsdi	adaleniha
much	it is confusing me	uh	so what	it beginning

ᏍᎩᎾ	ᎤᏲ	ᎢᏂᏗᎬᏩᎾᏛᏅᏕᎩ	ᎢᏴ	ᏃᎴ
sgina	uyo	indigvwandvhnadeg	iyv	nole
that	bad	poor condition	there	and

ᎮᏍᎦᏂᎨᏩ	ᏕᏥᎪᏩᏘᏍᎬ	ᎣᏏᏇ	ᎢᏳᏍᏗ	ᏄᎾᏛᎾᏕᎬ	ᎢᎨᎵ
hesganigehv	dejigowhtisgv	ohsigw	iyusd	nundvnadegv	igeli
nearer	that I see	fair	kind	they are getting along	I think

ᎤᏥᏘᏯᏃ	ᏔᎵᎭ	ᏄᎾᏓᎴ	ᏄᏂᏍ ᏄᏂᏍᏗ	ᎾᏆᎵᏍᏓᏁ
utsgwiyano	talaha	nundale	nuns-nunsd	nagwalsdahne
too much	two	different	[false start]	it seems to me

Durbin:

ᎳᏍᎪ	ᏍᎩ	ᏱᏄᏍᏗ	Ꭵ	ᏗᏤᏅᏒ
hlasgo	sgi	yinusd	v	dijenvsv?
not	same	situation	uh	where you are from

Wilbur:

Ꭵ	ᎥᏣᏃ	ᏍᎩᎦ	ᎠᏩᏓᎴᏅᏤᎮᏃ
v	vjano	sgiga	awdalecheheno
uh	no	that much	it is confusing me

Ꭵ	ᎠᏴ	ᏍᎩᎾ	ᏗᎦᎳᏫᏍᏗ	ᏗᏥᎳᏫᎩ	ᎯᎩ
v	ay	sgina	digalawisdi	dijilawig	higi
uh	I	that	council	counselor	I am

Ꭵ	ᎣᏣᏁᎳᏗᏍᎪ	ᏂᎦᏓ	ᏂᎬ	ᏍᎩᎾ
v	ojanelhdihsgo	nigad	nikv	sgina
uh	we try	all	all around	that

ᏙᏣᎦᏎᏍᏙᏔᏂᏓᏍᏗ	ᎤᏲᎢ	ᏱᏄᏛᎾ	ᏍᎩᎾ
dojaksesdohtanidasde	uyo?i	yinudvna	sgina
to watch over them	bad	in position	that

ᏬᏥᏃᎮᏍᎪ	Ꭵ	ᎠᏂᏩᏥᎾ	ᏚᎾᏓᏁᎸ	ᏚᎾᏙᎵᏒᎢ
wojinohehsgo	v	aniwajin	dundanelv	programs
we go and report it	uh	government	provision	programs

ᎦᎵᏐᏕ	ᏗᎾᏁᏍᎨᏍᎩ	ᎪᏍᏞ	social	service	ᏱᎩ
galsode	dinahnesgesgi	gosdle	social	service	yigi
house	builders	something	social	service	or

ᎠᏘᏗ	ᏥᎩ	ᏍᎩᎾ	ᎭᏂ	ᎬᏂᎨᏒ	ᏂᏙᏨᏁᎰ
atdi	jigi	sgina	han	kvnigehsv	ndojvneho
to say	when	that	here	to be known	to them

ᎣᏣᏁᎸᏗᏍᎪ	ᏍᎩᏃ	Ꭿ	ᏑᏓᎴᎩ	ᏥᎦᏗ
ojanelhdisgo	sgihno	hiʔ	sudaleg	jigadi
we try	and that	this	one thing	which I

ᎠᏴ	ᏄᎾᏛᏅ	ᎨᏍᏗ	Ꭺ	ᏯᏂᎩ
ay	nundvhnv	gesd	go	yanigiʔ
I	condition	not	something	they are not getting

Ꭽ	ᎭᎾᏗᎠ	ᎬᏉᏎ	ᎢᎦᏓ	ᎭᏂᏃᎮᏍᎬ
ha	handiʔa	gvgwose	igad	haninohesgv
[hesitation]	they say	say to me	some	they talk about

ᎨᏍᏗ	ᏱᎨᎦᏊᏎᏍᏓᏁᏍᎪ	ᏙᏳ	ᎤᏲᎢ	ᏄᎾᏛᏏ
gesd	yigegaksesdanesgo	doyu	uyoʔi	nundvhna
not	paid attention to	really	bad	their condition

ᎭᎾᏗ	ᎨᏍᏗᏃ	ᏱᏥᎪᏩᏓ	Ꭵ	ᏱᎪᎵᎦ	ᏍᎩᎾ	ᎭᏂ
handi	gesdno	yijigowd	v	yigolihga	sgina	hani
they say	and not	I did not see	uh	I don’t understand	that	here

Ꭿ	Ꭵ	ᏗᏂᎳᏫᎩ	ᎤᎾᏚᏓᎵ	ᏧᎾᏤᎵ
hiʔ	v	dinilawig	undudal	junjeli
this	uh	council members	they are responsible	their people

ᎬᏩᏑᏯᎩᏗ	ᎨᎲ	ᏓᏁᎲ
gvwsuyagid	gehv	danehv
elected by them	which is where	they live

ᏍᎦᏚᎩ	ᏕᎪᏒᏩᏗᏒᎢ	ᏧᎾᎦᏎᏍᏙᏗ
sgadug	degohsvhwadisv?i	junaksesdohdi
country	establishments	to look after

Durbin:

ᏍᎩᏗᏙ	ᏄᏍdi	i	ᏂᏗᎦᎵᏍᏙᏗᏍᎬᏃ	ᏍᏊ
sgidido	nusd	v	ndigalsdohdisgvhno	sgwu
that really	it is	uh	because and	also

i	ᎦᏲᎵ	ᎨᏒ	ᏱᎧᏃᎮᎵ	ᎥᏍᎩ	ᏣᎳᎩ
v	gayohli	gesv	yikanohelh	vsg	jalag
uh	some	which is	if you tell	that	Cherokee

ᎠᏂᏬᏂᏍᎩ	ᎨᏒ	Ꮎ	ᏣᎳᎩ	ᎤᏂᏬᏂᎯᏍᏗ
aniwonisgi	gesv	na	jalag	uniwonihisd
speakers	which are	that	Cherokee	their speech

ᎤᏂᎭ	ᏍᎩᏳᏍᏗ	ᎠᏂᏬᏂᏍᎩ	ᎤᏏᏴ	ᏂᏧᎾᏛᏏ	Ꮎ
unih	sgiyusd	aniwonisg	uhnayv	njundvnh	na
they have	that kind	speakers	out there	they are	that

ᏌᎷᏱᏴ	ᎠᏙᎯᏴ	i	ᏝᏃ	ᏳᎾᏚᎵᏍᎪ	ᏕᎦᏚᎲ
saluyiyv	adohiyv	v	hlahno	yundulisgo	degaduhv
woods	forest	uh	and not	they want	in town

ᏂᏙᏓᏳᎾᏛᏁᏙᏗ	i	ᏍᎩᏃ	ᏣᎳᎩ	ᎠᏂᏬᏂᏍᎩ
ndodayundvnhdohdi	v	sgino	jalag	aniwonisg
to come to	uh	that	Cherokee	speakers

Ꮩ	ᎠᏂᏣᎳᎩ	ᎨᏒ	ᎠᎭᏂᏃ	ᏚᏂᎸᏫᏍᏓᏁ
do	anijalagi	gesv	ahanihno	dunilvwsdaneh
real	Cherokees	which is	and here	they are employed

ᎤᏟ	ᎢᎦ	ᎠᏂᏲᏁᎦ	i	ᏍᎩᏃ	ᏍᏗᎩᏓ	ᏓᎾᏓᎴᎪ	ᏳᏍᏗ
udli	iga	aniyoneg	v	sgihno	sdikid	dandalego	yusd
more	amount	whites	uh	and that	a little	don’t agree	kind of

Wilbur:

VOᴕᏌGꙍᏒ	ᏗᏝᏍhᏫ	ꙍᏴᎾ	ꙍꙍᏝ	Ꮻh	RꙍSZ
donhiyusd	didaleniha? [ok]	sgina	osd	han	esganh
what	it begins	that	good	here	nearer

ᎾihᏝ	DhᏠᎩᏢ	ꙍb	GꙍᏒ	ꝙꙍᎷᴕ
na?vnige	aninegili	ohsi	yusd	nundvhvn?
nearer	dweller	fair	kind	they are

OᴕVG	ᏗᎾᏠ4ꙍᎩ	ᏕAꙍꙭ	TSᏝ	KꙍᏝ	ᏝhᏠᎩᏢ
udoyu	dinahnesesg	degoshv	igad	josd	daninegil
really	builders	exits	some	good	their homes

Oᴕ	ꙍᎩᎾ	T		ᏠG	ᎾhSMEᎾ	hᎩ	ꙍᎩᎾ
v	sgina	i		hiyu	wingaluhgvn	jig	sgin
uh	that	[hesitation]		there	arrived	has not	that

ᎾᏒᏝᏕᏠꙍᏝᏒ	OᴕᎾ	TBT
widigeganehsgehdi	una	iyv?
to be built for	there	degree of distance

Durbin:

i	TSᏝᎶ	ꙍꙭ	DhGWᎩ	hᎩ	ꙍꙭ	Ꮅ
v	igadadv	sgwu	anijalagi	jig	sgwu	hla
uh	some	also	Cherokees	which are	also	not

GᎾSᏢꙍA	Ꮅ	i	Ꮅ	GᎾSᏢ
yundulisgo	hla	v	hla	yunduli
they want	not	uh	not	they want

Wilbur:

DhᎾᏰꙍE
aninayesgv?
they fear

Durbin:

ᎥᏂ	ᏍᎩ
vhv	sgi
yes	that is it

Wilbur:

ᏣᏍᎪᏃ	ᏯᏁᎭ	ᎩᎶ	ᏗᏂᎳᏫᎩ	ᎣᏍᏓ	ᏫᏗᎬᏩᏃᏏᏐᏗ
chasgon	yaneha	kilo	dinilawig	ohsd	widigvwanosisohd
isn't there	living	someone	council	good	to explain

Durbin:

ᎩᎳᏃ	ᏍᎩᏴ	ᎣᏣᎯᎵᏙ	ᏓᏲᏣᎴᏅ	ᏍᎩ
kilahno	sgiyv	ojihilidoh	dayojalenv	sgi
just now	that	we are doing	we are going to	that

ᏃᏣᏛᏁᏂ	ᎣᏥᏃᎮᎵᏙᏂ	Ꮎ	Ꭵ	ᎥᏍᎩ
noja?advnehv	ojihnohehlidohv	na	v	vsgi
we are doing	reporting things	that	uh	that

ᎢᎬᏩᎵᏍᏙᏗ	ᎨᏒ	ᏍᏗᎯᏓᏃ	ᎣᎩᏍᎦᏃᎵ
igvwalsdohdi	gesv	sdihidhno	ogisganol
to happen	which	a little	we are slow

Wilbur:

i	what means	speech	not	I do not know	how to say it
v	what means	speech	not	I do not know	how to say it
yes	what means	speech	not	I do not know	how to say it

ᏳᏁᎦ	ᎤᏤᎵ	ᏓᎦᏙᎵᏏ	i	breakdown	communication	ᎢᏳᏍᏗ
yuneg	ujeli	dagatolsi	v	breakdown	communication	iyuhsd
what means	I am	going to borrow	uh	breakdown	communication	kind

ᎾᏆᎵᏍᏓᏁ	ᏍᎩ	Ꭿ
nagwalsdahne	sgina	hi
it seems before	that	this

Durbin:

ᏍᎩᏃ	i	ᏗᏓᎴᏅᎢᏍᏗ	ᎨᏒ	Ꮎ	i	ᏛᏟᏃᎮᏟᏙᎲ
sgihno	v	didalehnv?isdi	gesv	na	v	dvhlinohehlidohv
and that	uh	to differ	which	that	uh	in communication

ᏍᎩᎾ	ᎤᏟ	ᎢᎦ
sgina	udli	iga
that	much	more

Wilbur:

ᎠᏎᏃᎨ	ᎢᏥᎯᎵ	ᏍᎩᎾ	ᎣᏍᏓ	ᎢᏨᏁᏗ
asenoge	ijihili	sgina	ohsd	ijvnhdi?
but	you are continuing	that	good	to do

Durbin:

i	ᎣᏥᎯᎵᏛ
v	ojihi?lidv
yes	we are working toward it

Wilbur:

ᏔᎵᎭ	ᎾᏕᏘᏴ	ᏃᎴ	ᎡᎵᏍᏗ	ᏰᎵᏫ	ᏍᏗᎩᏓ
ta?liha	nadetiyv	nowle	elisd	yeliw	sdikid
two	years from now	I	suppose	possible	a little

ᎣᏍᏛ	ᎢᏳᎵᏍᏔᏂᏓ	ᎨᎮᏍᏗ
ohsdv	iyulstanid	gehesd?
good	become	it will be

Durbin:

i	about	five	maybe
v	about	five	maybe
yes	about	five	maybe

Wilbur:

maybe	never	ᏂᏗᎦᎵᏍᏙᏗᏂ	ᎠᏕᎳ	ᎧᏂᎦᏗ	ᏍᏭᏅ
maybe	never	ndigalsdohdihv	adel	kanigadi	sgwuhnv
maybe	never	because	money	lacking	and also

ᎠᏎ	ᎡᎳᏗ	ᏁᏨᏁ	ᎠᏕᎳ
ase	elad	nejvhne	adel?
probably	lowered	they are lowering	your budget

Durbin:

ᎢᎸᏍᎩᏛ	ᎢᏯᏂ	ᏕᎨᏥᏲᏌ	ᏚᏂᎸᏫᏍᏓᏁᎲ	ᎠᎭᏂ
ilvsgidv	iyani	degejiyos	dunilvwisdanehv	ahan
a few	of them	released	their working	here

ᎯᎠᏭ	ᏏᏅᏓ	ᏔᎵ	ᎢᏅᏓ	ᏥᎨᏒ
hi?agw	sinvd	ta?l	invd	jigesv
just this	month	two	months	much it was

Wilbur:

ᎡᎵᏍᏗ	ᏃᏊ	ᎦᏲᎳ	ᎢᏳᏍᏗ	ᏂᏗᎦᎵᏍᏙᏗᏍᎬ
elisdi	now	gayol	iyusd	ndigalsdohdisgv
it seems	now	small amount	kind	because

ᏍᎩᎾ	ᏍᎩᏳ	ᏫᏂᎦᎷᎬᎾ	ᎨᎲ	ᏍᎩᎾ	ᎣᏍᏓ
sgina	sgiyu	winiga?luhgvn	gehv	sgina	ohsd
that	there	it has not arrived	which	that	good

ᎢᏳᎾᎵᏍᏓᏁᏗ	ᏕᏥᎸᏫᏍᏓᏁᎲ	ᏃᎴ	ᏂᏗᎦᎵᏍᏙᏗᎭ
iyunalsdahne	dejilvhwisdanehv	nowle	ndigalsdohdiha
happen to them	you are working	and	because

ᎨᏍᏗ	ᏳᎾᏚᎵ	ᎤᏅᏌ	ᎭᏂᎾᏰᏍᎦ	ᏧᎾᏓᏂᎸᎢᏍᏗ	ᏍᎩᏍ
gesd	yunduli	unvhsa	haninayehsga	jundanilv?isdi	sgis?
not	they do not want	themselves	they fear	to accept	is that it

Durbin:

iᏇ
vhv
yes

Wilbur:

ᏜᎮD ꝗᏯᎫ ᏴᎾꝏ D4
sge?a nuhsd yvwiya ahse
that is it is Indian probably

that is the Indian way
that is the Indian way
that is the Indian way

DᏬᎫ TSᏝ
atdi gad
you might say some

Durbin:

D4ꝏᎩh DᏊ ᏏᏞꝏA ᏴᎾ i ꚉꝏᏝ ꚉᎫꙦZꙩ4W
asesgin agwu gelisgo ayv v osd yidikanosel
but nearby I think I uh good if you tell them

i TEᏇᏞꝏWhᏝꝏᎫ ᏏR ꚉZᏞᎩ ᏏᏞ
v igvwalstanidasdi gesv yanolhgi geli
uh what might be the which are they would understand I think
    possibilities

GᎾSW ᏗᎾᏝWᎫꝏᎫ
yunadul unteldisdi
they would want to join

Wilbur:

ꚉᏝᏏᏒGꝏWh DB Ꙩꝗꚉ DB ꝗꚉGᏏᏇ DEꚉ
yidahchilostani ay usoyi ay soy jigehv agvyi
as an illustration we same we same if was first

Ө	GOꞏW	mutual	help	program
na	janht	mutual	help	program
that	you know	mutual	help	program

ZꞶ	DB	ƲℱMⱯW	ꞶᏱ	GꞶᎪ	i	DEᏉ	ꞶꞶ
now	ay	wogiluhchel	sgi	yuhsd	v	agvyi	sgwu
when	we	it came to us	that	kind	uh	at first	also

DᏫꞶSTRT	ᏂꝋᏞ	DB	Ꞷᏹ	ᏉEꞮSW	GⱠrӨ	ꞶᏹӨ
agisduʔisvʔi	jiʔoli	ay	sgi	yigvgwadul	wajin	sgina
I opened	my mouth	I	that	I would not	get	that

ꝖꞶꝋ	ᏚꝋꞞTꞶᎪ	D4Z	DᏂZᏢꞶE	ᏂᏚᏁ	OꞋℰSᎮ	ꝖOꞋᏁꝋꝖ
nusdv	judvnvʔisd	aseno	anihnohesgv	nigad	uwoduhi	nunvnelv
type	provision	but	they talked about	all	pretty	they did

ꞶᏹӨT	OꞋᏏT	ᏂGꝋOꞋ	ᏕⱠᎷᏴꝖ	OꞶᏞ	ᏂᏞCꞦBᏞᏞ
sginaʔi	uyoʔi	nijadvhnv	dejingilv	osda	nidajvyvnel
that	bad	your situation	you dwell	good	we will do

Zꝺ	DℱᏉᎪ	ᏐR	ꞶᎪ	ᏞCℱᏴᏢᏏ
nole	akwiyhdi	gesv	sdi	dajakwiyvhesi
and	to pay	which is	little	you will pay

ZꞶZ	V	ᏉᏚᏒꞶᏞ	EℱᏉᎪ	ᏂᏐRO	Ꮙᏹ	SVᎮ
nownh	do	yigalsd	gvkwiyhd	nigesvna	yigi	gadoh
and then	what	would happen	to pay	without	if	land

DᏞᏞᏞ	Ꮙᏹ	SᏏC	GⱠrӨ		OꞋᏞᏞᏴᎪ	Ꮙᏹ	ꞶᏹӨ
adahnel	yig	gayohli	wajin		udanhtehd	yig	sgina
to give	if	little	U.S. government		authority	would be	that

SᏒᎿᏴ	ᎪӨᏞꞶᏂꞶᏹ	Ᏽℰ	Qualla	houses	DӨᎪꞶA	ꞶᏹᏞ
galsode	dinahnesgesgi	gehv	Qualla	houses	andisgo	sgihna
house	builders	which	Qualla	houses	they say	that

ᎠᏂ ᎤᎾᏤᎵ ᏂᎦᎵᏍᏗ ᏍᎩ ᎢᎦ ᏓᏲᏒ ᎦᎵᏐᏕ
an unjeli nigalsdi sgi iga dayohsv galsode
here theirs it becomes that much let go house

ᎠᏌᎲ ᎠᏀᏁᏍᎨᎲᎴ ᏱᎩ ᎯᎸᎯᏳ ᏃᏊ ᎠᏴ ᏆᏤᎵ
asahv anahnesgehvle yigi hilvhiyu now ay gwajeli
in addition to their building if never then I mine

ᎢᎬᏩᎵᏍᏙᏗ ᏯᎩᏄᎸᎿ ᎠᏆᏈᏴᏗ
igvwalsdohd yaginulvnh agwakwiyvdi
to happen if I fail for me to pay

ᎦᎵᏐᏕ ᎠᎩᏲᎱᏎᎸ ᏱᎩ ᎦᏙᎯ
galsode agiyohu slv yig gadoh
house lost if land

ᏱᏚᎾᏓᏂᎸᏨ that is just the Indian way
yidundanilvj that is just the Indian way
they accepted that is just the Indian way

ᏳᏁᎦ ᎬᎾᏗ ᎦᏬᏂᎯᏍᏗ
yuneg gvnhd gawonihisd
English with speech

Durbin:

ᎦᏙᎲ ᎢᏣᏛᏁᎴ Ꭵ ᎡᎵᏊ ᏚᎾᏓᏂᎸᏨ
gadohv ijadvnele v eligw dundanilvje?
what you did uh possible they accepted

Wilbur:

Ꭵ ᎢᎦᏓᏃ ᎤᎾᏧᏴ ᏚᏂᎩᏒ ᏃᏊ ᏍᎩᎾ
v igadno unatsuyv dunigisv now sgina
uh some were among they received then that

as time went on now ᎠᏂᎪᏩᏘᏍᎬ ᎣᏏ
as time went on now anigowhtisgv osi
as time went on now they saw all right

ᎨᎲᎢ	ᏃᎴ	ᏍᎩᎾ	ᎤᏩᏌ	ᎢᎬᏩᏅᏁᏗ	ᏃᏊ	ᎦᏌᏄ
gehv?i	nole	sgina	uwahsa	igvwanvn	now	gasanu
it was	and	that	self	to do it themselves	then	fast

ᎣᏍᏓ	ᎦᎵᏠᏕ	ᎬᏩᏂᎩᏍᏗ	ᎨᎲᎢ	ᏃᏊ	ᏓᏂᎪᏩᏘᏍᎬ	ᏃᏊ
ohsd	galsode	gvwanigisd	gehv?i	nogw	danigowahtisgv	now
good	house	they could get	was	now	as they saw	now

ᎠᏴᏗ	ᏃᏊ	ᏍᏊ	ᎭᏩᏚᎵ	ᏍᎩᏳᏍᏗ	ᏃᏊ	ᎠᏂᏔᏲᎲ
aydi	now	sgwu	hawaduli	sgiyusdi	now	anitayohv
I also	now	also	I want	that kind	now	they asked for

ᏃᏊ	ᎡᎵ	ᎬᏩᏂᎩᏍᏗ	ᏭᏟᏰᏮᏢ
now	eli	gvwanigisd	wuhliye?hlv
now	possible	they could get it	it got to the point

Wilbur:

ᏏᏇ	ᎪᎰᏍᏗ
sihke	gohusd?
still	something

Durbin:

ᎪᏪᎵ	ᏗᏣᏁᏍᏗ	ᏱᏦᏪᎳᏅ	ᏱᏍᎩᏁᎳ
gohwel	dijanesdi	yijohwelan	yiskinel
letters	where you get	if you write	if you give me

ᏱᏕᎾᏓᏙᏪᎳᏏ	ᎪᏪᎵ
yidendadohwelas	gohwel
we could write to each other	letters

ᎠᏜᎢᎵᏒ	ᏱᏣᏚᎵ
ahli?ilisv	yijaduli
sometime	if you want

Wilbur:

ᎣᏏᏊ	ᎨᏍᏗᏃ	ᏗᎪᏪᎵᏍᎩ	ᏱᎩ	ᏥᎦ	ᎭᏎᏃ	ᏰᎵᏊ
ohsigw	gesdno	digowelisg	yig	jiga	haseno	yeligw
good	and	written	not	much	but	possible

ᏍᎦᏃᎵ	ᎠᏉᏪᎶᏗ	ᎦᏲᏟ	ᏍᏊ	Ꮟ	ᎦᏙᎴᏆ	ᏗᏉᏪᎶᏗ
sganol	agwowelod	gayotli	sgwu	si	gadolehgwa	digwowelodi
slow	I could write	a little	also	still	I am learning	to write

Durbin:

ᏍᎩᏛ	ᎿᏛᏁᎲ	ᏱᏕᎭᏕᎰᎶᏆ	ᏔᎵᏍᎪ	ᏔᎵ	ᎢᏯᏆᏕᏘᏴᏓ	ᎨᏒ
sgidv	hnadvnehv	yidehadehlogw	ta?lsgo	ta?li	iyagwadetiyvd	gesv
that	as you do	you will learn	twenty	two	years old	was

ᏓᏆᏕᎵᏆ	ᏗᏉᏬᎶᏗ	I	learned	how	to	read	when
dagwadelhgwa	digwohwelodi	I	learned	how	to	read	when
when I learned	to write	I	learned	how	to	read	when

I	was	ten	ᏍᎪᎯ	ᏯᏆᏕᏘᏴᏓ	ᎨᏒ	ᏗᎩᎪᎵᎡᏗ
I	was	ten	sgohi	yagwadetiyvd	gesv	digigoliyedi
I	was	ten	ten	years old	was	to read

ᎠᏆᏕᎵᏆ	ᏗᏉᏬᎶᏗᏂᏃ	ᏔᎵᏍᎪ	ᏔᎵ	ᎢᏯᏆᏕᏘᏴᏓ	ᎠᏂᏲᏍᎩ
agwadelhgwa	digwohwelodinh	ta?lsgoh	ta?l	iyagwadetiyvd	aniyosgi
when I learned	and to write	twenty	two	years old	military service

ᏥᏯᎥ	ᎡᏣᏃ	ᏣᎨᏒ	ᏫᏓᏉᏬᎳᏁᎰ	ᏗᏣᎳᎩᎭ	ᏲᏁ
jiya?v	ejihno	jigesv	widagwohwelaneho	dijalagiha	yoneg
I was in	and my mother	who was	she would write to me	in Cherokee	English

ᎬᏗ	ᏕᎪᏪᎵᏍᎪ	ᏢᏴ	ᎠᏆᏓᎾᏢ	ᏣᎳᎩ	ᏙᏓᎪᏪᏔᏂ
gvhd	degowelisgo	dlvyv	agwadanhtehlv	djalag	dodagowelan
with	I wrote back	finally	I thought	Cherokee	I am going to write

ᏔᎵ	ᎾᏆᏁᎵᏔᏅ	ᏓᏆᏕᎳᏆᎥ	ᏗᏉᏪᎶᏗ
ta?li	nagwanelhtanv	dagwadelhgwa?v	digwohwelodi
two	attempts	I learned	to write

ᏍᎩ	ᏱᏂᏣᏛᏁᎵ	ᏍᏊ	ᏯᏕᎶᏆ	ᏗᏦᏪᎶᏗ
sgi	yinjadvnel	sgwu	hyadelohgwa	dijowelodi
that	if you do	also	you will learn	to write

Wilbur:

ᎠᏴᏗ	ᏅᎭᏍᎪ	ᏯᏆᏕᎲ	ᎤᎶᏒᏍᏗ	ᎡᎵᏍᏗ	ᎨᎮ	ᎩᎳ
aydi	nvhasgo	yagwadehyv	ulohsvsd	elisd	gehe	kil
I	forty	years old	past	probably	will be	until

ᏍᎩ	ᏱᎾᏆᏛᏁᎴ	ᎠᏂᏲᏍᎩᎢ	ᎤᏥᏅᎮ	ᏱᏭᎾᏓᎨᏎ
sgi	yinagwadvnele	aniyohsgi?i	ujinvhe	yiwundagese
that	if I did	military service	away	they would have thrown

ᏱᏮᎩᏍᏚᏃ	censorship	ᏳᏂᏲᏍᏔᏃᏁ	ᎪᏪᎵ
yiwvksduhnenh	censorship	yuniyostanohne	gowel
I would have been jailed	censorship	they would have torn up	letter

Durbin:

ᏱᏦᏪᎳᎾᏛ	ᏊᏪᎵ	ᏗᏣᏁᏍᏗ
yijohwelandv	gohwel	dijanesdi
if you will write	letters	where you get them

Wilbur:

ᎨᏍᏗ	ᎲᏍᏊ	Ꮵ	Ꭶ	ᏱᏥᏏᎾ	ᏗᏉᏪᎶᏗ
gest	hvsgwu	ji	ga	yijisina	digwohwelodi
not	also	much	quantity	I know	to write

ᏣᏁᎵᏁ	ᏩᏆᎴᎲ	ᎨᏍᏗ	ᏗᎩᏍᎦᏛ	ᏱᎩ
chaneline	wagwalehnv	gesd	diksgwadv	yig
eight	I have gone to	not	I have not finished	is

Wilbur:

ᏍᏱᏩᏧ   ᏂᎦ
sgigwuju   niga?
that is   all

Durbin:

i   ᏍᏱᏩᏛ   ᎬᏯᎵᏒᎵᏥᏏ
v   sgigwudv   gvyali?elichisi
yes   that is   I am thankful to you

Morpheme by Morpheme

Durbin:

kohi-ga^3-hno   dununhdi   tal-sgohi-ne^{34}-ka?
day this and   october   two ten Ord Ques

Wilbur:

v
yes

Durbin:

ta^{3}l-sgohi-ne^3 so^{3}hne-la^{3}du^3 isgo^{3}hitsgwi   ne^{23}l-sgo^{23} ta?l^3
two ten Ord   nineteen   hundred   eight ten   two

u-detiyv^{3}sadi^{3}s-v   jalag   u-weti   a-neh^{23} a-n^{23}-edoh^{32}
3 year-of exP   cherokee   3 old   3 dwell   3 Pl be-there

a-ni^{23}-ta^3?li-ha   galhja?di^3 j-u-do^{23}?id   sagwu^3
3 Pl two Num   bo   Pl 3 be-named   one

Wilbur:

a-lhjado^{32}hvs-g-i^{32}
3 preach Prog Ag

Durbin:

a-lhjado^{23}hv-s-g nihi-nh^3 gado de-^{23}j-a^{3}do^3?
3 preach Prog Ag you and what Pl 3 be-named

Wilbur:

wili^{3}m sigwoyi^{43}
wilbur sequoyah

Durbin:

wil^{23} sigwoyi^{43}
wil sequoyah

Wilbur:

wilimi^{43}
wilbur

Durbin:

wilimi^{43}
wilbur

Wilbur:

agvyi^{32}-no yo^{3}negu-hne^{32}?i-sd charles wilbur
first and white-person 3 tell Ins charles wilbur

sequoyah d-agw-ado^3 sgi^{3}na ayelh^3 d-agw-ado^{3}sd-v
sequoyah Pl 1 be-named that middle Pl 1 be-named exP

ji iga^3 vki-yani^{3}s-g-o wili^{3}mi^{42} gvgw-o^{3}seh-o
more of 1Pas call Prog Hab wilbur they-me call Hab

Durbin:

hila^{3}hv^3 yv sdi^3-luhj-e^3
when time you-two come-to repP

oklahoma?
oklahoma

Wilbur:

tali-ha^3 nuhsv^3 iyu^3 ji-geh-v^3
two Num   day   then   Pst be exP

uhsv^3 sohnel^{23} iyu^3 iyu^{3}wahnilv^3
at-night   nine   about   hour-of-day

Durbin:

ga^{3}go-hv^3 esdi-wahtvhi^{23}d-o?
who but   you-two visit Hab

Wilbur:

ay-hno^3 ges-v   a-ni-yvwi-ya   niga^{3}do-gw   de-ji^{3}w-ahtvhid-o^{32}
I and   be exP   3 Pl people pure   everyone just   Pl 1 visit Hab

ndigal^{3}sdoh^{3}di^3 hi?   agvyi^3 kil   g-edo^{32}
because   this   first   time   1 be-there

a^{3}han   oklahoma?   utsgwiya^3 ak-tvgan-v^3 hi
here   oklahoma   much   1 hear exP   this

sgina^3 ha   jalag   nana^3 han
that   interjection   cherokee   there   here

uweti^3 nda-y-u^3-noiloh^{3}s-v   a-n-eh-v^3 sgi-gw   agi-kdu^{3}nidoh-a^3
old place   this-way nonF 3   3 Pl live exP   that just   1 check Pres
          come exP

n-u-n-dvhna^{3}de-g-v^3 nole^3 iyuhsd^3 v   iyuhsd^3
Spec 3 Pl do Prog exP   and   what   uh   what

n-u-n-dvhna^{3}de-g-v^3 sgina^3 na-n
Spec 3 Pl do Prog exP   that   those and

a-ni-ne^{3}gil-v^3 a-ni-ne^{23}l-v^3
3 Pl live exP   3 Pl live exP

dudo^{23}da^{3}gwvd   iyuhsd^3 n-a-n-dv^{3}neli-doh-v^3 ino^3 j-u-dalehnv^{3}da-gw
daily   what   Spec 3 Pl do here-   then   Pl 3 different and
                                  and-there exP

sgi   igv^{3}walstanv^{3}da   sgwala^3 yi-ni-g-v^{3}nel^{34} hi?   yi-n-ji^{3}w-i
that   and-so-forth   short   nonF Spec 3 make   this   nonF Spec 1 say

iyuhsd^3 n-u-n-dvhnade^3-g-v
what   Spec 3 Pl do Prog exP

v   judo^{23}da^{3}gwvd   v
uh   daily   uh

a-ni-ne^{23}l-v^3 a-n-a^3?ihs-v^3?   ig
3 Pl live exP   3 Pl walk exP   day

judlehnvd   nole^3 v
different   and   uh

j-u-ni-lawi^{3}s-di   geh-o
Rel 3 Pl pray Inf   be Hab

sgwu^3 yvw   iyuhsd^3
also   people   what

ni-geg-adv^{3}hn-eh-v   sgi^3 nigad^3 igv^{3}walstanvd^{23} no^{23}wle^3
Spec for-them do Dat exP   that   all   and-so-forth   and

v   kanohed^{23} ges-o
uh   news   be Hab

y-a-n-h^{3}tvgi^4?-a   osd^3
nonF 3 Pl hear Pres   good

kanohed^{23} y-ig   sgina^3 ha   sgina^3
news   nonF be   that   interjection   that

ha   yi-gv^{3}walsta^{3}nv   sgi-w
interjection   and-so-forth   that just

yuhsd^3 hagi-kdv^{3}hnid-o^3 ay
what   1 check-on Hab   me

Durbin:

d-u-dalehna^3?ak-e^3 v
Pl 3 different repP   uh

a^{3}han   no^{23}le^3 di-j-e^{23}nv^{32}s-v?
here   and   Pl 2 come-from exP

Wilbur:

v^{34}-hano^3 ji   iga   sgina^3 yvw   nuhsd^3
yes and   more   quantity   that   people   is

u-n-a^{3}igis-di   ges-v
3 Pl that-way Inf   be exP

ja   dale^2 na^2-sgin
no   different   that but

v   iyuhsd^3 v   dodi^3 yuhsd-hno^3 y-vda   sgina^3
uh   that   uh   what   that and   nonF say   that

di^{3}ge   elishsd   v   nigad^3 geh-v^3 na
not   supposedly   uh   all   be exP   that

uhsd^3 vja
that   no

hi?   yi-d-u^{23}-da^{3}leh-a
this   nonF Pl 3 differ Pres

sgi-w
that just

iga^3 ni-gega-dv^{3}hneh-v^3
quantity   Spec for-them do exP

ji-de-g-al^{3}no^{3}h-el-do^{3}h-v
Pst Pl 3 converse Dat start exP

uhsv   i^{23}g   gvgwalenv^{3}da
yesterday   now   since

v   sdi^{3}kid-no^3 igad^3 gesd^{34}
uh   a-little and   all   not

v   iyu^{3}sdi
uh   that

i-ge^{3}g-adv^{3}hn-eh-d   ni-geg-a^{3}dvhn-e^3 iyusd^3 y-a-ni^3-gi^4?-a
Inf 3Pl Pas do here-and-there   Neg for-them do   that   nonF 3 Pl get Pres
  Dat Inf   Dat

igad^3 ohsi^3
some   fair

n-u-n-dvhv-nh   nole^3
Spec 3 Pl do and   and also

igad^3 u-yo?i^3 n-u^3-n-dvhn-v^3 g-atvgi^3?-a
some   3 poor   Spec 3 Pl do exP   1 hear Pres

sgi-hno   ji-g-adi   gesd^{23} ay
so and   Rel 1 say   not   I

yi-g-o^{23}lihg-a
nonF 1 understand Pres

si^3 agw-vhsa^3-no^3 di-ji-gahtol^{23} y-ahk-ta^{4}ne^3 yi-ji^3-gahtah-e^3
yet 1 self and Pl 1 eye nonF 1 use nonF 1 know repP

iyuhsd^3 v
that uh

di-d-a^3-lenis-g-v^3 g-eli^3
Dst Pl 3 begin Prog exP 1 think

si igad^3
set some

gesd^3 y-eli^3
not nonF be-able

v a-ni-so^3
uh 3 pl other

nunhsdv^3 iga^3 y-a-ni^{3}gi iyuhsd^3
condition that much nonF 3 Pl receive that

u-ni-gisd^3 ges-v^3 u-n-alhsdelh^{23}d-o ges-v^4?i
3 Pl receive be exP 3 Pl make-living Hab be exP

d-a-ni-ne^{3}gil-v uyo^3 n-u-n-dn-v^3
Pl 3 Pl live exP had Spec 3 Pl condition exP

a-n-di^{3}hs-g-o hi?
3 Pl say Prog Hab this

dlv^3 invhi^3 ges-v^3 a-doh^3 di-ge^{3}s-v
somewhere far-away be exP 3 be-in-woods Dst be exP

iyv^3 di-ni-ne^{23}l-i ges-v^3
distance Pl Pl live Ag be exP

e^{3}sga^3-gwu^3 hi
near just much

esga^{23}hni   di-ni-nel^{23} gadu^{3}hv   na?v^3-hnige^3 y-i^{3}gi
nearby   Pl Pl live   from   close more   nonF be

iyuhsd^3 g-atvgi^3 v^{3}ja-no^3 yi-ji^3-gaht-a^3 sgina^3
that   1 hear   not and   nonF 1 know Pres   that

ha   utswiya^3 agw-ada^{3}leche^{3}h-a   v
interjection   much   he/me hide Pres   uh

doni^{3}yuh^{4}sdi   a-da-leni^{4}h-a
so-what   3 Refl begin Pres

sgina^3 uyo^{34} in^{23}di^3-gvw-andvhnadeg^3 iyv^3 nole^3
that   bad   Pl 3 Pl be-poor Prog   there   and

hesgani^3 geh-v   de-ji^3-gowhti^{23}s-g-v
nearer   be exP   Pl 1 see Prog exP

ohsi-gw
fair just

iyusd   n-u-n-dvnade^3-g-v   i-g-e^{3}li^3
kind   Spec 3 Pl do Prog exP   Rep 3 think

utsgwiya^3-no   tala-ha^3 nundale^3 n-agw-alsda^{32}h-ne
much and   two Num   different   Spec it/me seem Dat

Durbin:

hla^3-sgo   sgi^3 yinusd^{23}
not Ques   that   kind

v   di-j-e^{23}nv^{32}s-v^3?
uh   Dst 2 be-from exP

Wilbur:

v   v^{34}jano^3
uh   not and

sgi^{23}-ga aw-da^{3}lechehe^{4}n-o^{3}
that much it-me hide Hab

v ay
uh I

sgina^{3} di-g-a-lawi^{23}s-di^{3} di-j-ilawig^{3} hi^{23}gi
that Pl 3 Pl council-member Inf Dst 1 be-council-member be

v oj-a^{3}nelhdih^{3}s-g-o
uh they-and-I try Prog Hab

nigad nikv sgina^{3}
all all around that

d-oj-aksesdoh^{3}ta^{4}nida-sde u-yo?i^{3}
Pl they-and-I watch-over Inf 3 bad

yinudv^{4}na sgina^{3}
in-position that

w-o-ji^{3}-n-ohehs-g-o^{3}
Tr they-and-I report Prog Hab

v a-ni-wajin^{3} d-u-n-da^{3}nel-v^{3} programs
uh 3 Pl govern Pl 3 Pl provide exP programs

galso^{23}de di-n-ahne^{23}s-g-i go^{23}sd-le
house Pl Pl build Prog Ag something

social service y-i^{4}gi
social service nonF be

a^{4}-tdi j-i^{3}gi sgina^{3} han kvni^{3} gehs-v^{3} n-d-oj-v^{3}neh-o^{3}
3 say Rel be that here visible be-exP Spec Pl they-and-I do Hab

oj-a^{3}nelhdi^{3}s-g-o sgi-hno^{3}
they-and-I try Prog Hab that and

hi?   sudaleg^{23} ji-g-adi^3
this   one-thing   Rel 1 say

ay   n-u-n-dvhn-v   gesd   go
I   Spec 3 Pl condition exP   not   something

y-a-n-i^{3}gi?
nonF 3 Pl get

ha   ha-n-di^3-a
interjection   3 Pl say Pres

gv-gwos-e^3 igad^3 ha-ni^{32}-nohe^{3}s-g-v
he/me say repP   some   3 Pl talk-about Prog exP

gesd   yi-geg-a^{32}-ksesda^{32}nes-g-o   doyu
not   nonF for-them pay-attention Prog Hab   really

u-yo?i^3 n-u-n-dvhn-a^3
3 bad   Spec 3 Pl condition Pres

ha-n-di   ge^{23}sd-no   v
3 Pl say   not and   uh

yi-g-o^{23}lihg-a^3 sgina^3 hani^{32}
nonF 1 understand Pres   that   here

hi?   v
this   uh

di-ni-lawig^3 u-n-dudal^{32} j-u-n-geli^3
Pl Pl council-member   3 Pl responsible   Pl 3 Pl people

gv-w-suyagid^{23} g-ehv^3 da-n-eh-v^3 sgadug^{23} de-g-oh^{3}svhwadi^{32}s-v^4?i
3 Pl choose   be exP   Pl 3 Pl live exP   county   Pl 3 establish-county
                                                                        exP

j-u-n-aksesdoh^{3}-di
Pl 3 Pl look-after Inf

Durbin:

sgidi^{3}-do   nusd^{23} v
that really   indeed   uh

n-di-g-al^{3}sdoh^{3}di^{3}s-g-v^{4}-hno^{3} sgwu^{3}
Spec Pl 3 happen Prog exP and   also

v   gayo^{23}hli
uh   some

ges-v^{3} yi-k-ano^{3}helh^{34}
be exP   nonF 3 claim

vsg   jalag
that   cherokee

a-ni-woni^{23}s-g-i   ges-v^{3}
3 Pl speak Prog Ag   be exP

na   jalag   u-ni-woni^{23}hi-sd
that   cherokee   3 Pl speak Inf

u-n-ih^{23} sgi-yusd^{23} a-ni-wonis-g^{23} uhna^{3}yv   n-j-u^{23}-n-dvnh   na^{3}
3 Pl have   that kind   3 Pl speak Prog   out-there   Spec Dst 3 Pl   that
                                                                        be-out-there

salu^{3}yi^{23}-yv   ado^{23}hi-yv^{3}
woods in   forest in

v   hla-hno^{3} y-u-n-dulis-g-o   de-ga^{3}du^{23}hv^{3}
uh   not and   nonF 3 Pl want Prog Hab   in-town

n-do-day-u^{3}-n-dvnh-doh^{3}-di
Spec Dst motion-toward 3 Pl come-start Inf

v sgino^3 jalag a-ni-wonis-g^{23}
uh that cherokee 3 Pl speak Prog

do
real

a-ni-jalagi^3 ges-v^3 a^{3}hani^3-hno^3 d-u-ni-lv^{23}wsdaneh
3 Pl cherokee be exP here and Pl 3 Pl be-employed

udli^3 i^{23}ga^3 a-ni-yo^{3}neg v
more much 3 Pl white uh

sgi-hno^3 sdi^{23}kid d-a-n-dale^{32}g-o^3
that and a-little Pl 3 Pl differ Prog Hab

yusd^{34}
kind

Wilbur:

donhi^{23}yusd^3 di-d-a^3-leni^{3}h-a sginv^{3}ga
what Dst there 3 start Pres that

osd^3 han esga-nh^{23}
good here nearer and

nahni^{3}ge a-ni^{23}-negili ohsi^3 yusd^{34}
nearer 3 Pl dwell fair kind

n-u-n-dvhvn?
Spec 3 Pl do

udoyu^3 housing dego^{3}shv^3
really housing department

igad^3 j-osd d-a-ni-ne^{3}gilv
a few Pl good Pl 3 Pl home

sgina^3 hiyu^3 wi-n-ga^{3}luhgv-n^{34}
that   there   Tr Neg 3 arrive Neg

wi-di-geganeh^{3}sgehdi
Trans Pl 3 Pl build-house Inf

una   iyv
there   distance

Durbin:

v   i^{23}ga^{3}dv^3
uh   some

sgwu^3 a-ni-jalagi^3
also   3 Pl cherokee

j-ig   sgwu   hla
Rel be   also   not

y-u^{23}-n-dulis-g-o^3 hla^3
nonF 3 Pl want Prog Hab   not

v   hla^3 y-u^{23}-n-duli
uh   not   nonF 3 Pl want

Wilbur:

a-ni-naye^{3}s-g-v
3 Pl fear Prog exP

Durbin:

vhv^3 sgi^{32}
yes   exactly

Wilbur:

cha^{3}sgon	y-a-n-e^{3}h-a	kilo^3	di-ni-lawig^3	ohsd^3	wi-di-gvw-ano^{3}siso-hd
is-it-not	nonF 3 Pl live Pres	someone	council	good	Tr Pl them explain-to-them Inf

Durbin:

kila-hno^3	sgi-yv^3	oji-hi^{3}li^{23}doh^{32}	day-o^{23}j-a^{3}lenv	sgi^3
now and	that exactly	they-and-I do	Fut they-and-I start	that

n-oj-adv^{3}neh-v^3	oji-hnohe^{23}hli^{3}do-hv
Spec they-and-I do exP	we Pl Ex going-around-reporting-things

na	v	vsgi
that	uh	that

ig-v^{23}-w-als-doh-di^3	ges-v^3	sdi^{23}hid-hno^3	o-gi-sganol^{23}
happen Pl Inf	be exP	a-little and	they-and-I Pl Ex slow

Wilbur:

v	yu^{3}neg
uh	white-man

u-hne^3?is-d	ge^3	iji-ga^{32}tah	i^{3}gvnhdi^3
3 utterance Inf	was	I do not know	how-say-it

yu^{3}neg	u-jeli^3	da-g-a^{32}tolsi^{32}
white-man	3 possessed	Fut 1 borrow

v	breakdown
uh	breakdown

communication	iyuhsd	n-agw-alsda^{32}hn-e^3
communication	kind	Spec it-me seem repP

sgina^3	hi
that	this

Durbin:

sgi-hno^3 v di-d-a-lehnv^3?is-di^3
that and uh Dst Pl differ Pl Inf

ges-v^3 na v
be exP that uh Dst

d-v-hlinohe^{23}hli^{3}doh-v^3
Pl 3 speak exP

sgina^3 udli^3 i^{23}ga
that much more

Wilbur:

ahs^{3}no^{3}ge iji-hiye^3 sgina^3
but you Pl work that

ohsd ij-vn-hdi?
good you-do Inf

Durbin:

v oji-hi?^{32}d-v
yes they-and-I work-toward exP

Wilbur:

ta?li-ha^3 nadeti^{23}yv no^{23}wle e^{34}lisd y-eliw^{23} sdi^{34}kid
two Num year away then supposedly nonF possible a-little

ohsdv^3 iyu-lstanidas-di
good 3 happen Inf

geh-esd^3
be Fut-Prog

Durbin:

v	about	five	maybe
yes	about	five	maybe

Wilbur:

maybe	never
maybe	never

ndi^{3}gal^{3}sdoh^{3}di^{3}hv^3	adel^{23}	ka-nigadi^3	sgwu^{23}-hnv^3
because	money	3 lack	also and

ase^3	elad
probably	lowered

n-e-jv^{3}hn-e	adel^{23}?
Spec 3 done repP	money

Durbin:

ilv^{23}sgi-dv^3	iya^{3}ni	de-ge^3-ji^{3}yos	d-u-ni-lv^{23}wsdaneh-v	a^{3}han
a-few Emp	of-them	Pl they fire	Pl 3 Pl work exP	here

hi?a-gw^3	sinvd^{23}	ta?l^3	invd^{34}	ji-ges-v^3
this just	month	two	month	Rel be exP

Wilbur:

e^{34}lisdi^3	now^{23}	gayol^{23}	iyusd^3	ndigal^{3}sdohdi^{3}sgv
it-seems	now	small-amount	kind	because-of-that

sgina^3	sgi^{32}yu	wi-ni-g-a^3?luhgvn^{23}	geh-v^3	sgina^3	ohsd^3
that	there	Tr Neg 3 arrive Neg	be exP	that	good

yu^{3}n-alsdahne^{3}di	de^3-ji-lv^{3}hwisda^{32}neh-v^3	no^{23}wle^3
they 3 Pl happen Inf	Pl you-Pl work exP	and

ndigal^{3}sdohdi^{3}ha	gesd^{23}
3 happen Pres	not

y-u^{23}-n-duli^3 u-n-vh^{4}sa ha-ni-nayeh^{4}s-g-a
nonF 3 Pl want   3 Pl self   3 Pl fear Prog Pres

j-u-n-dani^{23}lv^3?is-di^3
Pl 3 accept Inf

sgi-s
that-it Ques

Durbin:

vhv^3
yes

Wilbur:

sge^3?a nuhsd^3 yvwi-ya^3 a^{23}hse^3
that-is it-is   person real   probably

that's the Indian way
that's the Indian way

a^4-tdi   i^{23}gad^3
say Inf some

Durbin:

ase^{3}gin^3 agwu^3 g-eli^{32}s-g-o^3
but   close-by 1 think Prog Hab

ayv v osd^{23} yi-di-k-anosel^{34}
I   uh good nonF Pl 3 tell

v i-gv^3-w-alstani^{23}das-di^3
uh you/them happen Inf

ges-v^3 y-a-nolhgi^3 g-eli^{32}
be exP nonF 3 understand 1 think

y-u-n-adul^{23} u-n-teldis-di^{3}
nonF 3 Pl want   3 Pl join Inf

Wilbur:

y-idah^{3}chilosta-n^{3}di   ay
nonF give-example Inf   we

uso^{4}yi   ay^{3} soy^{3} ji-geh-v^{3}
same   we   same   Pst be exP

agvyi
first

na^{3} j-anht   mutual   help   program
that   you know   mutual   help   program

now^{23} ay   w-ogi^{3}-luhch-el^{23} sgi
when   we   Tr you-all-and-I come-to Dat   that

yuhsd^{23} v   agvyi   sgwu^{3}
kind   uh   first   also

a^{3}k-sdu^{3}ʔis-v   jiʔ-o^{23}li   ay   sgi
1 open exP   1Pos mouth   I   that

yi^{23}-gv^{3}-gwadul^{23} wajin^{3} sgina^{3}
nonF 1 want   u.s.-government/virginia   that

nusdv
type

j-u-dvnv^{3}ʔi-sd   ase^{3}no^{3} a-ni-hnohe^{23}s-g-v^{3}
Rel 3 provide Inf   but   3 Pl talk-about Prog exP

nigad^{3} u-woduhi^{3} n-u-n-v^{3}nel-v^{3} sgina^{3}ʔi
all   3 pretty   Spec 3 Pl do exP   that

u-yo$?$i^3 ni-j-advhn-v^3 de^3-ji-ngil^{3}v osd^{23} ni-d-ajvyv^{32}n-el^{23}
3 bad   you Pl in-situation Pl Loc 2 Pl good Fut we/you fix
     Pl   where-live   Dat

no^{23}le^3 akw-iyh-di^3 ges-v^3
and   1 pay Inf   be exP

sdi d-a-j-akwi^{3}yvhes-i^{43}
little Fut two pay Fut

nownh^3 do yi-g-alsd^3
and then what nonF 3 happen

gv-kwiyhd
to-pay

ni-ge^{3}sv^{34}-na y-i^{4}gi
Neg be Neg   nonF be

gadoh
land

a-da-hnel^{23} y-ig
if had-been-given nonF be

gay^{34}ohli wajin
few   u.s.-government

udanh^{23}tehd y-ig^{23} sgina^3
authority   nonF be that

galso^{23}de^3 di-n-ahnesge^{23}s-g-i
house   Pl Pl build Prog Ag

geh-v^3 Qualla
be exP Qualla

houses   a-n^3-di^{3}s-g-o   sgihna^3
houses   3 Pl say Prog Hab   that

an   u-n-jeli   ni-g-alsdi^3 sgi
here   3 Pl possess   ni 3 become   that

iga^3 d-a-yohs-v   galso^{23}de^3
much   Pl 3 let-go exP   house

asahv   a-n-ahne^{3}sgehv^{3}l-e
on-top   3 Pl build repP

y-i^{4}gi   hil^{3}vhiyu^3
nonF be   never

now   ay^3 gw-ajeli^3
then   I   1 possessed

ig-v^{3}walsdohd   y-agi^3-nulvnh^3 agw-akwih-di^3
1 happen   nonF 1 fail   1 pay Inf

galso^{23}de^3 agi-yohu^{3}sl-v^3 y-ig^{23} gadoh^3
house   1 lose exP   nonF be   land

sgi^3-ha   u-ni^3-tsgwis^3 a-n-inayes-g^3 sgi-no^3 usoy^{23}
that exactly   3 Pl much   3 Pl afraid Prog   that and   same

n-u-nasd-v^3 hi   ji-n-unasd^3
Spec 3 become exP   these   you Pl become-same

salu-y^3 di-n-eh^3 ch-adi^{3}h-a^3 sgina^3-ha   gesd^{23} gasanul^{23}
woods in   Pl Pl live   2 say Pres   that exactly   not   fast

yi-d-u-n^{3}danilvj^3
nonF Pl 3 Pl accept

that's   the   Indian   way
that's   the   Indian   way

yu^{3}neg   gvnhd^3 ga-wo^{3}nihis-d
english   with   3 speak Inf

Durbin:

gadohv^3 ij-adv^{3}nel-e^3 v
what   youPl do repP   uh

eligw^{23} d-u-n^3-danilv^{3}j-e^3
possible   Pl 3 Pl accept repP

Wilbur:

v   igad^3-no^3
uh   some and

u-n-atsu^{3}y-v   d-u-n-igi^{3}s-v   no^3 sgina^3
3 Pl be-among exP   Pl 3 Pl receive exP   then   that

as   time   went   on   now
as   time   went   on   now

a-ni-gowhti^{3}s-g-v   osi^3
3 Pl see Prog exP   ok

geh-v^{3}ʔi   nole^3 sgi^{3}na^3 u-wah^{3}sa   igv^{3}w-anvn^{3}di   o^3
be exP   and   that   3 self   3 do Inf   then

gasanul
fast

ohsd   galso^{23}de^3 gv-w-anigis-d
good   house   3 could-get

geh-v^{4}ʔi   now^{23}
be exP   now

d-a-n-igowahti^{23}s-g-v   now^{23} ay^{23}-di
Pl 3 Pl see Prog exP   now   I also

now^{23} sgwu^3 hawa-duli^3 sgi-yu^{4}sdi   now^{23} a-ni-tayoh-v^3
now   also   1 want   that kind   now   3 Pl ask exP

now^{23} eli^3
now   possible

gv-w-a-nigis-d   wuhliye^3?hlv
3 could-get   because

Wilbur:

sihke^3 gohusd?
still   something

Durbin:

gohwel   d-ij-anes-di^3 yi-j-o^{23}hwe^{34}lan
letter   Dst you-all get Inf   nonF 2 write

yi-ski^3-nel^{34} y-i-de-n^3-dadohwe^{23}las^{32}
nonF you/me give   nonF Pl you/I write each-other

ahli^3?ili^3 sv   yi-j-adu^{3}li
letter   sometime   nonF 2 want

Wilbur:

ohsi-gw^{23} gesd^3-no   di-g-owelisg^3
good just   not and   Pl 1 write

y-ig   j-iga^3 hase^{3}no   y-eligw^3
nonF bePl   quantity   but   nonF possible

sganol^3 agw-owe^{3}lod   gayolh^3 sgwu
slow   1 write   a-little   also

ki^3 g-adoleh^{3}gwa   di-gw-owelodi^3
just now   1 learn   Pl 1 write

Durbin:

sgi-dv^3 h-n-adv^{3}neh-v   yi-de^{23}-ha^{3}dehlogw^3 ta^{3}ʔl-sgo^{23}
that Emp   2 Spec do exP   nonF Pl 2 learn   two ten

taʔli^3 iya^{3}gwadetiyvd^{23} ges-v^3 d-agw-adel^{23}hgw-a
two   year-old   be exP   Pl 1 learn Pres

di-gw-ohwe^{23}lo^{32}-di
Pl 1 write Inf

I   learned   how   to   read   when
I   learned   how   to   read   when

I   was   ten
I   was   ten

sgoh^{23} y-a^{3}gw-adetiyvd^{23} ges-v^3 di-gi-goli^{23}ye^{32}-di^3
ten   nonF 1 year-old   be exP   Pl 1 read Inf

agw-adelh^{23}gw-a   di-gw-ohwe^{23}lo^{32}-di-nh^{23} taʔl^{32}-sgoh
1 learn Pres   Pl 1 write Inf and   two ten

taʔl^{32} iya^{3}gwadetiyvd^{23} a-n-iyo^{3}s-g-i
two   years-old   3 Pl be-soldier Prog Ag

jiy-a^{3}ʔ-v   e-ji^{23}-hno^3 ji-ges-v^3 wi-d-agw-o^{3}hwelaneh-o^3
1 be-in exP   1Pos mother and   Rel be exP   Tr Pl he/me write Hab

di-jalagi-ha^3 yo^{3}neg   do-d-ag-o^{32}we^{23}lan^{32}
Pl cherokee in   english   Fut Pl 1 write

gvhd^3 de-g-o^{32}we^{23}li^{32}s-g-o^3 dlv^{32}yv^3
with   Pl 1 write Prog Hab   finally

agw-adanhte^{23}hl-v^3 di-jalag
1 think exP   Pl cherokee

ta?l^{32} n-agw-a^{3}nelhta^{3}n-v^3 d-agw-adelhgwa^3?-v^3 di-gw-ohwe^{23}lo^{32}-di^3
two   n 1 attempt exP   Pl 1 learn exP   Pl 1 write Inf

sgi^3 yi-n-j-adv^{32}nel^{23} sgwu
that   nonF Spec 2 do   also

yi-de^{23}h-a^{3}dehlohgw^3 di-j-owe^{23}lo^{32}-di^3
nonF Pl 2 learn   Pl 2 write Inf

Wilbur:

ay-di^3 nvh^{3}a-sgo^3 y-a^{3}gw-adehy-v^3 ulohsvsd^3 e^{34}lisd
I also   four ten   nonF 1 year-old exP   past   probably

geh-e^3 kil
be repP   until

sgi^3 yi-n-a^{3}gw-adv^{3}nel-e^3 a-ni-yoh^{3}sgoi   uji^{23}nv^{4}h-u^3 yi-w-u^{23}-n-dages-e^3
that   nonF Spec 1 do repP   3 Pl be-soldier   away repP   nonF Tr 3 Pl throw
                                                              repP

yi-wv^{23}-ksduhnenh^3
nonF 1 would-be-jailed

censorship   y-u-ni^3-yostano^{3}hn-e^3 gowel
censorship   nonF 3 Pl tear-up repP   letter

Durbin:

yi-j-o^{23}hwe^{34}land-v^3
nonF 2 write exP

gohwel   di-j-anes-di^3
letter   Pl 2 receive Inf

Wilbur:

gest^3 hvsgwu^3 ji
not   also   much

ga^3 yi-ji^3-sin-a^3 di-gw-ohw e^{23}lo-di
quantity   nonF 1 know Pres   Pl 1 write Inf

chanel-ine^3 w-agw-alehn-v^3 gesd^{23}
eight Ord   Tr 1 go-to exP   not

d-iksgwa-dv^3 y-ig
1 have-finished   nonF

Wilbur:

sgi-gwu^3-ju^3 niga^3?
that just Ques   all

Durbin:

v   sgi-gwu^3-dv^3 gv-yali?e^{23}li^{32}chisi^{32}
yes   that just Emp   I-you thank

Syllabary

Durbin: ᎠᏬᏍᏃ ᏍᏂᎫ ᏫᏲᎠᏅᏁᎣ

Wilbur: i

Durbin: ᏪᏛᎣᎠᏅᏂ ᏉᏁᏫᏏ ᏔᏬᎠᏅᎣᎶ ᏂᏫᏬᎠ ᏪᏁ ᎤᏍᏣᏴᎤᎡᎡ ᏓᏫᏴ ᎤᏬᏣ
           ᎠᏂ ᎠᏁᏫ ᎠᎲᏪᎵᏉ ᏍᎩᏣᎫ ᏧᏫᏔ ᎤᏬ

Wilbur: ᎠᎵᏥᎢᎤᎶᎣᏫ

Durbin: ᎠᎵᏥᎢᎤᎶᎣᏫ ᎲᏅᏃ ᏒᏫ ᏍᏥᏫ

Wilbur: ᎤᎵᎯ ᏰᏫᏙ

Durbin: ᎤᎵ ᏰᏫᏪ

Wilbur: ᎤᎵᎯ

Durbin: ᎤᎵᎯ

Wilbur: ᎠᎥᏅᏃ ᎲᏁᏚ ᎤᎲᏚᏔᎤᏫ Charles Wilbur ᏰᏫᏙ ᏞᏥᏫ ᎣᏴᎾ ᎠᏘᏁ
           ᏞᏥᏫᎣᎮ ᎢᎡ ᏔᏚ ᎢᏳᎣᎲᎣᎠ ᎤᎵᎯ ᎬᏫᏉᏉ

Durbin: ᎯᎳᎲ Ᏼ ᏍᏗᎷᏤ ᎭᎦᎳᎨᎹ

Wilbur: ᏔᎵᏌ ᏄᏒ ᎢᏳ ᏦᎨᎲ ᎤᎲᏒ ᏌᏁᎳ ᎢᏳ ᎢᏳᏣᏂᏄ

Durbin: ᎦᎪᎲ ᎡᏍᏗᏩᏛᎯᏙ

Wilbur: ᎠᏴᏃ ᎨᏒ ᎠᏂᏴᏫᏯ ᏂᎦᏙᏉ ᎦᏦᏩᎲᎯᏙ ᏂᏗᎦᎵᏍᏙᏗ Ꭿ ᎠᎬᏭ ᎩᎳ ᎨᏙ ᎠᏌᏂ ᎭᎦᎳᎨᎹ ᎤᏦᏍᏊᏯ ᎠᏆᏛᎦᏅ Ꭿ ᏍᎩᎾ Ꮜ ᏣᎳᎩ ᎾᎾ ᏌᏂ ᎤᏪᏘ ᏂᏓᏣᏂᏣᏒ ᎠᏁᎲ ᏍᎩᏉ ᎠᎩᎦᏛᏂᏙᏌ ᏄᎾᏛᏖᎦᎬ ᏃᎴ ᎢᏳᏍᏗ Ꭵ ᎢᏳᏍᏗ ᏄᎾᏛᏖᎦᎬ ᏍᎩᎾ ᎾᏖ ᎠᏂᏁᎩᏄ ᎠᏂᏁᏄ ᏚᏙᏓᏋᏓ ᎢᏳᏍᏗ ᎾᎾᏛᏁᎵᏙᎲ ᏍᎩᏃ ᏧᏓᎴᏂᏅᏓᏯ ᏍᎩ ᎢᎬᏩᎵᏍᏔᏅᏓ ᏍᏆᎳ ᏭᏂᎬᏁᎵ Ꭿ ᏭᏂᏦᏫ ᎢᏳᏍᏗ ᏄᎾᏛᏖᎦᎬ Ꭵ ᏧᏙᏓᏋᏓ Ꭵ ᎠᏂᏁᏄ ᎠᎾᎢᏒ ᎢᎦ ᏧᏓᎴᏅᏓ ᏃᎴ Ꭵ ᏧᏂᎳᏫᏍᏗ ᎨᎮ ᏍᏯ ᏴᏫ ᎢᏳᏍᏗ ᏂᎨᎦᏛᏁᎲ ᏍᎩ ᏂᎦᏓ ᎢᎬᏩᎵᏍᏔᏅᏓ ᏃᎴ Ꭵ ᏑᏃᏢᏓ ᎨᏌ ᏯᎾᏛᎩ ᎭᏍᏓ ᏑᏃᏢᏓ ᏭᎩ ᏍᎩᎾ Ꮜ ᏍᎩᎾ Ꮜ ᏭᎬᏩᎵᏍᏔᏅᏓ ᏍᎩᏊ ᏳᏍᏗ ᏌᎩᏑᏛᏂᏙ ᎠᏴ

Durbin: ᏚᏓᎴᏖᎠᎨ Ꭵ ᎠᏌᏂ ᏃᎴ ᏗᏤᏅᏒ

Wilbur: ᎥᏌᏃ Ꮶ ᎢᎦ ᏍᎩᎾ ᏴᏫ ᏄᏍᏗ ᎤᎾᏂᎩᏍᏗ ᎨᏒ Ꮭ ᏓᎴ ᎾᏍᎩᏂ Ꭵ ᎢᏳᏍᏗ Ꭵ ᏙᏗ ᏳᏍᏗᏃ ᏴᏓ ᏍᎩᎾ ᏗᎨ ᎡᎵᏍᏗ Ꭵ ᏂᎦᏓ ᎨᎲ Ꮎ ᎤᏍᏗ ᎥᏝ Ꭿ ᏭᏚᏓᎴᏌ ᏍᎩᏯ ᎢᎦ ᏂᎨᎦᏛᏁᎲ ᏦᎦᎦᎵᏃᏢᎵᏙᎲ ᎤᏒ ᎢᎦ ᎬᏆᎴᏅᏓ Ꭵ ᏍᏗᎩᏓᏃ ᎢᎦᏓ ᎨᏍᏗ Ꭵ ᎢᏳᏍᏗ ᎢᎨᎦᏛᏁᏗ ᏂᎨᎦᏛᏁ ᎢᏳᏍᏗ ᏯᏂᎩᎠ ᎢᎦᏓ ᎭᏏ ᏄᎾᏛᏅᎯ ᏃᎴ ᎢᎦᏓ ᎤᏥᎢ ᏄᎾᏛᏅ ᎦᏛᎩᎠ ᏍᎩᏃ ᏦᎦᏗ ᎨᏍᏗ ᎠᏴ ᏭᎪᎵᎦ Ꮟ ᎠᏋᏈᏃ ᏗᏦᎦᏙᎵ ᏯᏋᎳᏁ ᏭᏦᎦᏔᏢ ᎢᏅᏍᏗ Ꭵ ᏗᏓᎴᏂᏍᎬ ᎨᎵ Ꮟ ᎢᎦᏓ ᎨᏍᏗ ᏰᎵ Ꭵ ᎠᏂᏌ ᏄᎾᏍᏛ ᎢᎦ ᏯᏂᎩ ᎢᏳᏍᏗ ᎤᏂᎩᏍᏗ ᎨᏒ ᎤᎾᎵᏍᎦᏄᏙᏗ ᎨᏒᎢ ᏓᏂᏁᎩᏄ ᎤᏥ ᏄᎾᏛᏅ ᎠᎾᏗᏍᎪ Ꭿ Ꮅ ᎢᏅᎯ ᎨᏒ ᎠᏙ ᏗᎨᏒ ᎢᏴ ᏗᏂᏁᎵ ᎨᏒ ᎡᏍᎦᏯ Ꭿ ᎡᏍᎦᏂ ᏗᏂᏁᎵ ᎦᏚᎲ ᎾᎥᏂᎨ ᏭᎩ ᎢᏳᏍᏗ ᎦᏛᎩ ᎥᏝᏃ ᏭᏝᎦᏔ ᏍᎩᎾ Ꮜ ᎤᏦᏊᏯ ᎠᏆᏓᎴᏤᏌ Ꭵ ᏙᏂᏳᏍᏗ ᎠᏓᎴᏂᏌ ᏍᎩᎾ ᎤᏥ ᎢᏂᏗᎬᏩ ᎾᏛᏖᎦᎩ ᎢᏴ ᏃᎴ ᏢᏍᎦᏂᎨᎲ ᎦᏦᎪᏩᏘᏍᎬ ᎭᏏᏯ ᎢᏳᏍᏗ ᏄᎾᏛᎾᎦᎬ ᎢᎨᎵ ᎤᏦᏊᏯᏃ ᏔᎵᏌ ᏄᎾᏓᎴ ᏄᏂᏍ ᏄᏂᏍᏗ ᎾᏆᎵᏍᏓᏁ

Durbin: ᎳᏍᎪ ᏍᎩ ᏭᏄᏍᏗ Ꭵ ᏗᏤᏅᏒ

Wilbur: Ꭵ ᎥᏝᏃ ᏍᎩᎦ ᎠᏩᏓᎴᏤᏢᏃ Ꭵ ᎠᏴ ᏍᎩᎾ ᏗᎦᎳᏫᏍᏗ ᏗᏦᎳᏫᎩ ᎯᎩ Ꭵ ᎭᏝᏁᎳᏗᏍᎪ ᏂᎦᏓ ᏂᎬ ᏍᎩᎾ ᏙᏝᎦᏎᏍᏙᏔᏂᏓᏍᏗ ᎤᏥᎢ ᏭᏄᏛᎾ ᏍᎩᎾ ᏡᏦᏃᏢᏍᎪ Ꭵ ᎠᏂᏩᏦᎾ ᏚᎾᏓᏁᏄ ᏚᎾᏙᎵᏒᎢ ᎦᎵᏌᎦ ᏗᎾᏁᏍᎨᏍᎩ ᎪᏍᏓ social service ᏭᎩ ᎠᏘᏗ ᏦᎩ ᏍᎩᎾ ᏌᏂ ᎬᏂᎨᏒ ᏂᏙᏣᏁᎮ ᎭᏝᏁᏄᏗᏍᎪ ᏍᎩᏃ Ꭿ ᏨᏓᎴᎩ ᏦᎦᏗ ᎠᏴ ᏄᎾᏛᏅ ᎨᏍᏗ Ꭺ ᏯᏂᎩ Ꮜ ᏌᎾᏗᎠ ᎬᏉᏎ ᎢᎦᏓ ᏌᏂᏃᏢᏍᎬ ᎨᏍᏗ ᏭᎨᎦᏑᏎᏍᏓᏁᏍᎪ ᏙᏳ ᎤᏥᎢ ᏄᎾᏛᏖ ᏌᎾᏗ ᎨᏍᏗᏃ ᏭᏦᎪᏩᏓ Ꭵ ᏭᎪᎵᎦ ᏍᎩᎾ ᏌᏂ Ꭿ Ꭵ ᏗᏂᎳᏫᎩ ᎤᎾᏚᏓᎵ ᏧᎾᏤᎵ ᎬᏩᏨᏯᎩᏗ ᎨᎲ ᏓᏁᎲ ᏍᎦᏚᎩ ᎦᎪᏒᏩᏘᏒᎢ ᏧᎾᎦᏎᏍᏙᏗ

Durbin: ᏍᎩᏗᏙ ᏄᏍdi Ꭵ ᏂᏗᎦᎵᏍᏙᏗᏍᎬᏃ ᏍᏊ Ꭵ ᎦᏲᎵ ᎨᏒ ᏜᎧᏃᏢᎵ ᎥᏍᎩ ᏣᎳᎩ ᎠᏂᏬᏂᏍᎩ ᎨᏒ Ꮎ ᏣᎳᎩ ᎤᏂᏬᏂᎯᏍᏗ ᎤᏂᎭ ᏍᎩᎶᏍᏗ ᎠᏂᏬᏂᏍᎩ ᎤᏏᏴ ᏂᏧᎾᏛᏏ Ꮎ ᏌᎷᏜᏴ ᎠᏙᎯᏴ Ꭵ ᏝᏃ ᏳᎾᏚᎵᏍᎪ ᎦᎦᏚᎲ ᏂᏙᏓᎶᎾᏛᏁᏙᏗ Ꭵ ᏍᎩᏃ ᏣᎳᎩ ᎠᏂᏬᏂᏍᎩ Ꮩ ᎠᏂᏣᎳᎩ ᎨᏒ ᎠᎭᏂᏃ ᏚᏂᏄᏫᏍᏓᏁ ᎤᏣ ᎢᎦ ᎠᏂᏲᏁᎦ Ꭵ ᏍᎩᏃ ᏍᏗᎩᏓ ᏓᎾᏓᎴᎪ ᏳᏍᏗ

Wilbur: ᏙᎾᎯᏳᏍᏗ ᏗᏓᎴᏂᎭ ᏍᎩᎤ ᎣᏍᏓ ᎭᏂ ᎡᏍᎦᏃ ᎾᎥᏂᎨ ᎠᏂᏁᎩᎵ ᎣᏏ ᏳᏍᏗ ᏄᎾᏛᎤ ᎤᏙᏳ ᏗᎾᏁᏎᏍᎩ ᎦᎪᏍᎲ ᎢᎦᏓ ᏦᏍᏓ ᏓᏂᏁᎩᎵ Ꭴ ᏍᎩᎾ Ꭲ ᎯᏳ ᏫᏂᎦᎷᎬᎾ ᏥᎩ ᏍᎩᎾ ᏫᏗᎨᎦᏁᏍᎨᏗ ᎤᎾ ᎢᏴᎢ

Durbin: Ꭵ ᎢᎦᏓᏛ ᏍᏊ ᎠᏂᏣᎳᎩ ᏥᎩ ᏍᏊ Ꮭ ᏳᎾᏚᎵᏍᎪ Ꮭ Ꭵ Ꮭ ᏳᎾᏚᎵ

Wilbur: ᎠᏂᎾᏰᏍᎬ

Durbin: ᎥᎲ ᏍᎩ

Wilbur: ᏣᏍᎪᏃ ᏯᏗᏁᎭ ᎩᎶ ᏗᏂᎳᏫᎩ ᎣᏍᏓ ᏫᏗᎬᏩᏃᏏᏎᏗ

Durbin: ᎩᎳᏃ ᏍᎩᏴ ᎣᏣᎯᎵᏙ ᏓᏲᏣᎴᎤ ᏍᎩ ᏃᏣᏛᏁᎲ ᎣᏥᏃᏢᎵᏙᎲ Ꮎ Ꭵ ᎥᏍᎩ ᎢᎬᏩᎵᏍᏙᏗ ᎨᏒ ᏍᏗᎯᏓᏃ ᎣᎩᏍᎦᏃᎵ

Wilbur: i what means speech not i do not know how to say it ᏳᏁᎦ ᎤᏤᎵ ᏓᎦᏙᎵᏏ i breakdown communication ᎢᏳᏍᏗ ᎾᏆᎵᏍᏓᏁ ᏍᎩ Ꭿ

Durbin: ᏍᎩᏃ Ꭵ ᏗᏓᎴᎤᎢᏍᏗ ᎨᏒ Ꮎ Ꭵ ᏛᏣᏃᏢᏣᏙᎲ ᏍᎩᎾ ᎤᏣ ᎢᎦ

Wilbur: ᎠᏎᏃᎨ ᎢᏥᎯᎵ ᏍᎩᎾ ᎣᏍᏓ ᎢᏨᏁᏗ

Durbin: Ꭵ ᎣᏥᎯᎵᏛ

Wilbur: ᏔᎵᎭ ᎾᎦᎫᏴ ᏃᎴ ᎡᎵᏍᏗ ᏰᎵᏉ ᏍᏗᎩᏓ ᎣᏍᏛ ᎢᏳᎵᏍᎳᏂᏓ ᎨᏢᏍᏗ

Durbin: i about five maybe

Wilbur: maybe never ᏂᏗᎦᎵᏍᏙᏗᎲ ᎠᎦᎳ ᎧᏂᎦᏗ ᏍᏊᎤ ᎠᏎ ᎡᎳᏗ ᏁᏨᏁ ᎠᎦᎳ

Durbin: ᎢᏄᏍᎩᏛ ᎢᏇᏂ ᎦᎨᏥᏲᏌ ᏚᏂᏄᏫᏍᏓᏁᎲ ᎠᎭᏂ ᎯᎠᏊ ᏏᎤᏓ ᏔᎵ ᎢᎤᏓ ᏥᎨᏒ

Wilbur: ᎡᎵᏍᏗ ᏃᏉ ᎦᏲᎳ ᎢᏳᏍᏗ ᏂᏗᎦᎵᏍᏙᏗᏍᎬ ᏍᎩᎾ ᏍᎩᏳ ᏫᏂᎦᎷᎬᎾ ᎨᎲ ᏍᎩᎾ ᎣᏍᏓ ᎢᏳᎾᎵᏍᏓᏁᏗ ᎦᏥᏄᏫᏍᏓᏁᎲ ᏃᎴ ᏂᏗᎦᎵᏍᏙᏗᎭ ᎨᏍᏗ ᏳᎾᏚᎵ ᎤᎤᏌ ᎭᏂᎾᏰᏍᎦ ᏧᎾᏓᏂᏄᎢᏍᏗ ᏍᎩᏍ

Durbin: ᎥᎲ

Wilbur: ᏍᎨᎠ ᏄᏍᏗ ᏴᏫᏯ ᎠᏎ that is the Indian way ᎠᏛᏗ ᎢᎦᏓ

Durbin: ᎠᏎᏍᎩᏂ ᎠᏊ ᎨᎵᏍᎪ ᏴᎾ Ꭵ ᎣᏍᏓ ᏱᏗᎧᏃᎯᏎᎳ Ꭵ ᎢᎬᏩᎵᏍᏔᏂᏓᏍᏗ ᎨᏒ ᏬᏃᎵᎩ ᎨᎵ ᏳᎾᎦᎳ ᎤᎾᏑᎳᏗᏍᏗ

Wilbur: ᏱᏓᏥᎶᏍᏔᏂ ᎠᏴ ᎤᏐᏱ ᎠᏴ ᏐᏱᏣᎨᏜ ᎠᎬᏱ Ꮎ ᏣᎤᏔ mutual help program ᏃᏊ ᎠᏴ ᏭᎩᎷᏙᎳ ᏍᎩ ᏳᏍᏗ Ꭵ ᎠᎬᏱ ᏍᏊ ᎠᎩᏍᎦᎢᏒᎢ ᏥᎣᎵ ᎠᏴ ᏍᎩ ᏱᎬᏆᎦᎳ ᏩᏥᎾ ᏍᎩᎾ ᏄᏍᏛ ᏧᏛᎤᎢᏍᏗ ᎠᏎᏃ ᎠᏂᏃᏢᏍᎬ ᏂᏕᏓ ᎤᏌᎦᎯ ᏄᎤᏁᏛᏅ ᏍᎩᎾᎢ ᎤᏲᎢ ᏂᏣᏛᎤ ᏕᏥᏁᎩᏅ ᏫᏍᏓ ᏂᏓᏨᏴᏁᎵ ᏃᎴ ᎠᏈᏱᏗ ᎨᏒ ᏍᏗ ᏓᏣᏈᏴᏢᏏ ᏃᏊᏃ Ꮩ ᏱᏕᎵᏍᏓ ᎬᏈᏱᏗ ᏂᎨᏒᎾ ᏱᎩ ᏕᏙᎯ ᎠᏓᏗᏁᎵ ᏱᎩ ᏕᏲᏟ ᏩᏥᎾ ᎤᏓᏗᏁᏑᏗ ᏱᎩ ᏍᎩᎾ ᏕᎵᏐᏕ ᏗᎾᏁᏍᎨᏍᎩ ᎨᏜ Qualla houses ᎠᎾᏗᏍᎪ ᏍᎩᏂ ᎠᏂ ᎤᎾᏙᎵ ᏂᏕᎵᏍᏗ ᏍᎩ ᎢᏕ ᏓᏲᏒ ᏕᎵᏐᏕ ᎠᏌᏜ ᎠᎶᏁᏍᎨᏜᎴ ᏱᎩ ᎯᏅᎯᏳ ᏃᏊ ᎠᏴ ᏆᏙᎵ ᎢᎬᏩᎵᏍᏙᏗ ᏬᎩᏅᏅᏂ ᎠᏆᏈᏴᏗ ᏕᎵᏐᏕ ᎠᎩᏲᎱᏍᏅ ᏱᎩ ᏕᏙᎯ ᏱᎦᎾᏓᏂᏅᏟ that is just the Indian way ᏳᏗᏁᏕ ᎬᎾᏗ ᏕᏭᏂᎯᏍᏗ

Durbin: ᏕᏙᏜ ᎢᏣᏛᏗᏁᎴ Ꭵ ᎡᎵᏊ ᎦᎾᏓᏂᏅᏟ

Wilbur: Ꭵ ᎢᏕᏓᏃ ᎤᎾᏧᏴ ᎦᏲᎩᏒ ᏃᏊ ᏍᎩᎾ as time went on now ᎠᏂᎪᏩᏘᏍᎬ ᎣᏏ ᎨᏜᎢ ᏃᎴ ᏍᎩᎾ ᎤᏩᏌ ᎢᎬᏩᎤᏁᏗ ᏃᏊ ᏕᏌᏅ ᎣᏍᏓ ᏕᎵᏐᏕ ᎬᏩᏂᎩᏍᏗ ᎨᏜᎢ ᏃᏊ ᏓᏂᎪᏩᏘᏍᎬ ᏃᏊ ᎠᏴᏗ ᏃᏊ ᏍᏊ ᏇᏩᎦᎵ ᏍᎩᏳᏍᏗ ᏃᏊ ᎠᏂᏔᏲᏜ ᏃᏊ ᎡᎵ ᎬᏩᏂᎩᏍᏗ ᏝᏟᏰᎶᎵ

Wilbur: ᏏᏢ ᎪᎱᏍᏗ

Durbin: ᎪᏪᎵ ᏗᏣᏁᏍᏗ ᏱᏦᏪᎳᎤ ᏱᏍᎩᏁᎳ ᏱᎦᎾᏓᏙᏢᎳᏏ ᎪᏪᎵ ᎠᎯᎢᎵᏒ ᏱᏣᎦᎵ

Wilbur: ᎣᏏᏊ ᎨᏍᏗᏃ ᏗᎪᏪᎵᏍᎩ ᏱᎩ ᏥᏕ ᏇᏎᏃ ᏰᎵᏊ ᏍᏕᏃᎵ ᎠᏉᏪᎶᏗ ᏕᏲᏟ ᏍᏊ Ꮟ ᏕᏙᎴᏆ ᏗᏉᏪᎶᏗ

Durbin: ᏍᎩᏛ ᏂᏛᏗᏁᏜ ᏱᏕᏇᏕᎨᎶᏆ ᏔᎵᏍᎪ ᏔᎵ ᎢᏬᏆᏕᏘᏴᏓ ᎨᏒ ᏓᏆᏕᎵᏆ ᏗᏉᏢᎶᏗ I learned how to read when I was ten ᏍᎪᎯ ᏬᏆᎠᏕᏘᏴᏓ ᎨᏒ ᏗᎩᎪᎵᎡᏗ ᎠᏆᏕᎵᏆ ᏗᏉᏢᎶᏗᏂᏃ ᏔᎵᏍᎪ ᏔᎵ ᎢᏬᏆᏕᏘᏴᏓ ᎠᏂᏲᏍᎩ ᏥᏬᎥ ᎡᏟᏃ ᏟᎨᏒ ᎾᏓᏉᏢᎳᏁᎨ ᏗᏣᎳᎩᏇ ᏲᏁ ᎬᏗ ᏕᎪᏪᎵᏍᎪ ᎵᏴ ᎠᏆᏓᎾᎵ ᏗᏣᎳᎩ ᏙᏓᎪ ᏪᎳᏂ ᏔᎵ ᎾᏆᏁᎵᎳᎤ ᏓᏆᏕᎳᏆᎥ ᏗᏉᏪᎶᏗ ᏍᎩ ᏱᏂᏣᏛᏁᎵ ᏍᏊ ᏬᏕᎶᏆ ᏗᏦᏪᎶᏗ

Wilbur: ᎠᏴᏗ ᎤᏇᏍᎪ ᏬᏆᏕᏜ ᎤᎶᏒᏍᏗ ᎡᎵᏍᏗ ᎨᏢ ᎩᎳ ᏍᎩ ᏱᎾᏆᏛᏁᎴ ᎠᏂᏲᏍᎩᎢ ᎤᏥᎤᏢ ᏱᏝᎾᏓᎨᏎ ᏱᏮᎩᏍᎦᏃ censorship ᏳᏂᏲᏍᏔᏃᏁ ᎪᏪᎵ

Durbin: ᏱᏦᏪᎳᎾᏛ ᏊᏪᎵ ᏗᏣᏁᏍᏗ

Wilbur: ᎨᏍᏗ ᏜᏍᏊ Ꮵ Ꮥ ᏱᏥᏏᎾ ᏗᏉᏪᎶᏗ ᏣᏁᎵᏁ ᏩᏆᎴᏜ ᎨᏍᏗ ᏗᎩᏍᏕᏛ ᏱᎩ

Wilbur: ᏫᎩᎰᏗ ᎯᏚ

Durbin: i ᏫᎩᏭᏉ ᎬᎯᏈᏒᏈᎭᏏ

English

Durbin: This is October 10th, isn't it?

Wilbur: Yes.

Durbin: October 10th, 1982. We have two visitors from North Carolina. One of them is "Bo."

Wilbur: He's a preacher.

Durbin: A preacher, and what is your name?

Wilbur: Wilbur Sequoyah.

Durbin: Wil Sequoyah.

Wilbur: Wilbur.

Durbin: Wilbur.

Wilbur: My first name in English is Charles Wilbur Sequoyah. I am called by my middle name mostly. They call me Wilbur.

Durbin: When did you arrive in Oklahoma?

Wilbur: Two days ago, around nine o'clock at night.

Durbin: Who are you visiting?

Wilbur: I'm just here to visit all the Indians. Because this is my first time to be in Oklahoma. I've heard a lot of stories from people who have come from North Carolina who live here. I'm just here to find out how people live here on a daily basis. I want to see what type of services they are receiving and whether or not they are hearing the gospel.

Durbin: Do you find much difference between here and North Carolina?

Wilbur: Not much. The lifestyles are not different but . . . how would you say? I guess there is not that big a difference. Just that I've been talking with others here regarding services. It seems some of them are not receiving what they should. Some are better off than others. I really don't understand this. Maybe as I see more, I'll begin to understand. Those that are farther away from here seem to be poorer than those close by.

Durbin: Isn't it like that where you're from?

Wilbur: Well, I'm a council member, and we try to reach all those in need and then repeat it to the tribal administrator. We provide them with information concerning public housing, social services, and so forth. Here I am being told that the people out there are not being informed.

Durbin: That' s true to some extent, because the Cherokee-speaking population who are monolingual are being left out on a lot of information.

Wilbur: I've noticed that there are services such as housing, but why doesn't it reach all the people?

Durbin: Some of the Cherokees would rather not receive such services.

Wilbur: They are afraid of it?

Durbin: Yes, that's it.

Wilbur: Aren't there council members who can go and communicate with them?

Durbin: I think we're just now realizing how important it is to communicate in Cherokee.

Wilbur: It seems there's a breakdown in communication.

Durbin: Yes. That's a big problem.

Wilbur: But you're correcting that situation?

Durbin: We are working on it.

Wilbur: Maybe within the next two years?

Durbin: Maybe about five.

Wilbur: Maybe never, because of budget cuts.

Durbin: There have been a few that have been laid off here.

Wilbur: I guess it hasn't picked up with the rest of them because they are afraid to accept those services. Is that it?

Durbin: Yes.

Wilbur: I guess that's just the Indian way.

Durbin: But I believe that if you gave them the complete information, they would accept it.

Wilbur: It was the same with us. They would tell us about all these services they had to offer, but I was the first to speak up against it.

Durbin: How did your people come to accept it?

Wilbur: There were a few who readily accepted, and then when others saw that it was working for them, the rest followed.

Wilbur: Anything else?

Durbin: If you would give me your address, we could correspond.

Wilbur: That would be all right, although I am just now learning.

Durbin: That's how you can learn. I was twenty-two years old before I started writing. I learned to read when I was ten, but I didn't learn to write until I was twenty-two. I was in the army, and my mother would write to me in Cherokee, and I'd write back in English. Then I made myself write in Cherokee. If you'll do that, you'll learn.

Wilbur: I think I'll be forty years old before I learn. If I had done that when I was in the military service, they would have torn up my letters and thrown me in jail.

Durbin: You can write your address here.

Wilbur: I can write very well; I've only finished the eighth grade. Is that all?

Durbin: Yes, that's all. Thank you.

Throw It Home

Mose Killer

In this story, Mose Killer of Greasy, Oklahoma, relates what happened when he attempted to play baseball without yet knowing the rules of the game. The result was comical but disappointing to the members of his team.

ᏣᎵ	ᎧᏃᎠ	ᎤᏦᏎᎲ	ᏣᏩᏰ	ᎬᏂᎭᏗ	ᏒᏚᎥ
jali	kanuna	ojosehv	jalagi	gvnhd	dudo?v
Charlie	Canoe	we called him	Cherokee	by means of	his name was

ᏣᎵ	ᎧᏃᎠ	ᏲᏁᎦ	ᎬᏂᎭᏗ
charlie	canoe	yoneg	gvnhd
Charlie	Canoe	English	in (by means of)

ᎫᏬᏆᏓ	ᎥᏚᎤᏲᎸᎥᏒ	ᏂᎪᎸ	ᎠᎧᏗ	ᎤᏲᏃᏎᎰ	ᎧᏃᎮᏢᎸᏗ
jojiyolh	dogatvsidisv	nigolv	gosd	ogihnoseho	kanohetlvdi
we children	as we were growing up	always	something	he would tell us	stories

ᎤᎿᏛ	ᏲᎦᏓᏕᏯᏍᏗ	ᎨᎲ	ᎤᎸᎩᏗᎤᏍᏯ	ᎨᎲ	ᎤᏬᏂᎯᏍᏗ
uhnadv	yogadadeysd	gehv	ulvkwdinsgwu	gehv	uwonihisdi
there is where	we would gather around	was	and he liked	was	him to talk

ᏔᎵ	Ꮑ	ᎾᏓᏗᏯ	ᏨᎨᎲ	ᏂᎨᏒᎾᏊᎴ	ᏱᎩ
ta?l	dlv	nadetiy	jigehv	nigesvnagwule	yig
two	about	years ago	when it was	or less than that	it may be

ᎤᏲᎱᏒ	ᏍᎩᏅ	ᎠᏑᏂᏙ	ᎨᎲ	ᏍᏊ	ᎣᎩᏃᏎᎸ
uyohusv	sgihnv	asuhnidoh	gehv	sgwu	ogihnoselv
he died	he	he a fisher	was	one	he told us

ᎤᏁᏦᏂᏙᎸ	ᎢᎦᏓ	ᎠᎾᏁᏣᎥᏍᎬ	ᎠᎾᏗᎰ	ᎢᎦᏓᏅ	ᎠᎾᎳᏍᎦᎵᏍᎬ
uhnejonidolv	igad	anahnejo?vsgv	andiho	igadanh	anlasgalisgv
his ball playing	some	playing sport	they say	and some	playing sport

ᎠᎾᏗᎰ	baseball	ᏍᎩᎾ	ᏌᏭ	ᏳᏩᎧᏗ	ᎣᎩᏃᎯᏎᎸ
andiho	baseball	sginh	sawu	yuwakd	ogihnohiselv
they say	baseball	and that	one	time	he told us

ᎢᎬᏱ	ᎠᏆᎳᏍᎦᎸᎭ	ᎠᏗᎲ	ᏏᎾᎴ	ᎠᏩᏗᏛᎲ	ᏣᏗᎲ
igvyi	agwalasgalvh	adihv	sinale	awdidvhv	jadihv
first	that I played ball	he said	early morning	I got up	he said

ᎠᏭᏅ	Ᏼ	ᎤᎾᏁᏦᏗ	ᎨᏒ	ᏣᏗᎲ	ᎣᏥᏁᎸ
awun	yv	uhnahnejodi	gesv	jadihv	ojinelv
and close	by	baseball diamond	was	he said	we lived

ᎠᎹᏳᎶᏗ	ᎨᎲ	ᎠᏭᏴ	ᎠᏆᏑᏅᏒ	ᏣᏗᎲ	ᏍᏗᏛ
amayulhd	gehv	awyv	aksuhnvsv	jadihv	sdid
close to water	was	close by	I went fishing	he said	a little

ᏒᎯᏰᏱ	ᏗᏜ	ᎠᏩᎦᏌᏔᏂᎸ	ᏣᏗᎲ	boy	ᏍᎩᏛ
svhiyey	didl	awaksatanihlv	jadihv	boy	sgidv
evening	toward	I came upon	he said	boy	that

ᏭᎵᏍᏛ	ᎤᎾᏓᎸᎬ	ᏴᏫ	ᎠᏭᏛ	ᏄᏍᏛ	ᎤᎾᎴᏅᏗ
wulistv	undalgv	yvwi	awdv	nusdv	unlendhi
to the end	there was a crowd	people	close	it was	for them to start

ᎤᎾᎳᏍᎦᎸᏗ	ᏣᏗᎲ	ᏴᏛ	ᎢᏗᏂᏅᎯᏛ	ᏕᏥᏁᎲ	ᎠᏂᎪᎳ
unlasgalhdi	jadihv	yvdv	idininvhid	deji?nehv	anigol
the game	he said	so much	length of	I had	perch

ᏣᏗᎲ	ᏑᏗᏅ	ᎩᎶ	ᏓᏳᏪᎸᏅ	ᏣᏗᎲ	ᏣᎵ
jadihv	suhdinh	kilo	dayuwehluhnv	jadihv	jali
he said	and a fishing pole	someone	yelled out	he said	Charlie

ˋᏓᏳᏛᏅ	ᏣᏗᎲ	ᎢᏍᎩᏍᏕᎳ	ᏌᏊ	ᎣᎩᎷᎶᏤ	ᎠᏁᏦᎥᏍᎩ
dayudvhnv	jadihv	isgisdela	sagwu	ogiluloche	ahno?ejo?vsgi
he yelled out	he said	help us	one	we are lacking	player

ᎤᏛᏅ	ᏣᏗᎲ	boy	ᏂᏥᎦᏔᎲᎾ	ᎠᏗᎲ	ᎠᏩᏁᏦᏗ
udvhnv	jadihv	boy	njigatahvn	adihv	awahnejodi
he said	he said	boy	I didn't know how	he said	to play

ᎢᎸᎯᏳ	ᎠᏆᏒᏂᎸ	ᏱᎨᎮ	ᏍᏆᏞᏍᏗ	ᏣᏗᎲ	ᏓᏩᎵᏨᏯᏍᏔᏅ
ilvhiyu	aksvhnilv	yigehe	sgwahlesd	jadihv	dawalchvyastanv
never	I touched	had not	ball	he said	I worked up some courage

ᏣᏗᎲ	ᎲᎥ	ᎦᏥᏲᎮᎸ	ᏏᎸ	ᏫᏗᏥᏅᏍ	ᎡᏥ
jadihv	hv?v	gajiyohelv	silv	widijinvs	eji
he said	all right	I told them	first	let me go give	mom

ᎯᎠᎾ	ᎠᏂᎪᎳ	ᎩᎳᏮ	ᎢᏥᎷᏨᎢ	ᎦᏥᏲᎮᎸ	ᏣᏗᎲ
hi?ana	anigola	kilaw	iji?luhjv?i	gajiyohelv	jadihv
these	perch	quickly	I will be back	I told them	he said

ᎠᏭ	ᏛᏓᏁᎸ	ᏣᏗᎲ	ᎡᏥᏅ	ᏧᏬᎶ	ᏣᏗᎲ
aw	dvdanelv	jadihv	ejinh	juwohlo	jadihv
close	the house	he said	and mother	was at home	he said

ᎪᎯᏛ	ᎢᏴᎥ	ᏣᏗᎲ	ᏄᎵᏍᏛᎷᏅ	ᎡᏥ	ᏣᏗᎲ
kohidv	iyv?i	jadihv	nulsdvhlunv	eji	jadihv
after a while	then	he said	she sat down	mom	he said

ᎣᏍᏛ	ᏂᏙᏓᏳᏩᏁᎸ	ᎠᏣᏗ	ᎣᎠᎴᏅᎲᏛᏍᏊ	ᎣᏣᎳᏍᎦᎵᎲ	ᏣᏗᎲ
osd	ndodayuwanelv	aja?d	o?alenvhvdvsgwu	ojalasgalihv	jadihv
good	she started to prepare	fish	we started too	playing the game	he said

ᎤᏗᏞᎬᏅ	ᎠᎩᏍᎦᏂ	ᏠᎨᏍ	ᏕᎭᏁᎶᏅᎢ	ᎬᏬᎮᎸ	ᏣᏗᎲ
udihlehgvhnv	agisgani	dloges	dehanlohnv?i	gvwohelv	jadihv
and it was hot	left	field	you play	they told me	he said

ᏐᏁᎵᏁᏛ	ᏙᏥᏴᎯᎲ	ᏣᏗᎲ	ᎭᏛ	ᎫᏍᏗ
sohnelinedv	dojiyuhihv	jadiha	hadv	gusd
and the ninth	inning we were going into	he said	and not	something

ᏱᏙᎢᎾᎡ	ᏍᎩᏛᎾ	ᏭᎵᏍᏛ	ᏙᎠᎨᏍᎸ	ᏣᏗᎲ	ᎤᏂᎾᏩᏍᏛᏅ
yido?ina?e	sgidvna	wulstav	do?ageslv	jadihv	uninawsdvhnv
we had not scored	and that	to the end	we were playing	he said	they were roaring

ᏣᏗᎲ	ᏐᏁᎵᎮᏅ	ᎤᎵᏍᏆᎸᏗ	ᎤᏅᏂᎸ	ᏣᏗᎲ
jadihv	sohnelihehnv	ulsgwalhd	unvhnilv	jadihv
he said	and the ninth	last	they hit	he said

ᏔᎵᏁᏅ	ᎤᎩᎶ	ᏣᏗᎲ	ᏔᎵᏅ	ᏗᎦᏄᎪᏫᏛ	ᏳᏂᏅᏅ
ta?lnenh	ukilo	jadihv	ta?linh	diganugohwid	yuninvn
and on second	he was on	he said	and two	were out	if they scored

ᎪᎢᎶᏍᎬ	ᏫᏓᏆᎧᏁᎾᏅ	ᏣᏗᎲ	ᎡᏥ	Ꮟ	ᎣᏍᏓ
go?ihlosgv	widagwakahnananh	jadihv	eji	si	osd
they would beat us	when I looked	he said	my mother	still	good

ᏂᏙᏗᎬᏁᎰ	ᎠᏣᏗ	ᎪᎯᏛᏴ	ᏣᏗᎲ
nidodigvneho	aja?d	kohidvyv	jadihv
she was preparing	fish	after a while	he said

ᏄᎵᏍᏈᏙᏏᏰᎥ	ᎤᏕᎩ	ᏣᏗᎲ	ᏭᏗᏅᎲ	ᏓᏳᏩᏂᎸ	ᏗᏥᏙᎬ
nulsgwidosiye?v	udeg	jadihv	wudinvhv	dayuwahnilv	dijidogv
he contorted	pitcher	he said	he pitched	he hit	where I was standing

ᏥᏳᎪᏗ	ᏌᏊ	ᏳᏓᏗᏅᏛ	ᎠᎢᏂᏴᎲ	ᏣᏗᎲ	ᎩᎶ
jiyukodi	sawu	yudadinvd	a?iniyvhv	jadihv	kilo
straight to	one	bounce	I caught it	he said	someone

ᏫᎤᏩᎸᎰᏅ	ᏣᏗᎲ	ᎠᏗᏝ	ᎣᏣᎵᏣᎰᎥ	ᏍᎩᏪᎾᎥ	ᏒᎵᏍᏗᎥ
dvʔuwehluhnv	jadihv	adidl	oʔaliʔohv	sgiwhnv	wulstv
he yelled	he said	toward that way	our teammate	and that	to the end

ᏩᏍᏗᏙᎵᏓᏫᏗᏎ	ᏍᎣᎥᎥᏎᎬ	ᏣᏗᎲ	ᏍᏲᎤᏎᎬ	ᏣᎵ	ᏓᏳᏛᎲᏅ
wasdidoldawdisv	ganvʔvsgv	jadihv	ogihlosgv	jali	dayudvhnv
he was racing toward	he was scoring	he said	we were losing	Charlie	he said to me

ᏣᏗᎲ	throw	it	home	ᏓᏳᏛᎲᏅ	boy
jadihv	throw	it	home	dayudvhnv	boy
he said	throw	it	home	he said	boy

ᏩᎩᎩᏒ	ᏣᏗᎲ	ᏍᏆᎵᏍᏗ	ᎠᏆᎧᏔᎲᏒ	ᏣᏗᎲ	ᏗᏓᏁᎵᏫ
wagigisv	jadihv	sgwahlesd	awaktahvsv	jadihv	didanelv
I took	he said	the ball	I turned	he said	to the house

ᏩᏩᏗᏅᏒ	ᎠᎴ	ᎤᏂᏥᏍᎫᎮᎥ	ᎡᏥ	ᎠᏣᏗ
wawadinvsv	ale	winjisguhyv	eji	ajaʔd
I threw it	almost	I hit her on the head	my mother	fish

ᏍᏏᏓ	ᏂᏙᏛᎩᎾᎮᏫ	ᏣᏗᎲ
osda	ndodgvnehv	jadihv
good	preparing	he said

Morpheme by Morpheme

jal²³i kanuna
charlie canoe

oj-oseh-v³ jalagi³
they-and-I call exP cherokee

gvnhd d-u-doʔ-v
in Pl 3be-named Exp

charlie   canoe   yo^{3}neg   gvnhd
charlie   canoe   english   in

j-oji-yolh^{23} d-og-atvsi^{23}-di^{32}s-v   nigo^{23}lv^3
Pl they-and-1Pos child   Pl they-and-I grow Inc exP   always

gosd^{23} ogi-hnose^{23}h-o
something   they-and-I tell Hab

kanohetlvdi
stories

uhna^3-dv^3 y-og-a^{3}d<u>a</u>deysd   geh-v^3
there Emp   nonF they-and-I gather   be exP

u-lv^{23}kwdi-n-sgwu   geh-v^3 ga-woni^{23}hi^{3}s-di
3 like and just   be exP   3 speak Inf

ta?l   hlv^3 nadetiy^{23} ji-geh-v
two   about   years ago   Rel be exP

n<u>i</u>-ge^{3}s-v^{32} na-gwu^3-le^3
Neg be exP   Neg just or

y-ig   <u>u</u>-yohus-v^3 sgi-hnv^3
nonF be   3 die exP   that and

a-su^{23}hni^{3}doh   geh-v^3 sgwu^3 <u>o</u>gi-hnos-e^{23}l-v
3 fish   be exP   also   he-them-and-me say Dat exP

u-hnejo^{3}ni-do^{32}-v   igad^3 a-n-ahnejo^3?vs-g-v   a-n-di^{23}h-o^3
3 play-ball here-and-there exP   some   3 Pl play-contact-sport   3 Pl say Hab
                                          Prog exP

i^{23}ga^{3}da-nh^3 a-n-la^{32}sg<u>a</u>li^{23}s-g-v   a-n-di^{23}h-o^3
some and   3 Pl play Prog exP   3 Pl say Hab

baseball   sgi-nh^3 sawu^3
baseball   that and   one

yuwakd^{23} ogi-hnohi̲s-e^{23}l-v^3
time   he-them-and-me Dat exP

igvyi^3 ag-wala^{32}sgal-v-h^{23} a̲-di^{23}h-v^3
first   1 play exP and   3 say exP

si̲na^{3}le   aw-didvh-v^3 j-a-di^{23}h-v
early-in-morning   1 get-up exP   Pst 3 say exP

a^{3}wu-n^3 yv   u-nahnejo-di   ges-v
close and   by   3 play-baseball Inf   be exP

j-a-dih-v^3 oji-ne^{23}-v^3
Pst 3 say exP   they-and-I live exP

a̲ma-yulhd^{23} geh-v^3 aw^{3}yv   ak-su̲^{23}hnv^{32}s-v^3 j-a-di^{23}h-v   sdid^3
water near   be exP   close-by   1 fish exP   Pst 3 say exP   little

svhi-yey^{23} didl^3 awa-ksa̲tani^{23}hl-v^3
evening   toward   1 come-upon exP

j-adih-v^3 boy   sgi-dv^3
Pst 3 say exP   boy   that Emp

w-u-l^{23}i̲st-v^3 u-n-dalh^3-g-v^3
Tr 3 to-the- end exP   3 Pl crowd Prog exP

yvw   aw^{3}dv^3 nusdv^3 u-n-len-d-hi^3
person   close   it-was   3 Pl start Inf

u-n-lasgalh^3-di   j-a-di^{23}h-v^3 yv^{23}dv
3 Pl play Inf   Pst 3 say exP   so-much

idininvhid   de-ji^3?-hen-v^3 a-ni-go
length-of   Pl 1 have exP   3 Pl perch

j-a-di^{23}h-v^3 suhdi-nh^3 kilo^3 day-u-we^{3}hluhn-v^3
Pst 3 say exP   fishing-pole and   someone   Dst 3 yell exP

j-a-di^{23}h-v^3 jali
Pst 3 say exP   charlie

day-u-^{23}dv^{3}hn-v^3 j-a-di^{23}h-v^3 i̲sgi-sde^{23}l-a   sagwu^3
Dst 3 yell-out exP   Pst 3 say exP   you-them-and-me help Imp   one

ogi-lu^{23}lo^{32}ch-e^3 a-hne^{23}joʔvs-g-i
they-and-I lack repP   3 play Prog Ag

u-dvhn-v^3 j-a-di^{23}h-v^3 boy
3 say exP   Pst 3 say exP   boy

n-ji-ga^{32}tahv-n^{23} j-a-di^{23}h-v^3
Spec 1 not-know exP and   Pst 3 say exP

a-wahnejo-di
3 play Inf

ilvhyu   ak-svhnil-v^3 yi̲-ge^{3}h-e^3
never   1 touch exP   nonF be repP

sgwahlesd^3 j-a-di^{23}h-v^3 d-a^{3}wa-lchv^{23}ya^{32}stan-v^3 j-a-di^{23}h-v^3
ball   Pst 3 say exP   Pl 3 say exP   Pst 3 say exP

hvʔv^4 gaji-yoh-e^{23}-v^3 si^{23}lv^3 wi̲-di-ji-^{23}nvhs^4 e-ji^3 hiʔa^3-na^3
okay   I-them tell Dat exP   first   Tr Dst Pl go   1Pos   this and
                                                                         mother

a-ni-gola^4 kilaw^3 i^{23}-ji^{3}ʔ-lu^{3}hj-vi^{43} ga-ji-yoh-e^{23}l-v^3 j-a-di^{23}h-v^3
3 Pl perch   quickly   again 1 arrive exP   I-them tell Dat exP   Pst 3 say exP

aw^3 dvda̲^{3}nelv^3 j-a-di^{23}h-v^3 eji-nh^{23} j-u^3-wo^{3}hl-o^3 j-a-di^{23}h-v^3
close   house   Pst 3 say exP   mother and   Rel 3 be-home   Pst 3 say exP
                                                                               Hab

k<u>o</u>hi^{23}-dv iyu?v^3 j-a-di^{23}h-v^3 n-u-lsdvhlu^{3}n-v^3
after-a-while Emp then Pst 3 say exP Lat 3 sit-down exP

e-ji^3 j-a-di^{23}h-v^3
1Pos mother Pst 3 say exP

osd^{23} ndodayu^{3}wa^{3}nelv^3
good start 3 prepare exP

aja?d o?-alenvhv^{23}d-v^3-sgwu^3
fish 3Pl start exP Aff

oj-ala^{32}sgali^{23}h-v j-a-di^{23}h-v^3 u-dihleh-g-v^{23}-hnv asgini
they-and-I play exP Pst 3 say exP 3 be-hot Prog exP and left-side

dloges de-h-a^{32}nlo^{23}hn-v^3?i gvw-<u>o</u>h-e^{32}l-v j-a-di^{23}h-v^3
field Pl 2 play Imp they-me tell Dat exP Pst 3 say exP

so^{3}hneli-he-dv^3 now^{23} dojiyuhihv^3 j-a-di^{23}h-a^3 hadv^3 gusd^{23}
nine Ord Aff now inning Pst 3 say Pres and-not something

yi-d-o?<u>i</u>^{3}-na?-e^3 sgidv-na w-u-^{23}lstan-v d-o?-<u>age</u>^{3}s^4-v^3
nonF Pl they-and-I have repP that and Tr 3 to-end exp Pl they-and-I play
exP

j-a-di^{23}h-v^3 u-ni-na^{32}wsd-v-nh^{23}
Pst 3 say exP 3 Pl roar exP and

j-a-di^{23}h-v^3 so^{3}hneli-ne-hnv^3 u^{23}lsgwalhd u-n-vhni^{3}l-v^3 j-a-di^{23}h-v^3
Pst 3 say exP nine Ord and last 3 Pl hit exP Pst 3 say exP

ta?l-ne^{23}-nh u-ki^{3}lo^3 j-a-di^{23}h-v^3 ta^3?li-nh^3 diganugo^{23}hwid y-u-n-i^{3}nvn
two Ord and 3 on Pst 3 say two and Pl out nonF 3 Pl
exP score

g-o?-<u>i</u>hlos-g-v^3 w<u>i</u>-d-a^{3}gw-akahnan-a-nh^3 j-a-di^{23}h-v^3 e-ji^3 si^3 osd^{23}
they-us beat Tr Pl 1 look Pres and Pst 3 say 1Pos still good
Prog Pst exP mother

ni-d-odi-gv^{32}neh-o^3 aja?d
Spec Pl they-and-I prepare Hab   fish

kohi^{3}dvyv^3 j-a-di^{23}h-v^3
after-a-while   Pst 3 say exP

n-u-lsgwi̲do^{32}siy-e^3?-v^3 u-de-g^3 j-a-di^{23}h-v^3 w-u-di^{23}nv^{32}h-v^3
n 3 contort exP   3 pitch Prog   Pst 3 say exP   Tr 3 pitch exP

day-u-wa^{3}hnil-v^3 di-ji̲-do^{32}?-v^3
Fut 3 hit exP   Dst 1 stand exP

jiyukd^{32} sawu^3 yu-da̲^{3}di^{3}nvd^{23} a?i-^{3}n-iyvh-v^3 j-a-di^{23}h-v^3 kilo^3
straight to   one   3 bounce   1 catch exP   Pst 3 say exP   someone

dv^3-?uw-ehluhnv^3 j-a-di^{23}h-v^3 a^{3}didl^3 o?ali^3?ohv^3
Rep 3 yell exP   Pst 3 say exP   toward-that-way   they-and-my teammate

sgiw^3-hvn   w-u-l^{23}st-v
that and   Tr 3 to-the-end exP

w-a-sdi^{3}doldawdi^{3}s-e^3 g-anv^3?vs-g-v^3
Tr 3 race-toward repP   3 score Prog exP

j-a-di^{23}h-v^3 ogi-hlos-g-v
Pst 3 say exP   they-and-I lose Prog exP

jali   day-u^{23}-dv^{3}hn-v^3
charlie   Fut 3 say Fut-Imp

j-a-di^{23}h-v^3 throw   it   home   day-u^{23}-dv^{3}hn-v^3 boy
Pst 3 say exP   throw   it   home   Fut 3 say Fut-Imp   boy

w-agi̲-gi^{3}s-v^3 j-a-di^{23}h-v^3 sgwahlesd^3 aw-aktahv^{3}s-v^3
Tr 1 take exP   Pst 3 say exP   ball   1 turn exP

j-a-di^{23}h-v^3 dida̲^{3}nelv^3 w-awa-di^{23}nv^{32}s-v^3
Pst 3 say exP   toward house   Tr 1 throw exP

ale^{3} wi-n-jisgu^{32}hy-v^{3} e-ji^{3}
almost Tr Pl hit-on-head exP 1Pos mother

ajaʔd
fish

osd^{23} ndod-g-v^{32}neh-v^{3} j-a-di^{23}h-v^{3}
good 3 prepare exP Pst 3 say exP

Syllabary

ᏣᎵ ᎧᏄᎾ ᎣᏦᏎᎭ ᏣᎳᎩ ᎬᏅᏗ ᏚᏙᎥ ᏣᎵ ᎧᏄᎾ ᏲᏁᎦ ᎬᏂᏗ ᏦᏥᏲᏟ ᏙᎦᏛᏏᏗᏒ ᏂᎪᏄ ᎪᏍᏗ ᎣᎩᏃᏎᎲ ᎧᏃᎮᎵᏗ ᎤᏏᏛ ᏲᎦᏓᎦᏯᏍᏗ ᎨᎭ ᎤᏄᏯᏗᎤᏍᏯ ᎨᎭ ᎤᏑᏂᎯᏍᏗ ᏔᎵ Ꮅ ᎾᎦᏧᏴ ᏥᎨᎭ ᏂᎨᏒᎾᏯᏬ ᏱᎩ ᎤᏲᎱᏒ ᏍᎩᏅ ᎠᏘᏂᏙ ᎨᎭ ᏍᏯ ᎣᎩᏃᏎᏄ ᎤᏁᏦᏂᏙᏄ ᎢᎦᏓ ᎠᎾᏁᏣᎥᏍᎬ ᎠᎾᏗᎲ ᎢᎦᏓᏅ ᎠᏅᎳᏍᎦᎵᏍᎬ ᎠᎾᏗᎲ baseball ᏍᎩᎾ ᏌᏊ ᏳᏩᎧᏗ ᎣᎩᏃᎯᏎᏄ ᎢᎬᏱ ᎠᏆᎳᏍᎦᏄᏈ ᎠᏗᎭ ᏏᎾᏬ ᎠᏩᏗᏛᎭ ᏣᏗᎭ ᎠᏊᏅ Ᏼ ᎤᎾᏁᏦᏗ ᎨᏒ ᏣᏗᎭ ᎣᏥᏁᏄ ᎠᏘᏳᎶᏗ ᎨᎭ ᎠᏊᏴ ᎠᏆᏋᏅᏒ ᏣᏗᎭ ᏍᏗᏛ ᎡᎯᏰᏱ ᏗᏜ ᎠᏩᎦᏌᏔᏂᏄ ᏣᏗᎭ boy ᏍᎩᏛ ᏊᎵᏍᏛ ᎤᎾᏓᏈᎬ ᏴᏫ ᎠᏊᏛ ᏄᏍᏛ ᎤᎾᏬᏅᏗ ᎤᎾᎳᏍᎦᏄᏗ ᏣᏗᎭ ᏴᏛ ᎢᏗᏂᏅᎯᏛ ᎦᏥᏁᎭ ᎠᏂᎪᎳ ᏣᏗᎭ ᏋᏗᏅ ᎩᎶ ᏓᏩᏇᏄᏅ ᏣᏗᎭ ᏣᎵ ᏓᎶᏛᏅ ᏣᏗᎭ ᎢᏍᎩᏍᏚᎳ ᏌᏯ ᎣᎩᎷᎶᏤ ᎠᏁᏦᎥᏍᎩ ᎤᏛᏅ ᏣᏗᎭ boy ᏂᏥᎦᎳᎭᎾ ᎠᏗᎭ ᎠᏩᏁᏦᏗ ᎢᏄᎯᎶ ᎠᏆᏒᏂᏄ ᏱᎨᎵ ᏍᏆᏞᏍᏗ ᏣᏗᎭ ᏓᏩᎵᏨᏯᏍᎳᏅ ᏣᏗᎭ ᎭᎥ ᎦᏥᏲᎮᏄ ᏏᏄ ᏫᏗᏥᏅᏍ ᎡᏥ ᎯᎠᎾ ᎠᏂᎪᎳ ᎩᎳᏉ ᎢᏧᎷᏨᎢ ᎦᏥᏲᎮᏄ ᏣᏗᎭ ᎠᏊ ᏛᏓᏁᏄ ᏣᏗᎭ ᎡᏥᏅ ᏧᏑᎶ ᏣᏗᎭ ᎪᎯᏛ ᎢᏴᎥ ᏣᏗᎭ ᏄᎵᏍᏛᎷᏅ ᎡᏥ ᏣᏗᎭ ᎣᏍᏛ ᏂᏙᏓᎶᏩᏁᏄ ᎠᏣᏗ ᎣᎠᏬᏅᎭᏛᏍᏯ ᎣᏣᎳᏍᎦᎵᎭ ᏣᏗᎭ ᎤᏗᏞᎬᏅ ᎠᎩᏍᎦᏂ ᏌᎨᏍ ᎦᏈᏁᎶᏅᎢ ᎬᏑᎮᏄ ᏣᏗᎭ ᏈᏁᎵᏁᏛ ᏙᏥᏴᎯᎭ ᏣᏗᎭ ᏈᏛ ᎫᏍᏗ ᏱᏙᎢᎾᏒ ᏍᎩᏛᎾ ᏊᎵᏍᏛ ᏙᎠᎨᏍᏄ ᏣᏗᎭ ᎤᏂᎾᏩᏍᏛᏅ ᏣᏗᎭ ᏈᏁᎵᎮᏅ ᎤᎵᏍᏆᏄᏗ ᎤᏅᏂᏄ ᏣᏗᎭ ᏔᎵᏁᏅ ᎤᎩᎶ ᏣᏗᎭ ᏔᎵᏅ ᏗᎦᏄᎪᏫᏛ ᎶᏂᏅᏅ ᎪᎢᎶᏍᎬ ᏫᏓᏆᎧᏏᎾᏅ ᏣᏗᎭ ᎡᏥ Ꮟ ᎣᏍᏓ ᏂᏙᏗᎬᏁᎲ ᎠᏣᏗ ᎪᎯᏛᏴ ᏣᏗᎭ ᏄᎵᏍᏬᏙᏏᏰᎥ ᎤᎦᎩ ᏣᏗᎭ ᏊᏗᏅᎭ ᏓᎶᏩᏂᏄ ᏗᏥᏙᎬ ᏥᏩᎪᏗ ᏌᏯ ᎶᏓᏗᏅᏛ ᎠᎢᏂᏴᎭ ᏣᏗᎭ ᎩᎶ ᏛᏅᏇᎷᏅ ᏣᏗᎭ ᎠᏗᏟ ᎣᎠᎵᎣᎭ ᏍᎩᏉᏅ ᏊᎵᏍᏛ ᏩᏍᏗᏙᎵᏓᏩᏗᏒ ᎦᏅᎥᏍᎬ ᏣᏗᎭ ᎣᎩᏌᏍᎬ ᏣᎵ ᏓᎶᏛᏅ ᏣᏗᎭ throw it home ᏓᎶᏛᏅ boy ᏩᎩᎩᏒ ᏣᏗᎭ ᏍᏆᏬᏍᏛ ᎠᏩᎦᎳᎭᏒ ᏣᏗᎭ ᏗᏓᏁᏄ ᏩᏩᏗᏅᏒ ᎠᏬ ᏫᏂᏥᏍᏗᏴ ᎡᏥ ᎠᏣᏗ ᎣᏍᏓ ᏂᏙᏗᎬᏁᎭ ᏣᏗᎭ

English

We called him Charles "Bullfrog" in Cherokee. His name was Charlie Canoe in English. When we were growing up, we would gather around him, and he would always tell us stories. He died about two years ago, maybe even less than that. He really liked to fish. He told us stories about how he played baseball. He said when he played baseball for the very first time, he had gotten up early one morning and had gone fishing. He said there was a stream close to where they lived, and their house sat next to a baseball diamond.

He was returning one afternoon from fishing when he found a big crowd of spectators at the baseball diamond, and the players were just about ready to start the game. He was walking toward the house with a long string of perch and a fishing pole in his hand when he heard someone yell to him, "Charlie! Come and help us. We need one more player." "Boy," he thought, "I don't know how to play baseball." He hadn't even touched a baseball. Bravely, he told them, "Okay, let me go and take these perch to Mom, and I'll be right back." Their house was just a few yards from the baseball diamond, and his mom was at home. After they had started the game, he saw his mom sit down on the porch and begin to clean the fish.

The game started, and the weather was hot. "Play left field," Charlie was told. So he played left field, and at the bottom of the ninth inning, both teams were scoreless. It was a tough game! The crowd was roaring! Someone came up to bat with two men out and a man on second base. If they scored, Charlie's team would lose. Charlie looked and saw that his mom was still cleaning the fish. His mind back on the game, he saw the pitcher contorting, getting ready to pitch. The pitcher delivered the ball, and the batter connected one straight toward Charlie in left field. One bounce, and Charlie had the ball in his hand. Someone from his team was yelling at him. The man on second base had rounded third and was racing toward home base to score. "Charlie!" they yelled. "Throw it home." Charlie took the ball, turned, and threw it toward the house, almost hitting his mom in the head!

References

American Bible Society. 1860. *The New Testament in the Cherokee Language.* New York: American Bible Society.

Conley, Robert. 1984. *The Rattlesnake Band, and Other Poems.* Cherokee translations by Durbin Feeling. Muskogee: Indian University Press.

Cook, William Hinton. 1979. "A Grammar of North Caroline Cherokee." PhD diss., Yale University.

Feeling, Durbin. 1994. *A Structured Approach to Learning the Basic Inflections of the Cherokee Verb.* Muskogee: Indian University Press, in cooperation with Bacone College.

Feeling, Durbin, Christine Armer, Charles Foster, Marcellino Berardo, and Sean O'Neill. 2010. "Why Revisit Published Data of an Endangered Language with Native Speakers? An Illustration from Cherokee." *Language Documentation and Conservation* 4: 1–21.

Feeling, Durbin, and William Pulte. 1975a. *Cherokee-English Dictionary.* Tahlequah: Cherokee Nation of Oklahoma.

———. 1975b. "An Outline of Cherokee Grammar." In Feeling and Pulte, *Cherokee-English Dictionary*, 235–355.

———. 1977. "The Nineteenth Century Cherokee Grammars." *Anthropological Linguistics* 19 (6): 274–79.

Hardy, Heather K., and Janine Scancarelli, eds. 2005. *Native Languages of the Southeastern United States.* Lincoln: University of Nebraska Press, in cooperation with the American Indian Studies Research Institute, Indiana University, Bloomington.

Pulte, William, and Durbin Feeling. 2002. "Morphology in Cherokee Lexicography: The *Cherokee-English Dictionary*." In *Making Dictionaries: Preserving Indigenous Languages of the Americas*, edited by William Frawley, Kenneth

C. Hill, and Pamela Munro, 60–69. Berkeley: University of California Press.

Walker, Willard. 1984. "The Design of Native Literacy Programs and How Literacy Came to the Cherokees." *Anthropological Linguistics* 26 (2): 161–69.

Walker, Willard, and James Sarbaugh. 1993. "The Early History of the Cherokee Syllabary." *Ethnohistory* 40 (1): 70–94.